Advance praise for **Parents with Inconvenient Truths about Trans**

"This book questions society's willingness to abandon a generation of children to the dictates of a global political movement. It challenges what it means to be 'kind' and blows apart the activist ideology you're supposed to believe. Essential reading for every parent, lawmaker, and teacher, and for everyone who cares about the welfare of children and the importance of truth."

—*Stephanie Davies-Arai BEM, Founder and Director, Transgender Trend*

"In the controversy over pediatric gender medicine, some of the most important voices are often the ones least heard. This collection of essays features highly compelling first-hand observations by parents on the front lines of the gender wars. The authors write with sensitivity, nuance, and a deep understanding of the issues. *Parents with Inconvenient Truths about Trans* is a critical resource for teenagers, medical professionals, journalists, policymakers, and most of all, other parents."

—*Leor Sapir, Fellow, Manhattan Institute for Policy Research*

"A much-needed and long-awaited set of narratives that should be considered essential reading for anyone either directly or indirectly affected by gender dysphoria, including trans-identifying teenagers and their parents, and for those who work with gender dysphoric patients, including teaching and clinical staff."

—*Dr. Az Hakeem, Consultant Psychiatrist and Specialist in Gender Dysphoria*

"These urgent and often heartbreaking testimonies document the pain, suffering, and hope of parents desperately trying to resist family fragmentation and the alienation of troubled but much-loved children."

—*Bernard Lane, Journalist,* Gender Clinic News

"Parents were the first to point out the unprecedented medical scandal that has been playing out before us, and they have been widely demonized for doing so. Most parents love their kids and are more invested in their flourishing than anyone else. Therefore, parents have been quick to spot an agenda that promises happiness but is likely to deliver confusion, distress, and dissociation from one's body. This book brings their important stories to a wider audience. This book should be required reading for anyone who works with children and teens."

—*Lisa Marciano, LCSW, NCPsyA, Jungian Analyst*

"This collection of essays offers a raw, informative, and incisive critique of youth gender medicine from the perspective of parents. At a time when parental concerns and questions about their children's gender distress are often belittled or dismissed as 'transphobia,' this book couldn't be more important. These stories remind us that the investment, love, and concern a parent has for her child is simply unmatched. And the resulting emotions are powerful: there is terrible grief when a close child suddenly decides to estrange; there is rage when physicians rush medical interventions with a poor evidence base; and there is also a great deal of love when parents are able to lean in and protect their child with care and caution. This anthology is timely reading for parents with gender-questioning children, and in years to come, it will provide some answers when society looks back to understand what happened during the scandal of pediatric gender medicine."

—*Sasha Ayad, M.Ed., LPC, Cohost,* Gender: A Wider Lens Podcast

Parents

with Inconvenient Truths about Trans

Tales from the Home Front in the Fight to Save Our Kids

Edited by Josie A. and Dina S.

Foreword by Stella O'Malley

PITCHSTONE PUBLISHING
DURHAM, NORTH CAROLINA

Pitchstone Publishing
Durham, North Carolina
www.pitchstonebooks.com

The views and opinions expressed in the parent essays in this volume are those of the authors alone and do not necessary reflect the official positions of Genspect. Nor do the views and opinions expressed in the parent essays necessarily reflect the views of the publisher, editors, or other parent contributors to the volume. As a collection of stories by parents from a wide range of personal and professional backgrounds and with a wide range of experiences and viewpoints, this volume is intended for informational purposes only, and the publisher, editors, and contributors disclaim any liability or responsibility for any errors or omissions in the information provided.

The names of some individuals in this book have been changed to protect their privacy. All parent essays in this volume were previously published on the Parents with Inconvenient Truths about Trans Substack (pitt.substack.com). For links to the original essays, see the "credits" section of this volume. In addition, part of this volume's introduction was originally published on the PITT Substack as "Why We Write about Gender Ideology (aka Trans)," July 20, 2021, pitt.substack.com/p/why-we-write-about-gender-ideology.

Library of Congress Cataloging-in-Publication Data

Names: A., Josie, editor. | S., Dina, editor.
Title: Parents with inconvenient truths about trans : tales from the home
   front in the fight to save our kids / edited by Josie A. and Dina S. ;
   foreword by Stella O'Malley.
Description: First edition. | Durham, North Carolina : Pitchstone
   Publishing, [2023] | Includes bibliographical references. | Summary:
   "Parents of trans-identified children share their real-life experiences,
   describing how their children were introduced to gender ideology, how
   they navigated a medical and mental health system that preaches
   affirmation-only care, and what, if any, strategies successfully led to
   the desistance of their children"— Provided by publisher.
Identifiers: LCCN 2023013670 (print) | LCCN 2023013671 (ebook) | ISBN
   9781634312462 (paperback) | ISBN 9781634312479 (ebook)
Subjects: LCSH: Parents of transgender children. | Gender identity
   disorders in children—Social aspects. | Transphobia.
Classification: LCC HQ759.9147 .P37 2023 (print) | LCC HQ759.9147 (ebook)
   | DDC 306.874—dc23/eng/20230417
LC record available at https://lccn.loc.gov/2023013670
LC ebook record available at https://lccn.loc.gov/2023013671

This book is dedicated to all of the parents who chose to tell their stories. Your bravery is a light to guide the path for others unfortunate enough to walk this path behind us. There is no force stronger than a parent's love, and we are proud to provide a stage for your voices.

Contents

Foreword *by Stella O'Malley*   11

Acknowledgments   15

Preface   17

Introduction: The Parent Experience   22

Parents on Community Capture

1. Parental Dysphoria   33
2. When the Village Turns on You   36
3. The World Needs All Kinds of Boys   40
4. Letter to a Well-Meaning Bystander   43
5. Dear Parent: Do You Really Know What's Best for My Son?   48
6. The Shunning   52
7. A Heap of Hatred   55

Parents on Community Influences:
Peer Groups, Teachers, and Schools

8. Pronoun Bullying at School   61
9. Schools Are Ground Zero of the Trans Epidemic   66
10. How Our Spirited Daughter Boarded the Trans Train   79
11. I Sponsored a High School GSA, and Then . . .   83
12. $30K a Year—and My Kid Can't Tell
the Difference Between a Boy and a Girl   87
13. A Pat on the Head   91
14. I Am Not the Same Teacher   96

Parents on Online Influences: Porn, Anime, and Social Media

15. Brainwashed: Yes, the Internet (and School)
    Did Make My Kid "Trans"   103
16. Gender Dysphoria's Undeniable
    Connection to Pornography   108
17. Crazy Like a (Trans, Gay) Fox (Girl)   113
18. Porn and Grooming   115
19. A Clusterfeck of Internet Indoctrination
    and Doctor Failures   121
20. An Internet-Fueled Crisis   128
21. A Death Cult with Anime and Unicorns   131

Parents on Gender Ideology

22. Why Our Smart Kids Think They're Trans:
    The Idiotic Reasons They've Given Us That
    Come Straight from the Gender Cult   137
23. An Ideological Threat to My Daughter,
    My Family, and Women's Healthcare   140
24. Testifying and Repenting: A New Cult   144
25. I Was a True Believer   148
26. This Debate Is Too Important for Political Divides:
    As a Liberal, I Think the Right Is Right   155
27. The Argument for Transitioning Children
    Is Based on Faith in Gender Ideology
    —Not on Facts or Scientific Evidence   159

Parents on the Betrayal of the Medical System

28. Think My Kid Is Trans? You'd Better Prove It   169
29. Parents Deserve Real Answers   171
30. Doctors, Stop Gaslighting
    Our Gender-Confused Children   178
31. Parental Disempowerment by the Gender Industry   181
32. A Letter to My Son's Affirmative Therapist   186

33. The Madness of "Gender Specialists" 189
34. Why I Can't Reveal My Son's Therapist's Name 193

Parents on Family, Love, and Loss

35. My New Identity, Not By Choice 201
36. Reflections on Time in the World of Trans 203
37. Reflections on Pain
     and Things That Break Our Hearts 206
38. Mourning the Living 209
39. Kills Me Every Time 213
40. The Abyss 216
41. Behind the Curtain:
     The Reality of Gender Transition in a Family 220
42. When Love Is Called "Abuse" 224
43. Ambiguous Loss 230
44. Unmade Memories: A Mother's Sadness 233
45. A Foolish, Pointless War 235
46. How Trans Destroyed My Family 237
47. Layers of Sadness 240
48. I Wish I Didn't Know 244

Parents on the Parent Underground

49. Parents: The New Resistance of the Twenty-first Century 249
50. Let's Go All the Way to Protect Our Kids 252
51. Waiting for Change 257
52. Yes, There Are Clear Patterns among Male Adolescents
     with Rapid-Onset Gender Dysphoria 261
53. Parents, Journalists, and Therapists—
     You Can Still Do the Right Thing 266
54. The "Lived Experience"
     of Rapid-Onset Gender Dysphoria 268
55. Gender Dysphoria: The Science Is Not Settled 272
56. Real Conversations, One at a Time 277

Parents on Parenting Through Trans

57. How to Be a Trans-Educated Rational Parent   285
58. A Tragedy in Slow Motion   298
59. To Help My Son, It's Time to Rediscover Myself   310
60. A Mother's Letter to Her Child   312
61. Not a Desistance Story   316
62. Finding Hope on the Road to Ruin   319
63. Becoming a Light for Our Wayward Son   323
64. Reflections of a Father   327
65. The Gender-Critical Parents' Guide to Trans   333

Parents on Desistance

66. Just a Phase   341
67. The One-Way Street   344
68. To My Daughter's Therapist: You Were Wrong   346
69. The Trans Detour   351
70. Saying Bye to the Gummy Bear Cult   355
71. In Like a Lion, Out Like a Lamb   361
72. Our Story of Desistance   364
73. Anger, Shame, and Then Pure Happiness   368
74. A Letter to My Daughter   372
75. Is Desistance Rare?   376

References   379
Resources   384
Credits   388
About PITT

Foreword

A medical scandal is unfolding. The main victims of this medical scandal are vulnerable, socially awkward, and naïve kids. Right behind them are their parents, wringing their hands in anguish as they watch their kids fall for a promise that they can one day become a different person. Perhaps they can; perhaps medical transition will deliver the promise of a new identity, but for many parents, the medical procedures feel too risky, and it all feels like using a sledgehammer to crack a nut.

Politics is very heightened these days, and identity politics is highly controversial, so although it might seem like a war is raging, we do well to remember that the main source of disagreement in this context is that these kids and parents don't always agree about which treatment path will make the kids feel better. These children may want medical treatment that will help to physically alter their gender expression, while their parents may favor talk therapy that can help to bring about their self-acceptance. Likewise, gender identity theory tells us that we have an unfalsifiable identity somewhere within us and we need to access medical procedures if this sense of gender identity is unaligned with our physical body; meanwhile, a developmental model of understanding suggests that some people develop gender distress as a result of some unresolved trauma in their lives.

These kids are often academically clever, but they're also gullible and tend to have other challenges, such as autism spectrum disorder (ASD), attention-deficit/hyperactivity disorder (ADHD), obsessive-compulsive disorder (OCD), anxiety, and eating disorders. They often feel left out, on the social fringes. They usually hate their bodies and hate themselves. Just like most teens of their generation, in times of distress, they turn to

11

Google. Typically typing in something like "I hate my body" or "I don't want to be me," a cascade of events takes place when the teen, who never before showed any signs of gender distress, becomes enraptured with the idea that their sense of gender is the start, middle, and end of all their problems and begins to believe that all they need to do is fix this one thing and everything else will resolve.

It can feel very relieving to be told that there is a very specific pathway to follow that will lead to a happier life. The teens become enthralled by the idea that they can be somebody else—a whole new person, with a new identity, and nobody will ever be allowed to refer to their old shameful self ever again. Indeed, this is perhaps one of the most beguiling promises that could be offered to an unhappy teenager.

While the teenager is busy in their bedroom, online, tending to their new identity like an avid horticulturist would a Bonsai tree, their loving parents often become increasingly terrified that their geeky and lovable child has been taken in by a false promise. I know these parents. As founder of Genspect, I have come across thousands of parents in this exact position over the last few years. Some of them I know very well, while some of them I may have only met during a crowded Zoom call. Although I, as a psychotherapist, have worked with a lot of people suffering from trauma, the deep well of devastation that I have witnessed during therapeutic support meetings for parents is harrowing.

I remember being in tears after I facilitated my first such parental support meeting on Zoom. It was shocking to see how society had lost its way so badly. These kind, loving, and engaged parents who simply wanted the best for their children had been summarily dismissed as transphobic bigots. Their kids, who were almost always neuro-diverse, had been placed on a fast track to medicalize their gender identities with aggressive interventions, no matter how vulnerable or how ambivalent they were or how many other diagnoses they already had.

The main crime that these parents are accused of is "transphobia." Yet, as one parent said to me, "If wanting to proceed cautiously and make sure that your immature teenager receives the most appropriate healthcare is transphobia, then so be it." These parents are, in the main, educated, involved, and open-minded people. Many of them smiled along when someone else's child was going through medical transition. They happily waved rainbow flags and took part in Pride marches.

However, we are often most conservative about the things that are most precious to us, and when their own child announced out of the blue that they were transgender, without ever having shown signs of gender nonconformity before, many of these parents immediately went about making sure that their child received the best treatment possible. The problem was that these announcements typically came after the teen had experienced some distress, and there was no high-quality evidence to support the aggressive and irreversible medical interventions so often and readily prescribed.

Most parents are initially skeptical but also open to the idea of medical transition. They believe that if their teen needs medical transition, then they, as good parents, should make sure that these procedures are accessed. But these parents are also very engaged, and it is only when they have studied all the information they are given, when they have read everything they can get their hands on, that they are willing to give consent to the medicalization of their teen's gender identity.

The mythical suicide statistics are often central to the parents' response. Many parents have heard frightening statistics taken from unreliable online studies that lead them to believe that they should immediately put their children on an irreversible medical pathway or they will be at risk of suicide. Often, these same parents will then read the peer-reviewed studies and realize that this isn't an accurate account of the situation. Although their teens are vulnerable, they are no more likely to die by suicide than other adolescents with conditions such as ASD, anxiety, and OCD. Then, like a ball of wool, these diligent parents keep reading the medical literature and discover a wealth of shoddy research that leaps to inappropriate conclusions and ignores significant warning signs about the health implications. They read studies where high numbers of the participants are "lost to follow-up," and so the reported regret rate is wholly unreliable. They read about infertility, sexual dysfunction, cardiac problems, and osteoporosis.

This is often when everything starts to unravel.

Some parents have been horrified by the low-quality care their kids received from mental health professionals, and other parents have been shocked by poor-quality studies: the majority of parents come to believe that medical transition will not help their kids. Their kids are certainly distressed, but their other challenges, their neurodiversity or the trauma they have recently suffered, have been overshadowed by gender issues, and this doesn't make sense to the parents. Many of these teens have repressed their sexuality, and plenty seem to be ignoring the fact that they are gay, lesbian, or bisexual. Lots of them are deeply disappointed by the reality of life. These kids are well loved and well cared for. But they believed the Disney films they grew up with and find the sharp shock of reality difficult to bear.

The parents have sought out other options and asked the care providers about different types of psychotherapy. Medicalizing their kids' perfectly healthy bodies in a way that will give rise to many more medical issues feels like too drastic a solution, and so they try to help their child to engage in real-life activities rather than allowing them to remain online, narrowly focused on one single proposed solution.

A horrible aspect of this medical scandal is that parents are so badly shamed by medical professionals when they seek any option for their child that does not involve medicalization. Parents of detransitioners I know poignantly describe how they were cruelly dismissed and shamed when they raised their concerns to doctors and therapists. One mother described to me how she was in the doctor's office with her precious child, and even though the doctor had promised high-quality care, after a forty-minute consultation, he suggested immediate medical intervention, without giving any consideration to the impact of the child's ASD, OCD rumination, and extreme immaturity—or to the risky nature of these difficult procedures. The mother reported that it felt like she was in a horror movie where the doctor ripped off his mask to reveal that he was actually the monster all along.

The stories you read in this book are filled with sadness. But they are filled with love too. As you read through this book, you will come upon many different viewpoints and many different parenting styles, yet there are some common threads that unite these parents: they love their vulnerable kids, and they only want what is best for them. As the poet Philip Larkin reminds us, "What will survive of us is love."

Stella O'Malley

Acknowledgments

All proceeds of this book are donated to Genspect to continue its work on behalf of parents. We are forever grateful for its public presence and constant advocacy, as well as for the expertise, advice, and hope given by Genspect's founder, Stella O'Malley, leadership team, and affiliates to so many of the contributors to this book, including Josie and Dina. Because of you, we can remain anonymous while ensuring our voices are a force to be reckoned with.

While this book contains selected essays from Parents with Inconvenient Truths about Trans (PITT), there have been many, many other contributors to PITT, all of whom deserve to be honored for their bravery and commitment. In allowing us to publish their stories, they are helping countless others find their way. We'd like to individually acknowledge all those whose essays have appeared on the PITT Substack, a subset of whom have essays in this volume (even if we can refer to them only by their pseudonyms): Gigi LaRuc, Lynn Chadwick, Jean Driscoll, Anne Mitchell, Chris C., Mothers Grim, Beth Lacy, Vera Lindner, Samuel Alfred, Victoria G., Mary L., Daisy W., Eleanor McEvoy, Derek D, Samantha Durand, Julie Capilano, Nettie Stevens, Ruth W. Simeon, Beth D., Stacy R, Angeles Green, Michele B., Florabelle Higgins, Hanna Vasilieva, Concerned GA Mom, Hippiesq, Juliet Nevasta, Cara Bee, Ruth P., Lizzie Purefoy, Liz Green, StoicMom, Fathyma Parker, Carol Bird, MamaAin'tPlayin, Betty Ventura, Molly Weasley, Camille LEBRETON, Jennifer Comer, Struggling South African mom, Elliot Swimmer, Rafael C., Emily and John Gordon, Maggy Goldsmith, Psy.D., Denton Yoga-Carter, Lydia Smith, Anita Green, Camille R., Jennifer Van Outer, Capri H., Felice J Killer, Jolene Brown, latin american mom,

Andrea Dalhouse, Rette Diekinder, Charlie S., Zelda Linda, Mama of lesbian, Lettie Parker, Jessica Vala, A. Palacios, notgivinguponher, Donna M., Katherine Parker, Alex Cleary, W. E. Pede, SK, Bill Ockham, Kevin Ingalls, RCW, Marie Borealis, PT, K. Fyfe, Consuelo Pan, Amy S., A. Gency, Mum_of_ROGD_son, Maria T., and many others who asked not to receive any recognition.

Preface

Parents with Inconvenient Truths about Trans (PITT) is a Substack (pitt.substack.com) founded by the editors of this volume, Josie A. and Dina S. (both pseudonyms). We are two moms whose lives were irrevocably altered by our own personal brushes with gender ideology.

We met back in the dark days of 2020 through the so-called parent underground—in our case, through a support group for parents of boys caught up in rapid-onset gender dysphoria, or ROGD. For the majority of parents, the culture wars are political hot buttons with little impact on daily life. However, for a small but growing cohort of parents, one aspect of the culture wars in particular—gender identity—is far from theoretical and impersonal. All parents that question the gender narrative first find themselves questioning their own sanity in a world where affirming a child's gender identity (i.e., agreeing with and encouraging a child's self-diagnosis that they are transgender) is considered the only socially acceptable path. We thus don't use pseudonyms or terms like "parent underground" lightly. Most of us need to protect our identities not only for fear of social and professional backlash but also to protect our children and other family members from public scrutiny. Prior to joining this support group, we had both spent some months suffering in isolation, each having doubts about our respective child's self-diagnosed transgenderism and dysphoria.

By the time parents find their way into one of the Parents of ROGD Kids (PROGDK) network support groups at parentsofrogdkids.com, they have often already been isolated and ostracized from their peer groups and social networks and sometimes have even been estranged from their extended and immediate families over this hot-button issue.

The mental strain can be overwhelming, even to the point of contemplating self-harm or suicide (ironically, the same threat often employed by kids if their parents do not go along with their newfound identity). Our very small group of parents of boys suffering from ROGD (just around fifteen parents at first and now close to three hundred) represented this sense of isolation to the extreme, as most parents of ROGD kids are parents of girls. We quickly found that we had an enormous amount in common in terms of experience in the crazy world of affirmation— and that our kids had a tremendous amount in common as well. It was almost immediately clear to us that our society had become brainwashed and that our children were on track to pay the price. The extent of this societal capture was both obvious and shocking.

One of our main drivers for launching PITT was the fact that we were moms of boys. It was apparent that our sons were quite different from the cohort of boys who are convinced they are girls from a very young age. Our boys had much more in common with the girls referenced in Abigail Shrier's *Irreversible Damage*, with very little gender-stereotype nonconformity and a sudden teenage emergence of their trans identity, often after extended exposure to online material. Our boys were almost universally intelligent, quirky, and socially awkward, with a high prevalence of autism spectrum disorder (ASD) and ASD-like traits, as well as attention-deficit/hyperactivity disorder. They had less exposure to trans-identified peer groups than the girls, who seemed to become infected in packs, and in most cases had "come out" as trans only after a period of intense online immersion in Reddit, Discord, and porn.

We were concerned that our boys were being overlooked in the already minimal ROGD research being conducted or written about, as most of the info out in the ether regarding ROGD was focused on girls. This focus was understandable given the explosive growth of teen girls identifying as trans in recent years. Yet, just as this steep rise in trans identification in girls was completely at variance with everything that had been witnessed in earlier generations, when transgender identification was typically associated with a small number of feminine boys, so too was the trans identification of our sons at odds with this earlier trans profile. We were seeing first-hand that ROGD was a problem for boys, too. Indeed, most of our boys did not have gender issues in childhood, and many of our boys are not same-sex attracted or feminine. While many of the journalists and researchers we contacted were very sympathetic to our cause, we failed (for the most part) to interest them in writing about or studying our boys. There was simply not enough available data out there, and there was already significant pushback to any research or writing on the growing ROGD crisis among girls.

We soon realized that if we wanted to be heard, there was no point in waiting around for someone to do it for us; we were going to have to help our boys ourselves. So, in an attempt to combat misperceptions about our boys and to build interest in our cohort of children, a small group of us decided to take matters into our own hands. None of us were writers or activists. We were parents and professionals with full-time jobs. But we decided to take a leap into the unknown and try our hand at writing and advocacy, activities that for the most part occur on the margins of our daily lives. In the spring of 2021, in coordination with Angus Fox's series in *Quillette* on ROGD boys (which was based on our boys—Angus was embedded with our parent group), we wrote a number of personal stories and essays about our experiences parenting ROGD boys that were published by New Discourses and Counterweight and on *Mercatornet* and *Medium*.

As we wrote, our floodgates burst. We had so many stories to tell, and we realized how important it was for other parents that we collect these stories and make them available on a single platform, because mainstream media and news organizations were entirely unwilling to do anything other than promote a trans-activist agenda.

In June 2021, we launched the PITT Substack to tell these stories. At first, our focus was on stories of our boys, written largely by Josie and Dina. Soon we realized that we could be a platform for parents in the world of transgender on a broader scale, so we asked parents we knew to write their stories, and they did. We grew through word of mouth in the parent underground, with Josie focused on gathering stories and getting the word out and Dina focused on writing and editing—all of this was done an hour here and there as time allowed. Our one or two stories a week quickly turned into a collection of stories so large that we could only get them all out by publishing five days a week. Clearly, many other parents had been struggling alone just as we had been, and now that there was a forum, they were ready to speak out.

By June 2022, we had told over 250 stories, with more pouring in every day from moms and dads (and even a grandparent or two) from all over the world, including the United States, the United Kingdom, Australia, Ireland, Canada, Spain, South Africa, France, Italy, New Zealand, and several countries in Latin America.

PITT authors, in addition to telling their personal stories, also began to share suggestions and recommendations with other parents. As subsequent stories demonstrated, these other PITT parents were paying attention. They not only used this advice to better counter the influence of trans ideology within their families but also often built on this earlier advice. Parents started to realize not only that they were not alone and not crazy but also that they had a well of information and experience to draw upon to develop their own opinions before, say, going to a gender clinic and following potentially devastating advice. With the passage of time and the transmission of this hard-won knowledge, we found that many of our children also began to desist and no longer identified as transgender. This further accelerated and amplified the cycle PITT had created, as parents of these children spread their stories and the hope of desistance to other parents who, for so long, had been brainwashed into believing that trans was a permanent state of being and that desistance and detransition were mythical.

Once a platform was available for parents to speak out, they did—in multitudes. We made and continue to make our best efforts to represent the breadth and depth of the parent experience in the world of trans, as we see it. To be clear, our overarching point of view is quite specific. Taken as a whole, PITT is the testimony of a group of parents, growing by the day, who are united in a shared belief that today's "trans" epidemic among youth stems from a social/psychological sickness that has captured our world's collective imagination. It is due to contagion—plain and simple—and not to some sudden change in material reality or biological fact. We believe that the medicalization of children, teens, and young people in the name of trans ideology is morally wrong, damaging to our children's physical and mental well-being, and, on top of all that, ineffective at improving outcomes. We believe that no one should be supporting a delusion. And, as parents of these troubled children, teens, and young people, we are the ones continuously keeping the long-term best interests of these affected individuals in mind. We are the parents. We have the most to lose. And the most to fight for. We will not stand by and allow our children to be offered as sacrifices to the gods of the gender religion while all of society cheers them on and celebrates.

We had to make some difficult decisions about which essays to include in this anthology given the sheer number of stories we have received. Each and every one is unique and valuable and deserves to be read. The essays contained herein have been selected to represent the range of topics that parents have chosen to address, with an emphasis on stories that communicate their own lived experience. They show a parent population that has grappled first with bewilderment and confusion, then anxiety and anger, then sadness and mourning—but that now has become a group of action, reclaiming their power and place as the head of their families, responsible for raising the next generation with calm confidence in the face of frenzy. Some parents write with a clinical or scientific lens, while others write with raw, unapologetic emotion, as evidenced by their choice of words and language. Some are themselves doctors, scientists, or mental health professionals, while others have working-class jobs or are full-time caregivers to their children. Some are politically liberal, while others are politically conservative. Some are nonreligious, and some have a deep level of religious faith.

Despite these differences, we are all working toward a common goal. We have explored the causes of trans identification, personal and societal. We have conducted our own informal studies when no scientists or researchers would come to our aid. We have experimented with angles to fight back, pressure points to push, and arguments to advance. We all understand the hard realities about trans that so often go unstated and unacknowledged in public conversations and debates about gender dysphoria in youth—including in all-important policy discussions. And now, with new tools in hand, we are fighting back. We believe that this toxic force that is gender ideology must not win. Our children are worth fighting for. We hope that you take the time to read these first-person accounts of parent life in this world gone mad—and check out the hundreds of other first-person essays that we continue to record on the Substack—and maybe question your own assumptions about what it means to be "kind." You cannot raise strong, healthy children by telling lies. Often this means we must tell inconvenient truths.

Introduction: The Parent Experience

Parents of trans-identified children started out like the rest of the parent population. Like most everyone in our politically and culturally charged environment, we'd read news articles about transgenderism and grappled with obscure new words (e.g., "menstruators," "pregnant people," etc.) and concepts (e.g., "cis gender," "pansexual," etc.). Maybe we had even been subjected to a pronoun announcement ritual at work or in our religious institution. Like most of the general population, we unwitting parents shook our heads and thought it was all harmless, maybe even progressive and kind.

But on the day your child tells you, most likely in a letter or text, that they are trans, all that changes. Your life is irreversibly knocked off kilter, and you enter a strange, dark upside-down world where everything you believed to be objectively true and real about your family, friendships, schools, doctors, and politicians was called into question. It is a world where nothing is as it seemed on that blissfully ignorant day before the grand trans pronouncement.

A parent's first reaction is invariably shock—after all, the vast majority of trans pronouncements come out of the blue. Most youth in this category showed zero signs of gender dysphoria or dissatisfaction with their biological sex in childhood. Parents describe feeling as though the wind has been knocked out of them, as though the bottom has fallen out of their world. From that second on, you begin to question your entire reality. How is it that this child you raised, who was indisputably and observably male or female from birth, was really the opposite "gender" all along? How could you, a loving parent, have missed such an enormous truth about your child? What the hell is going on?

Parents who write for PITT are what we call trans-educated rational parents (TERPs). None of us started out as TERPs. Just as trans-identified youth follow clear patterns in identifying as trans, so too do their parents tend to follow a common pattern. To become a TERP, you must move through a life cycle of understanding, a progression of stages that resemble the five stages of grief: denial, anger, bargaining, depression, and acceptance. In our cycle, though, it's more like disbelief and confusion, depression and loneliness, anger and fact-finding, and resistance. At first, parents struggle to wrap their minds around what has happened. They research the phenomenon. They explore and test various causal factors, try to understand the risks of medicalization, and dive deep into the philosophy of gender ideology—a cult-like religion and mind-worm—with all of its deep-seated illogic and inconsistencies.

Parents who have never peeked under the hood of gender ideology are immediately confronted by a society that has adopted a true-believer mentality about transgenderism, with neighbors trying to be kind and accepting and with doctors and therapists who either believe in gender ideology wholesale or are too afraid of legal repercussions to speak against it. But when your child is on the line, you are forced to dig deeper and ask the hard questions, such as: How is it that one "just knows" they are trans? How do you know what it feels like to be the opposite sex? How can a doctor tell if someone is trans? Can you prove it one way or the other? Does my child's premature birth have something to do with this? Are transgender brains the same as those found in the opposite sex (or, worded differently, can you have a male brain in a female body, or vice versa)? It is common during this first phase for parents to frantically seek information and scour the Internet for clues. It can come to entirely dominate your life for months or even years.

Some spend time deconstructing the logic of trans or determining whether there's an argument to be made that transition will benefit children—particularly because the very first thing a parent in this situation will hear is the standard refrain, "Would you rather have a living (son/daughter) or a dead (daughter/son)?" In other words, to stand in your child's way—to prevent even medical transition—is to inevitably lead to your child killing him- or herself. Of course, doctors and therapists will always say this directly in front of your child, both adding to the emotional manipulation of the parent by the child and medical or mental health professional and increasing the odds of suicide, which is well known to be highly prone to contagion and suggestion.

Invariably, after weeks or months of research, PITT parents conclude that their experience is not at all uncommon and that their children are reading and acting from a script. This form of trans is not an organic development or innate, as some might tell you. You will read story after story showing how the trans coming-out ritual is the same across many families—this is unsurprising since they often follow the same online playbook. One day, PITT parents begin to realize that most medical and mental health professionals will offer no other answers and that this whole transgender thing really is illogical. It's an eye-opening, eureka-moment experience when you learn you have been duped into believing nonsense. There are no statistically significant studies that back up core claims and no real proof of anything. It's worse than that, though, because it's nonsense rife with ideological fervor. You try to articulate these facts, while searching for the real reasons for this sudden change in your child. And, suddenly, unexpectedly, you are very far removed from the glitter, rainbows, and unicorns and in a dark place filled with pornography, groomers, and trans cheerleaders, as well as peer groups and overreaching schools and activist teachers who are telling your children that they can save them from you.

Parents in this stage often discover the real reason or trigger why their child began to feel he or she is "trans." They might find it happened at school. Without their permission or knowledge, the school might have encouraged their child to adopt an alternate identity or name and has purposefully concealed this from them, the "dangerous" parents by definition, since the prevailing view is that parents who do not support immediate social and medical transition are abusive. More often, parents will find that the trans identity emerged from the Internet—particularly from social media, peer-group echo chambers, and TikTok videos. Some PITT authors have also recounted harrowing discoveries related to porn and grooming. While searching for the root cause of this rapidly emerging trans identity, parents frequently delve into academic and medical research, questioning the "scientific" underpinnings of transgenderism. When they find that the evidence is shaky at best, some are inspired to write for PITT to bring this awareness to other parents.

On PITT, some parents choose to write about their confusion, fear, and disbelief over their child's sudden personality shift. Some delve into their frustration and terror after realizing that the medical and therapeutic communities that they had once trusted as "experts" are no help and only encourage medical pathways. Others explore the philosophy and logical fallacies of trans ideology to point these issues out to readers, to try to understand how their children fell into the trans logic trap (often through schools, online forums, and peer groups), and to see if they can map a route out of it. Still others try to understand the science—or lack thereof—underpinning the idea of trans, and the medical risks of transition that remain willfully unstudied. Parent writers have also used the forum provided by PITT to rail against the institutions that prop up the trans regime—Planned Parenthood, the American Civil Liberties Union, medical associations, prominent newspapers, and even governments. And still others imagine what comes next—a future when everyone will see this immense scandal as we do. Like all of the other PITT authors, our own experiences inform our writing, work, and mission.

Josie's Story

My son became trans-identified back in 2019 at the age of fifteen. He was a typical boy, and I didn't believe he was trans. I knew something else was going on. I started researching and joined groups of parents and realized how many other parents were going through the same thing or had the same story. I couldn't believe how indoctrinated my son was in his belief and that I couldn't talk him out of it no matter how hard I tried. He is my only child, and I refused to let trans ideology destroy my son and my family. I couldn't just wait around for the inevitable to happen. It was like watching a slow-moving train coming right at me. I had to do something. I was listening to a podcast by two therapists with expertise in this subject, Stella O'Malley and Lisa Marchiano, and they said the only way to stop trans ideology was for parents to organize. I heard this cry, and I decided I had to fight.

Abigail Shrier had just published *Irreversible Damage*. Then Keira Bell, who had been prescribed puberty-blocking drugs at the age of fifteen, won her case against Tavistock in the United Kingdom. Things seemed to be moving in the right direction, but I realized much of the discussion centered around girls. Lost in the emerging discussion was any mention of boys.

I became an accidental activist after my story titled "My Son Doesn't Want to Be a Man," which I wrote together with Angus Fox, got published and noticed. Eventually, my writing, along with essays written by others in my group, was relocated to PITT, and we put out the word to other parents in our internal networks that we would publish their original essays if they had something to say about their experiences in the world of transgenderism. I always thought that even if I couldn't save my own son, I could help other parents and call attention to what was really going on with gender ideology. That was and always has been the driving force behind my founding of and involvement with PITT. Writing and developing PITT has been very cathartic for me.

It gives me a great deal of satisfaction to help other parents. I do not want them to experience the pain that trans ideology has inflicted on my family and me. My story continues to evolve, and my son is still trans-identified. I would do anything to save him. Even if I can't, he can never say I didn't try everything to keep him from harm. I wish I had been able to read about stories such as mine when gender ideology first hit my family, and I wonder, if I had, would my family's story be any different today? Regardless of the outcome in my family's case, I'm glad we are now here to help others until this entire medical scandal ends.

Dina's Story

My son announced he identified as "trans" in July 2020 at the age of thirteen. From that moment on, my life was forever changed. I spent countless hours down the Internet rabbit hole learning (or so I thought) everything I could about trans, and why my son thought this applied to him, a typical, nonfeminine boy who had never exhibited any signs of dysphoria or stereotypical cross-sex interests or behaviors. There were no signs of hope on the Internet back then, just story after story of how affirmation and transition were the only options for my son. His sudden announcement was to be considered permanent and irrevocable.

After several disastrous brushes with affirmative therapists, our family decided to take the "watchful-waiting" approach and to let our son experience his childhood without the complications of social transition. At the same time, we blocked all outside trans influences, redirected our son to real-life activities, and cracked down on Internet and game usage to give him space to grow up without toxic interference.

While this was all going on, I managed to find the PROGDK group, specifically its support group for parents of boys, where I found kindred spirits. Back then, I vowed that, if my child and family came through this crisis intact, I would share my story with others. I could not stomach the thought of a single other parent going through the hell that I had been through. Eventually, with Josie and others in that group, I was able to find my voice through PITT. A year and a half later, my son desisted. In a gradual process that extended over months, he grew into his body and mind and found a new confidence in himself. With my own desistance story, I'm now able to make good on my promise to help others who are navigating their own crises and to embolden those who want to help fight the institutionalized evil and corrupt force that is gender ideology.

Why We Write about Gender Ideology

There are three types of people that are threatening and, therefore, absolutely intolerable to the trans ideology narrative: *desisters* (people who thought they were trans but then stopped thinking that way), *detransitioners* (people who "transitioned" to the other sex and are now reverting back), and parents who question.

We are part of the third group. We are parents who do not go along with the affirmative model, whereby children who say they are a different sex than their biology indicates must be agreed with, celebrated, and then physically and socially modified to support their delusion—making them lucrative medical patients for life. This model, against all reason, is the currently accepted way of thinking in most liberal Western societies.

The writings on PITT are by a number of moms and dads of all different political and religious persuasions who found each other through underground support groups across the world. We have just one thing in common—we all have children who, suddenly, out of the blue, announced they were "trans." After learning more, we came to realize that something was rotten in the state of Denmark, and some of us decided to work together to consolidate our voices and speak our minds in a forum where we could speak as directly and bluntly as necessary.

We are not writers. We are not activists by profession. We're your neighbors—regular people with regular jobs who have found ourselves secretly whispering into phones to journalists and penning emotional anonymous essays and first-person accounts as we fight for our children's mental and physical well-being in the shadows.

Why are we doing this all anonymously and in secret? Simple— we are scared that you will take away our kids, dox us, and destroy our livelihoods and, much more importantly, our families. Think we're being overly dramatic? Just ask anyone who's dared to publicly question trans ideology. This is exactly what is happening as our so-called liberal societies become increasingly illiberal, anti-free speech, and anti-family.

The easy thing to do would be to go along. But we've been inspired by vocal detransitioners like Sinead Watson, Grace, Garrett, Tullip, Helena, and more, who have been bravely speaking out about how they were let down by the medical community. We've decided that we are not going to stand silently by while our children are experimented on and misled by a quasi-religious cult ideology. We're not going to let our children down, like our society has let detransitioners down. We are the adults in the room, and we're not going away.

It's way past time for the world to understand that all three of these counter-ideology groups exist, that parents have been silenced for years, emotionally blackmailed and held hostage by threats to take away our kids, and that today's narrative of trans as a biological fact has gone unquestioned and has been permitted to run amok, with unfettered access to our schools, government, and media for far too long.

So, what do we hope to accomplish with our writing and this book? **We write so that you know we are here.** For every glitter/rainbow mom you see on the news repeating harmful stereotypes about girl and boy behaviors, gushing about how their little girl is a boy (or vice versa), and rejecting any fair-minded questions as cruelties that deny their child's very existence, there are ten, twenty—maybe even hundreds of us—unable to speak publicly but working hard behind the scenes to expose the complete lack of evidence and science behind trans.

We write so that you can see that the things people say never happen, do happen, and we can prove it because they happened to us. *"No teen would ever receive 'wrong-sex' hormones on their first visit without exhaustive exploration!"* Not true. Some of our kids have easily obtained wrong-sex hormones on their very first visit to a clinic. Doctors and clinics even readily give hormones to kids with well-documented physical and mental health conditions that should make them ineligible. How do we know this? This has happened to our own kids, many of whom have other serious physical and mental health conditions.

"No one would ever be censored for writing about their experiences in the United States—free speech is alive and well, and reports to the contrary must be hoaxes!" Not true. A number of us have been censored on *Medium* and other platforms when writing about trans topics, us included.

"Trans kids just know who they are!" Not true. Some of our kids thought they were trans, passionately and vocally, and have since changed their minds. And we know first-hand that our teens are no different than the average teen—immature, impulsive, changeable, risk-taking, and prone to making decisions and acting in a way they later regret.

"No one would ever take away your child just because you disagree about ideology!" Oh yes, frighteningly, they would, and that, too, has happened within our parent group. In many locations, schools, government bureaucrats, and courts currently exercise free rein to usurp parental prerogative and safeguarding when it comes to trans.

We write in the hopes that our stories open your eyes. We hope that our stories will lead you to think critically about the prevailing narrative and raise questions in your mind that you seek to answer. When you seek those answers, we hope you will see the vast multitudes of people and communities that are pushing back against trans ideology. Once your eyes are open, you will see them everywhere. Feminists, the LGB community, medical professionals who know their profession has been overrun by politics and ideology and is now causing harm instead of helping. Detransitioners who were irreparably harmed after going down an "affirmation" track. Journalists, academics, and writers who speak out with reasonable concerns and questions and who risk cancellation for so doing. And other parents, like those of us from PITT.

We write so that you might see that when parents do not agree that their kid is trans, it is not abusive, neglectful, or evil. There are thousands of parents like us who saw their child's trans identity emerge suddenly, after immersion in porn, Internet chat groups, and anime or following strong influence from peers who had already taken on a trans identity. We are nothing like the "horrible" unaffirming parents described in mainstream media. We love our kids. We don't beat them or throw them out of the house. Quite the opposite. We protect and shield them and give them the space to be kids as they work through their kid issues in a world trying with all its might to thrust them into adult situations with adult problems. We lovingly support our children while holding the line against "affirmation" because, unlike other modes of teen expression like emo and goth, trans comes at a much higher cost—drugs and surgeries are a central part of this fad. We know that elective cosmetic surgeries on sex organs for no physical reason, with myriad known side effects and a lifetime of required medication, are not good for our children's long-term health. Helping your kid grow up healthy in body and mind and comfortable in their own skin is good parenting, not child abuse.

We write because maybe, just maybe, our stories will be the straw that breaks the camel's back for you. That it brings about that peak moment where you say, "Okay, now this gender thing has gone too far, and I don't want any part of it anymore—maybe my blind faith in the idea of trans as noble and inclusive was misplaced." Maybe we can help you see that there are other viewpoints and that disagreeing with or being skeptical of trans ideology is not synonymous with bigotry and that that one-sided attitude has stigmatized even having a conversation about these very real and serious concerns.

We write so you have the courage to join us and speak up, knowing that you are not alone. Trans ideology falls apart like a house of cards under even the most superficial scrutiny. If you see us—with our children and families at stake—speaking out, maybe you will feel brave enough to speak up too—after all, your child may very well be the next kid captured by this new ideological fad.

We write because we believe that, with our voices and our writing, we can do our part to change how the public sees trans ideology and its associated corrupt medical practices before our children's lives are forever damaged.

Parents on Community Capture

1

Parental Dysphoria

I suffer from parental dysphoria.

Parental dysphoria is a new condition, growing in frequency as the transgender trend that is indoctrinating our children picks up steam. Specifically, it's the discomfort with your sense of self and view of reality that results from your child's sudden announcement that he or she is transgender. Parental dysphoria commonly results from the immense societal pressure to unquestioningly support your child's "gender journey," up to and including social transition to the opposite gender (or nonbinary), wrong-sex hormones, and surgeries.

Parental dysphoria involves the extended state of having to stay silent about something that you know will lead to tragedy, because you don't want to lose your child, your friends, your extended family, and your marriage—everything you've worked to build. You do this to preserve some small chance of having an impact, to keep your child close enough to eventually help them find their way out of this delusion. It's living with fear—fear of loss, fear of estrangement, fear of losing your own mind, fear of losing your integrity by denying your own instincts. Those who suffer from this condition, myself included, know this to be the most awful feeling you've ever experienced in your life.

If you suffer from parental dysphoria, you wish to say, "You were not born in the wrong body—that's impossible!" But you also know your child wants so badly to believe this that you aren't sure whether to lie or tell the truth about how you see things. So, instead, you say very little and pray every day that your child will find peace in their own body before it is too late, before your child denies and destroys their own sexual function and fertility and poisons their own body with synthetic hormones.

It's the pain surging through your very being as you pray this ideology will release your child from their delusion and give you your child back. It's the tears you choke back as you do your best to support your child despite their best efforts to push you away. It's holding your breath, not even knowing how you can carry on. It's a feeling of hopelessness you have never felt before.

It's the horror of being told by your other child, the one who serves as the pronoun police in your own home, that YOU are the one who isn't loving and supportive. It's the shame of realizing that you've lost your ability to be the adult in the room. It's feeling that the liberal, progressive values you instilled in your children are being used against you in a way you could never have seen coming. It's disheartening, destabilizing, and destructive.

Parental dysphoria is what happens when you are advised by a professional to call your child by a new name, one that represents to you a symbol of their deep pain, a name that is more likely to have its origins in Pokémon than in the family heritage you tried to pass on to them. It is the dissonance of having to validate a decision to transition at school made by a child going through a very confusing and difficult time in their life. It's the out-of-body experience of hearing your child say, "I am not the person you raised—I am someone else entirely." It's the loneliness of being the only person who thinks all of this is damaging to your child, rather than it being brave and liberating.

It's insane, actually, this parental dysphoria. It's insane to live with and to live through. It makes you gradually lose your own tether to reality, bit by bit, day by day.

We should all want to know why so many kids are declaring a trans identity. We should not simply accept this as normal, and we should certainly not teach it, nor enshrine it into law, until someone can demonstrate through unassailable longitudinal studies that any of it is valid in the first place! At what point will we collectively stop and question this? It's truly like living in an alternative universe! So many of these young people are being led astray by the very people who are supposed to protect them. Doctors and psychologists are no longer experts to be trusted.

Teachers and schools have not only betrayed their most vulnerable students by encouraging them down a path of self-sacrifice but have also destroyed the sacred bond they hold with parents to ensure the healthy growth and development of their children.

What is a parent to do when they suffer from parental dysphoria? Lean into the lie, hoping it will make it easier to keep the lines of communication open with our children as they mature, hoping that all the little questions you peppered in there along the way will help them to use their judgment and not their pain to make decisions about their own lives? Or do you try to cure your own dysphoria with action to repair the rift and to heal your child, despite the risks?

Parental dysphoria is to be told you are wrong when you know your instincts come from the deepest place a mother can ever draw from—the instinct to protect her own child. Our children, our friends, and our society are being groomed to believe a harmful ideology, and they aren't even aware that this is happening. Even though it's hard, I choose to treat my parental dysphoria rather than to live with, affirm, or validate it. That means I must keep speaking up. I must believe. I must never stop believing that my child's dysphoria can be healed, as can my own, that this cultural phenomenon will pass, as all trends pass, and that our children will come back to us, hopefully all still in one piece.

2

When the Village Turns on You

"It takes a village to raise a child," we are often told. Many interpret this saying to mean a community must work together to create a safe environment that allows for the mental and physical growth of all children. Today, unfortunately, in Canada, that village is working to separate children from their parents. Safeguarding protections have been cast aside, and community institutions and members such as public schools, teachers, hospitals, doctors, psychologists, social workers, mainstream media, and the legal system are preventing parents from protecting their children from a lifelong dependency on chemical and surgical interventions and the inherent risks that come with them.

The situation is often even worse for parents of children on the autism spectrum, parents like me who are trying to protect their already vulnerable child. Autism spectrum disorder (ASD) varies greatly from one child to the next, but common characteristics include black-and-white thinking, sensory challenges, and difficulties with interpreting social cues, processing language, planning, physical coordination, and proprioception. For girls on the spectrum, the process of menstruation can be extremely difficult to adjust to and manage, especially if extreme hormonal shifts, imbalances, or endometriosis accompany their monthly cycles. It is not uncommon for individuals on the spectrum to have digestion issues and food sensitivities that result in chronic stomach discomfort. Communication challenges associated with autism and poor mind-body connections can make it difficult for young people with

36

ASD to articulate their physical symptoms. In a nutshell, there are many reasons why a teen with autism may feel uncomfortable with his or her body, even before introducing confusing concepts like gender identity.

Children on the spectrum are especially vulnerable to a theoretical concept that suggests a person can be born in the wrong body and that identifying and transitioning to the opposite sex could relieve the individual from all the mental pain and physical discomforts they have been experiencing. Gender ideology conveniently avoids the obvious, that an individual's biological sex cannot be changed and that medical interventions are purely cosmetic and come with health risks, many of which are still unknown due to lack of research.

As a child growing up in Canada, I benefited from the "village." Before I started kindergarten, my retired neighbor read to me in English because my immigrant parents could not. The first time I ever put on a pair of ice skates or visited a museum was on a school field trip, and it was the librarian at my local public library who helped me fill out an application for a library card. These experiences complemented the efforts of my parents to positively impact my overall development.

Things are so different now. My child and I experienced a radically different village, a threatening one that actively sought to work against my efforts to protect and nurture my autistic daughter in her teen years. This village interpreted her nonconformity to gender stereotypes, her quirkiness, and her same-sex attraction as things that needed to be fixed medically. In order to be part of the community, she needed to fit a specific box, even if it meant taking lifelong medications and undergoing multiple surgeries. Because she wasn't mainstream, it wasn't okay for her to stay in her natural state. Meanwhile, I accepted and loved her differences and wanted to give her time to see if she could love and accept those differences in herself.

The "village" turned on me and tried to prevent me from fulfilling my responsibility to protect my daughter. The first stop was my daughter's public school, where gender ideology was introduced into the anti-bullying/sex education curriculum, not as a theoretical concept but as fact. The school curriculum told my vulnerable daughter that individuals who feel uncomfortable with their bodies and whose preferences and behavioral traits fit the stereotypes of the opposite sex are transgender and introduced the concept of "being born in the wrong body."

The next stop was the medical community. After she learned of the concept of trans and determined that it applied to her, we sought professional help. Every single one of the clinicians involved with my daughter instantly affirmed and confirmed her self-diagnosis of being trans and her belief that she required testosterone and a double mastectomy to survive. Keep in mind: this was back in 2016–2017. The medical community not only dismissed my concerns about the risks involved and the lack of assessment inherent to the affirmation model but also told me my questions were not supportive and were detrimental to my daughter's mental health. The "village" was telling me I was wrong and negligent for trying to weigh the benefits against the risks and for considering other less invasive methods of treatment. I quickly learned that I could not safely ask questions about these procedures. Nor could I demand that these clinicians evaluate the root causes of my daughter's distress and treat any coexisting conditions first, without the risk of having social services involved. Like the school system, the healthcare and social services system further ingrained into my child the concept of "being born in the wrong body" and the need for medicalization.

At that time, the gender clinic inside the children's hospital where my daughter was seen still acknowledged biological sex in their consent form for testosterone, making it clear that any medical interventions could only go so far, not to the point of literally changing a person's sex. It included the following language, "Even though I think of myself partially or completely as male, I am genetically, biologically and physically female." Today, the language in those consent forms no longer includes the words "male" and "female." They now refer to "masculine" and "feminine" traits, resulting in even less clarity and less reasonable possibility of informed consent.

Even at the time of my daughter's visits, important information was withheld from patients and their families before medical interventions were introduced. For example, none of the clinicians told me that, prior to the affirmation model, under the watchful-waiting approach to gender confusion, approximately 80 percent of patients with childhood gender dysphoria desisted and eventually accepted their biological sex and that many, if not most, grew up to be gay, lesbian, or bisexual. This was kept from me even after I told them my daughter was unsure of her sexual orientation. What does it say about a "village" that doesn't allow such children to realize their sexual orientation naturally, knowing that many would otherwise grow up to be gay, lesbian, or bisexual?

I was also not informed of the documented overlap of gender dysphoria with autism and other coexisting conditions despite the concerns I expressed about my daughter's black-and-white thinking, immature social skills, and body dysmorphic comments. What does it say about a "village" that immediately accepts a teenage girl's declaration that she is a boy without first considering whether she had experienced sexual trauma, suffered from an eating disorder or body dysmorphia, experienced painful periods, or was neurodiverse—or without first questioning or discussing any other potential causes of her distress?

It means the "villagers" have chosen to look away from the truth: that homophobia exists, that children and adult females are the predominant victims of sexual assault, that social media exacerbates body image issues, that the medical community has not poured time and energy into researching gynecological issues such as endometriosis, and that some people's brains just work differently.

Parents are undermined in other ways as well. There are cases of schools proceeding with the social transitioning of children despite the objections of parents who think a watchful-waiting approach is what their child needs. Parents who have not affirmed their child's gender identity have had their child removed from their care, and two court cases in British Columbia ruled against parents objecting to the gender-affirming medicalization of their child due to prior mental health concerns that had not been addressed under the affirmation model of care. The mainstream media further undermines parents by presenting affirmation as the only viable treatment and way a parent can show their love and support while at the same time refusing to report on the growing number of detransitioners.

It is hard to protect your child when the other "villagers" are holding your arms behind your back.

My daughter's gender dysphoria gradually resolved without medical interventions over a two-year period as she began to accept her bisexuality and learned how to better cope with the sensory and social challenges of autism. I shouldn't have had to fight "the village" to allow my kid time to do that.

3

The World Needs All Kinds of Boys

My son came out as trans to me by text message almost three years ago. His message basically said, "I am trans, and I need hormones." He had been "feeling this way" only for about a month prior to that and had found answers on the Internet. From there, he planned a quick medical transition over the summer between his ninth- and tenth-grade years in high school, based only on his self-diagnosis and following very closely along with the plans of one of his friends who wanted to do something similar.

Like many other examples, this came totally out of the blue—so much so that I thought he was joking. There were no signs of gender nonconformity before this. Like the other boys following a similar path, he is brilliant, sensitive, creative, quirky, kind, and empathetic, and he loves animals. He is gifted in computer programming, security, and hardware. This last trait has the unanticipated downside of limiting our ability as parents to meaningfully monitor and regulate his computer usage.

One of the most harmful things about gender ideology is that it pushes sex and gender stereotypes to extremes. It is not liberating; it is enslaving. It tells our delightful sons that since they like cute animals, are slight in build, prefer bright-colored hoodies, and are kind and compassionate, they must be girls trapped in boy bodies. It then forces them into the role of "woman" at a critical time when our society needs men like our sons. If you believe transwomen are truly women, then we are saying society does not need men like our sons. Effectively, they are being cast out of society and reinvented as "women," which will result in an erasure of the brilliance of what some men can do for humanity.

Our sons are brilliant. Like many other gender-confused young men, my son is gifted. He is very likely highly gifted, though he has not had an IQ test. He is so talented with a computer it is astonishing not just to his proud parents but also to his teachers and our academic friends. He has what it takes to do things like: safeguard humanity from dangerous proliferation of AI by unscrupulous people, enhance privacy and security for everyone using the Internet, sound the alarm about the dangers of social media and implement solutions to this challenge . . . the list goes on. He has the skills, knowledge, ethics, and morals to help us all if tech goes dangerously awry. Like many other boys in his situation, his intellect, skills, morals, values, and compassionate heart give me hope for our future.

Our sons are sensitive, kind, empathetic, and compassionate people. I am not sure why society wants to associate those traits only with women these days. Being female, I can attest that not all of us are naturally that way—we are human, after all, with all of our individual variations. I feel really sad that men are not supposed to have those traits, or they are called feminine, or they are teased for it as children. I think that it is time that the idealized stereotype of the hypermasculine, gun-toting, emotionless, and brawny macho man goes away. We need men who are like our sons to balance out society. Men with those qualities will make measured, thoughtful, and caring leaders who could help guide us through the challenging times ahead, with climate change, social upheaval, and the other perils that face us. They may take a more compassionate approach rather than just adopt the stance of warriors.

Society needs both men and women and the unique traits, skills, and talents each contributes. Without one or the other, we would be off balance, and the worst attributes of the dominant sex would be amplified. When men and women work together in a complementary way, the best attributes of the human species are realized. Similarly, we need the natural variations that exist within our separate sex-based groups. If all women are hyperfeminine, adhering to rigid gender roles and only participating in stereotypically female pursuits, we miss out on the talented female physicians, politicians, scientists, and others in traditionally male professions. If all men are hypermasculine, we miss out on the caring teachers, nurturing fathers, male nurses, and other men working in stereotypically female professions. The end result would be a stagnation of society that is polarized in the extreme.

Gender ideology is pushing this extreme segregation on our children. It is not progressive; it is regressive in the extreme. I don't want to live in a world where all boys and men who have so-called feminine traits or are softer in temperament than what we deem typically "masculine" are pushed to become trans women. I want to live in a balanced world where we accept men and women for all of our wonderful natural variations. The future of humanity depends on it.

4

Letter to a Well-Meaning Bystander

Dear Friend,

I appreciate the concern expressed for my daughter and any difficulties that she and our family might be facing. I know your sympathy is sincere, and you would like to be helpful if possible. I thank you for your suggestion of [embracing "his" new identity, finding a gender counselor, joining PFLAG or Gender Spectrum, giving unqualified support to "trans rights," working to ensure that society accepts "him as he truly is," seeking out an affirming religious congregation] because of the spirit in which it was made—it was motivated by your care and compassion. I value our friendship and will trust in your ability to entertain an honest response from me that you may not have expected, to trust that I also sincerely mean well.

What would actually be most helpful to our family right now, and to many other people who are in or are soon to be in similar situations, is your open-minded, slow-paced, and careful consideration that maybe much of what you've heard about gender identity and transgender youth is actually wrong. That the recent enthusiasm for encouraging young people along a path of opposite-sex make-believe, proceeding step by step into sterility and lifelong medical dependency, is not simply a generous extension of recognition and acceptance to a long-oppressed minority. Rather, it's a dangerous embrace of a new faith in preference to and denial of objective reality, tangled up with a contagious moral certainty, that has jumped the rails of good sense. In this respect, it looks like just another in the series of retrospectively bizarre cultural manias that punctuate history: the lynching of heretics, the worship of miraculous relics of martyrs, the creation of utopian communities with free sex or no sex at all, the spread of multilevel marketing and pyramid schemes and the exuberance behind financial bubbles in general, the belief in recovered memories and ritual satanic abuse, the fervor of movements like the Children's Crusade of 2012, the promise of spiritual discovery through LSD, etc., etc. Eventually, this craze too will burn out, but not before leaving many thousands of people badly injured who were unlucky enough to be emotionally vulnerable and suffering from one of the perennial anguishes of being human at the moment when a new magical solution swept through the popular imagination.

Charles MacKay, in *Extraordinary Popular Delusions and the Madness of Crowds*, wrote that "men, it has been well said, think in herds; it will be seen that they go mad in herds, while they only recover their senses slowly, and one by one." Although many claims made today would have baffled nearly anyone twenty years ago, the herd now has largely accepted, or at least submitted to not publicly doubting, the following:

1. Everyone has an innate gender identity that is independent of biological sex and can only reliably be recognized by oneself through introspection.

2. Gender identity forms very early in life, is unaffected by social influence, and is thereafter stable. A child can accurately identify their own gender identity without fear that they may change their mind later in life.

3. Gender identity can be completely male, completely female, or some intermediate or fluctuating blend of characteristics traditionally associated more often with one sex. Any such gender identity is perfectly natural and just as healthy as another. Transgenderism is not a mental disorder nor a symptom of any such disorder.

4. Any psychological distress or maladaptive behavior that a transgender person exhibits should be attributed first to the minority stress of not being accepted by society for who they truly are. Only after full

medical and social accommodation has been made for their gender identity does it make sense to inquire into any other possible causes of psychological distress.

5. Psychological gender identity takes precedence over mere physical sex in two critical ways:

    a. Where they are in conflict, it is assumed that the mental self-image is more essential and immutable, more susceptible to accidental damage and permanent suffering than the body, so that it is the body that must change, through drugs and surgery. No psychological therapy that might question gender-identity claims can be permitted.

    b. Where society has seen fit to provide single-sex accommodations, the defining categories must now be reframed from objective physical definitions to subjective mental self-definitions. Anyone can choose their own category.

6. Although transgender identification in itself is completely normal and healthy, it demands aggressive, irreversible, and experimental medical intervention that should be paid for by others, as though it were a rare and life-threatening disease.

7. Questioning any of these claims is an expression of hate that will only contribute to the incredibly high suicidality of these perfectly healthy people and delay the life-saving medical and social interventions they require.

You've probably never seen it laid out quite like this, but I don't think this is an unfair mischaracterization of the essential logic behind the "affirmation-only" theory that has swept through many institutions recently. The conclusion all of the above is supposed to buttress is that immediate and unquestioning affirmation, including social and then medical transition, is the only helpful or ethical response to a claim of transgender identity by a young person. As gender-affirmation theory has gained currency over the past decade, we've gone from almost no one having heard of a transgender child to laws being passed against "gender-identity conversion therapy" and schools socially transitioning children without their parent's knowledge. Yet, I believe that if one spends enough time carefully considering each of the claims above, it's not hard to see that they are all quite doubtful, at best.

I don't actually know what you personally think of all of this. I suspect most people are reluctant to speak with full candor on this topic. Perhaps your life has been minimally touched by this issue so far, so you haven't been compelled to think deeply about it or do any independent research. Maybe you've heard that science stands behind gender affirmation and have seen no reason to question that. Maybe you have noticed some contradictions or inconvenient unexplained facts, but politeness, agreeableness, and a desire to avoid unnecessary trouble have led you to nod along with the herd. Maybe it has hit your life hard, through a family member, and in your desperate love for that person, hearing only from experts who advise it's the only way, you have gone along with transition and embraced the new religion because you need to believe that things will work out for the best.

Whatever you really think, I do not expect or even hope to affect your opinions quickly through argument. That's not how people work, including, of course, myself. Once formed, from whatever origin, opinions are sticky things. They become bound up with our ego, our delicate self-regard. It takes time and privacy to slowly reexamine inconsistencies that pop up among our beliefs and decide how best to grind them against one another and eventually prune them back into respectability. We need to find our own way, our own narrative, out of that thicket. That's why, although people go mad in herds, they recover their senses only slowly and individually.

What I do hope is that the concern and generosity that led to your expression of support could extend into doing me the favor of reading some things of which you might not have been aware and seeing where that leads, including, among many other sources, *Material Girls: Why Reality Matters for Feminism* by Kathleen Stock, *Trans: When Ideology Meets Reality* by Helen Joyce, and the Parents with Inconvenient Truths about Trans (PITT) Substack.

Please take your time.

Although it's easy to miss if you're not looking for it, there is a rapidly growing group of dissidents from the dominant narrative about gender identity and affirmation. This group is much more ideologically diverse than its opponents would like to portray and, in my experience, substantially from the left/liberal side of their national cultures. People tend to fall out of the dominant belief and into the dissident camp via one of four routes: as medical or mental health professionals whose direct experience leads them to question affirmation-only therapies; as parents of gender-conforming teens who suddenly adopt a transgender identity and pursue medical transition under obvious social and ideological influence; as feminists or gay rights supporters who see mission drift in the evolving LGBTQ+ as undermining and damaging what their movements previously stood for; and as people who adopted a transgender identity themselves, for some months or decades, and who eventually found their way out of it or wish to dampen the current enthusiasm. All of these dissidents have things to say that you might find surprising, informative, or compelling, and they are just the tip of the iceberg.

Sincerely,

A Loving Parent

P.S. Nothing is more important to most parents than the welfare of their children. There's an urgent reality to having a child who decides that they want medical sex transition that cuts through the idealistic generalizations pushed by "experts." Many parents with science backgrounds have done more and better investigation of the research basis for gender affirmation than the educators, therapists, and doctors engaging in it. As noted, an excellent starting place is PITT's Substack. An early prominent voice in the wilderness was U.S.-based 4thWaveNow. In the United Kingdom, Transgender Trend became a similar rallying point. Worldwide there are now many grassroots parent organizations with their own websites. Recently Genspect has formed as something of an umbrella group. It's a deliberately fostered misconception that "gender affirmation" is backed by solid science. Although there's a large body of publications by "affirmation" advocates, the literature is very low quality and rife with shoddy methodology and unchallenged confirmation bias. The Society for Evidence-Based Gender Medicine offers a critical review of gender medicine's scientific claims. Meanwhile, Thoughtful Therapists is a group of mental health practitioners who work with the relevant patient group and are skeptical of affirmation-only recommendations.

5

Dear Parent: Do You Really Know What's Best for My Son?

Dear Parent of My Child's Friend,

I'm so thrilled that you asked about continuing our conversation about the medical decisions we have made for our child and your very relevant opinions about said decisions. I am confident that you came away from our meeting knowing that, despite our obvious ignorance and bigotry, we are decent-enough people and may be capable of being enlightened by a "well-informed" educator such as yourself.

After all, you've had at least five interactions with my child in the past four months since our kids became . . . friends? What does one call a relationship where, with your approval, your daughter purchased estrogen made by a "bathtub brewer" who concocts his mixtures in what is surely a sterile environment in his home and sells it online to anyone willing to pay, and then injected it into my son? I know your highest priority is to keep my son safe. I mean, not safe from illegal, unregulated substances that will sterilize my child within four months, but safe from meddling, backward parents like us. As you said, isn't it better, given that my fifteen-year-old kid is dead-set on starting hormones, that he do so in your home? I mean, if he were playing Russian roulette, I'd rather him pull the trigger in the safety of your living room than just about anywhere else. Having you overseeing that is immensely comforting. It takes a village!

As for my simpleton viewpoint on medicalizing children who adopt a gender identity, I know the year and a half I have spent tirelessly searching for the latest and highest-quality research and articles regarding hormones and blockers, and hearing from therapists, endocrinologists, biologists, physicians, gender clinicians, young detransitioners, and trans adults, can't compare to all the (likely two or three) trans people you know well who are all really happy with their transitions. Obviously, their experience is a mirror image of my child's. And despite the words of detransitioners about how they told others how happy they were at every step of their transition even while keeping their own mounting regret at bay, I'm sure those you're close to couldn't possibly be questioning whether committing to being a lifelong medical patient with a future of known health issues, the loss of their fertility, and an existence based on convincing others you are something you never can be is a great way to live out your days. Why let the recent shifts in Sweden and Finland—two of the most trans-friendly countries in the world who have severely restricted medical transition for those under eighteen because of the high risk of negative effects and growing concerns about regret, and the lack of evidence that medicalization is effective for managing dysphoria—color your opinions, which are clearly unbiased by facts? And how could my meager, desperate concern for my vulnerable and mentally fragile child hold up against your innate knowledge that, as an academic, you simply know better. Clearly, you're willing to sacrifice your career (and the best interests of your family) by overstepping your bounds and running roughshod over our parental authority in your righteous indignation. Your daughter knows better, too, because, as she said, lots of her friends have done it. Who would ever doubt the sage wisdom of an eighteen-year-old?

I can understand your significant frustration that we will no longer let our child spend time in your home. I'm sure those two or three times you had him over for dinner (and an injection!) were wonderful. No doubt our kid spared you the insults, the anger, the unwillingness to lift a finger, the disdain, the casual but consistent reminder that he DOES NOT CARE about you. You probably heard an earful about how abusive we are, despite us making sure that he eats well and has nice clothes and a comfortable, safe home, that he gets to and from activities, and that he has ample access to music lessons, extracurricular activities, and anything else he's willing to participate in that gets him out of his own head—despite our working with his teachers and school administrators to make sure he gets the support he needs. It's incredible he's survived this long in our hateful environment.

At the same time, I can't help but wonder why you weren't there at his bedside as I was for the three days in a row just a few short years ago when he was admitted on a 5150 (the first time). You know, that time when he had five months of therapy in the intensive outpatient program, when there was no mention of gender dysphoria and no referral to the in-house gender clinic? I don't remember seeing you when we rushed him to the hospital after he fell and split his forehead open after he slipped on the concrete, refusing to let his collection of pinecones fall. I missed you at all of the dentist appointments when the staff had to hold him down to clean his teeth. And who could forget that night when he ripped out his own newly cemented orthodontics because he didn't like the feeling of metal in his mouth? Remember how exciting that was? No? I missed you essentially every night of his childhood, when he and I would snuggle in his bed, reading and talking and then waiting until he finally fell asleep so that I could start my night's work. You must have been busy all of those long nights when we were helping him finish his science fair projects and prepare for his exams. I also note that you were unable to patiently sit with him as he worked through new pieces of music or find time to make it to just one of his countless band performances. We certainly missed you at all of the concerts and plays we went to, all of the trips to exciting faraway places. So sorry you couldn't be there on the countless grocery-store runs, when I would take his hand when he started running wild in the aisles and feel his little body relax, relieved to be unburdened of his freedom.

Surely you have insight into our child that we couldn't dream of, and I am eager to take in all that you have to share. Truly I am. Because if there's one thing I am dedicated to, it's finding out what is best for my beloved child—the path forward that will keep him safe from his own worst impulses and allow him the space to grow and explore and develop into the fullest version of himself. If you hold the answer that has eluded me all of these years, I want to hear it. If my child has confided the true source of all of his distress, please let me in on his secret. If you have solved the mystery of how to tell who will and won't benefit from the magical transformation from male-looking person to female-looking person, I eagerly await this revelation (as do thousands and thousands of other parents dedicated to the health and well-being of their child).

If not, I have heartfelt advice for what you can do with your know-nothing opinions, and I'm definitely looking forward to sharing it with you.

Sincerely,

The Parent of Your Child's Friend

6

The Shunning

This is written for my family and friends who have not supported me or been by my side during the hardest time of my life.

My son told us two years ago that he was "transgender." I immediately knew that something was off, that something else was going on with him. I researched, for endless hours, as all parents in this scenario do, and what I found out—that this is a social contagion and that kids on the autistic spectrum are especially vulnerable to the trans ideology—only reinforced my skepticism.

When tragedy strikes, you find out who your real friends are.

I shared with friends what had happened. They were hesitant to believe me. They said there have always been trans people. Even though they have known my son his whole life, it didn't matter. Even though my son had never had any signs of gender confusion and was a typical boy, they doubted me. They blamed my parenting or my husband for not having stricter boundaries. They made me feel awful, more than I already did.

If my son had cancer, my friends and family would not tell me that his cancer was due to my parenting. Rather, they would ask what they could do to help me. They would read up on the literature. They would write letters or make calls for me. They would care. They would be worried about me. Not so with trans. Once you make the mistake of telling your family and friends about your predicament, you are treated like the worst human being. All your political and social capital, all that history, is tossed aside. There is only trans, and you are a bad parent if you do anything but throw a party—and if you do throw that party, you are now brave in the eyes of those you love. You will make them so proud.

Now some members of my former social support network have said they do support me. But, they do nothing to help, aside from patronizingly telling me how I should feel or suggesting that I medicate myself for anxiety or depression. They are upset that I'm not myself. They tell me to stop feeling sorry for myself. It's hard to be around them. They make it even worse.

I avoid everyone. I worry about being judged or called out when I don't use the girl name. The name I will never use.

What is it really like to have a trans-identifying child? It's the worst feeling you can ever imagine. Your child, who you raised and loved, now tells you everything you knew about them is wrong, even when you know you are right. You are the parent, after all, charged with the most important job of your lifetime—raising your child to be a healthy, responsible adult. Now you can't do that. You know in your head this is wrong, but everyone around you tells you that you must affirm.

The doctors are atrocious. They have no sympathy for you. You are on the same level as a murderer, likely to cause the death of your fragile child. You will never see such disregard or disrespect as a parent as you do when you question trans ideology in the context of your child. Your feelings don't matter. They no longer carry weight, even though, just the day before, you were a respected member of society and well liked in your social circles. You will be told you need to get over it. You're the problem. You have a daughter now. Accept it, or your child will kill "herself." And it will be your fault.

Your friends shun you. Your family blames you. You're lucky if your spouse is on the same page. You have no one. You imagine killing yourself to escape. Meanwhile, your child changes his name at school and receives accolades from the school's staff—thugs and overreachers who believe they are being righteous. Keeping secrets from parents used to be called predatory. Now society sees these enabling, abusive usurpers as your child's comforters and safety net while you are the enemy.

You cannot sleep, but you must because it's your only escape. Your last thought is this nightmare. It is also your first thought when you wake up. How will you keep your child safe when the world is against you, even those you thought were on your side, even your siblings, even your spouse? You plot your next move. All you think about is saving your child.

When this nightmare ends, and it will, how will you get those years back? How will you ever trust again? How will you ever feel emotionally safe in your home, in your community? Will your friends and family apologize and admit they were wrong? Will the doctors and schools apologize and admit their mistakes? Will they just pretend they were there for you and you were to blame because you were too difficult to be around? Because you were not any fun anymore, too anxious, too depressed, too hard on yourself?

This has changed me forever. Part of my heart has been taken from me, and my anger is unbearable. But what have I learned? Only one lesson: I will never trust those same people ever again.

7

A Heap of Hatred

Parenting a child caught in ideological thinking who adopts drastically changing social tones and uses manipulative language that obscures truth requires one to hold on tight to their sanity, with both hands.

Since my fourteen-year-old daughter has taken the path of trans identification, I have walked, jogged, and run on a parallel path of my own, full of reading, research, podcasts, YouTube watching, information gathering, support seeking, hate receiving, attempted indoctrination, blatant dismissal as a parent, and endlessly heedful conversations with my child. To say that this is stressful is a gross understatement.

To imply that the peaked parents of otherwise "affirmed," love-bombed, and pedestalled kids might be having a hard time is an enormous underestimation. We are not okay! I am not okay, but I have decided to take the hurt and anger, the disrespect and negation, and the insults and unjustified reprimand that I receive on a daily basis and use them to fuel the fire that will keep me pressing forward in my efforts to help derail this dangerously fast-moving train.

Through the commitment I have made to the preservation of my child's mental and physical health, I have been showered with hostility and disapproval. In trying to keep my daughter grounded in reality and open to thoughts and ideas other than those provided to her by the irrational ideology she has adopted, I have been peppered with ridicule and censure. Because I refuse to get my daughter a place in line for her share of the puberty-blocking drugs, cross-sex hormones. and amputations being actively introduced to all children, I have been called unloving, unsupportive, and unfit as her mother.

I have received more negativity and attacks on my character in the short time my daughter has been saying she's a boy than I have at any other time in my life, from those who know me and from those who don't. These insults and barrages have not been in response to any actual neglect or abuse of her. Rather, they arc in response to my lack of instructed celebration of my kid's perceived transgenderism, my refusal to boast about her stunning bravery for being a trans kid, and my hesitance to medically transition a minor. Further animosity has been thrown in my direction for my noncompliance with the doctrine of a religion that I don't believe in.

I have been vilified to both of my children by their all-affirming father—but to my credit, and by my luck, this has not been enough to break the bonds my children and I share. I have been undermined by my "concerned" sister for expressing to her my worry over the medical and mental health issues that my child may be facing, and thus I have been forced for the first time to feel like I need to protect my child from her aunt. I have been placed in the category of "potentially unsafe parents" by my child's school while they hide details about her, details that I am fully aware of, in a misguided and underhanded effort to "protect" her or out of fear for their livelihoods.

There have been times that I have felt like giving up, calling her "he," and letting the mystified individuals and the delusory sect that have surrounded my daughter win. I have had moments of anguish over the thought that others suddenly consider me villainous in my otherwise reputable story. While I have never had reason to question my mental health, the steep uphill battle toward my child's emancipation from a cunning club that would like to see her drug addicted and surgically modified as soon as possible has given me one. But it is not enough to knock me down completely, and every time I get back up, it is with a rejuvenated passion to see the walls around a fallacious fad fall.

This heap of hatred, this pile of perpetual reproach, is not big enough to smother my spirit or to quiet my voice. I will take ill-founded comments like "you can have either a live son or a dead daughter" and wrap them in the reality that I want a healthy, happy, and whole child instead. I'll drown the threats of losing my child to social services or to her father in the knowledge that gender ideology will eventually be exposed for its widespread mind-wash and its mass medical malpractice. The people who have turned against me will receive easy forgiveness upon waking up from the nightmare they had deemed a progressive and inclusive dream.

As parents who can see the wolf inside the proverbial sheep's clothing, we are faced with the daily struggle to do right by our children while deflecting the poison arrows that are constantly flying toward them and ourselves. With jobs and responsibilities, brave faces, and exhaustion, we continue to work toward the common goal of abolishing a noxious ideology and helping to save the remainder of a battered generation of youths.

Parents are drawing from their diminished wells of energy and their depleting emotional reservoirs to hold on to the truth and our sanity with both hands. Tired fingers return change-affecting emails, send out important tweets and posts over social media, and write truthful accounts of the damaging effects of gender ideology on their children and our society. Wary eyes read unnerving and astonishing articles and books that they would rather not read to build an informed arsenal that may help save our children from the inevitable mental and physical decay of experimental medical transition.

As the social and political tables begin to turn, ever so slightly, we can pull the strength we need to finish this fight from the awareness that we have already made a difference. We can gain much-needed confidence through the knowledge that lawsuits against butcherous gender clinics and devious school boards are beginning to create a wave of redress. The time is coming that our children will begin to hear whispers of truth in their social circles and start to shed the shackles of their "gender" indoctrination. The ever-growing community of vocal and determined detransitioners are purposefully serving as living proof of the devastating effects of youth transition, blowing the whistle on rushed affirmation by mental health and medical professionals, and sounding the alarm to end this maiming practice.

I will not come through this battle for child protection, the restoration of parental rights, and the return to rationality unscathed—but if my daughter does because I wouldn't quit, I will be okay.

Parents on Community Influences:
Peer Groups, Teachers, and Schools

8

Pronoun Bullying at School

I applaud all parents who have done so much to bring the concerns and needs of our children—our quirky, unusual, brilliant, awkward children—to light. These are strange times we are living in, and I think it's much harder to grow up in the weird online garden of social media and virtual communication than it was back in the days of playing in the streets and woods with one's friends. Teachers and schools are reacting to this difficulty, and though I know their response always comes from a good place, sometimes their solutions create problems of their own.

One thing that's made me uncomfortable lately is the introduction of "personal pronoun choice" to elementary school kids. I learned recently that this is being done at my child's school by a new teacher and that it is presented in the part of the curriculum that's about respecting and loving other people.

Very nice, to respect and love other people. All types of people are worthy of love and respect, including people not like us and people we disagree with. But are we sure that this measure is respecting and loving people? And all people, not just some people? And is introducing this in elementary school at all reasonable?

Kids of elementary school age make things up. If you were to ask a classroom of elementary school students to raise their hands if they play the piano, more arms would go up than kids who actually play the piano. If you were to ask how many are acrobats, half the kids who've ever botched a cartwheel will raise their hands. Depending on the day, you might even encounter kids claiming to be another species, like a cat, a dog, or a tiger. Is it really reasonable to ask kids that age what their preferred pronouns are?

Let's set aside the fact that we're talking about elementary school kids who barely know what a pronoun is and who may be unclear on the actual biological difference between boys and girls. The potential for grammatical confusion is there. In another time, their answers would have been widely seen as funny. What I'd like to talk about is not so funny, though: the use of the pronoun question as bullying. I'd like to be able to say to my daughter's well-meaning teacher that, in many cases, asking a school-age child what her pronouns are isn't nice in the least—it is, to the contrary, opening a new door for cruelty.

There is more than one way the pronoun question may appear as bullying. The first, which will fly under the radar of well-meaning administrators and teachers, is that it calls out the odd kids. When you ask boys and girls who are seen as odd or who do not conform to gender norms (e.g., kids like mine), the question, "What are your pronouns?" may make them feel singled out. Other kids may take to asking this question on purpose to single them out and get away with it ("I was just trying to be inclusive!"). They aren't going to ask this of the little girl who performs girlishness perfectly or the little boy whose boyishness is impeccably demonstrated. They are going to ask the weird kids, the tomboys, the twee. My kids.

I am relieved that my daughter is not a tomboy. Not because I don't like tomboys, but because I think these are absolutely horrible times for a tomboy. Feminists (like my mother) fought for generations to secure for their daughters the right to things previously restricted to men: property, bodily autonomy, adequate math instruction, etc., and with one clever question, our girls can be thrust right back into that little gender box. The question, "What are your pronouns?" says to a tomboy, "You are acting too much like a boy." It says, "Are you a lesbian?" It says, "You're a freak" or "Stop acting like a boy." And it suggests, to that tomboy, that she ought to consider altering herself medically so that she might fit in better. The forced pronoun question can cause the child to feel a sense of disconnection from her body, which can be interpreted as gender dysphoria; in this, it is grooming for the transgender delusion.

As a geek from a long line of geeks, I am glad I didn't have to put up with this when I was a kid. It was probably better for me, in the long run, that other boys just called me "weirdo" instead of pushing me to question whether I was really a boy at all. I'm also glad that my mother didn't have to put up with modern gender ideology when she was crossing gender lines in her work. She was lucky: she was from a generation where women felt they were doing important work by expanding into a man's role—and not from a generation where a woman expanding into a man's role has her very sex questioned. Will my daughter be so lucky if she turns out to be a math nerd like her grandmother?

A second type of pronoun bullying is the sort my son has encountered repeatedly in camp, high school, and college: the pronoun gauntlet. On the first day of class or camp, all the students are called out front and center: they have to say, in turn and in front of all the other students, what their pronouns are. Teachers and professors may imagine this is a neutral, disinterested question, but that's not what it looks like from the other side. For some students, it's a moment of intimidation: it's a statement by the professor or teacher that the class is going to be run according to gender ideology and that skepticism or criticism will not be welcome. It's bad enough for the male students who have to say, "My pronouns are he, him, his," and be scowled at by the social justice warriors in the class. It's worse for the kids who don't want to answer that question for any number of reasons—they don't believe in the premise of the question, they think it's nobody's business, they don't feel their essence is encapsulated in pronouns—but who give an answer anyway because they fear if they pass on the question they will be treated worse. Indeed, for many kids questioning their gender or trying to understand their sexuality, like my son, it can make the situation worse. This ritual is hurting the people it purports to protect.

For the socially awkward, this can be an excruciating moment: they are called out on the carpet to explain personal things about themselves and to take a political position on one of the biggest controversies in the spaces they inhabit. Everybody is looking and listening—what will they answer? My son has found that if he responds "he/him," some students—especially those in the alphabet mafia—won't address him anymore in class because he's been marked as a "cis het" (i.e., straight man). If he responds "they/them," then his classmates will consider his opinion more, stop accusing him of mansplaining, and express more interest in conversing with him.

The pronoun gauntlet shoves kids into gender boxes that come with their own forms of punishment and reward. A girl who uses "she/her" pronouns and conforms to gender roles might be criticized for "performing for the patriarchy," and a boy who uses "he/him" pronouns and similarly conforms to gender roles might be criticized for "abusing male privilege." Meanwhile, a kid who conforms to the gender ideology of the alphabet mafia by using the right language and pronouns is rewarded. For example, if a boy answers "she/her," then he grabs the brass ring and wins the immunity token of oppressed status. Again, this system is grooming children into the transgender delusion.

For a time, my son suffered under the transgender delusion, and the pronoun gauntlet did indeed help to normalize that delusion in him. My son has never dressed or acted in a typical fashion for a boy (he conforms neither with straight men nor with gay men), not even when he was tiny, and classmates have always found him confusing. He's found that by using "they/them" pronouns and saying he's nonbinary, he can defuse some of the animosity that would otherwise be directed at him if he were to use "he/him" pronouns and say he's bisexual. In short, when faced with the pronoun gauntlet, he has sought to avoid bullying—but not by the sexist, homophobic dolts of yesteryear but by a cooler, more empowered group of sexist homophobes.

We are lucky that our son desisted. The self-rejection of transgenderism in children leads to an increase in self-loathing and, sometimes, a lifetime of medical complications. Desistance has come with a new set of problems, however. My son is now, secretly, an apostate from woke ideology. He can't talk about this with most of his peers or in classes, and it frustrates him. He feels that the LGBT community, which should be there to support a bisexual man like him in his love and in his difference, is not there for him. It's there even less for lesbian girls. If you don't toe the line of transgender ideology, you are no longer welcome under the rainbow . . . but that can be fixed if you play the pronoun game right.

We should all be kind to those adults who identify as transgender. To want to accommodate those few children who identify as transgender is an admirable impulse. But, when applied to children, kindness is not what the question "What are your pronouns?" achieves. The proportion of children who are gay, odd, or idiosyncratic, or who do not otherwise conform to gender expectations, is, has been, and will always be higher than the proportion of children who identify as transgender. Pushing them back into a different box isn't kindness. It isn't acceptance either—it's just a new kind of conformity. Even those children who feel they may be transgender don't want to be called out with that question all the time. So please, teachers and administrators, stop calling children out on the carpet to talk about their pronouns. Woke bullying is still bullying.

9

Schools Are Ground Zero of the Trans Epidemic

Our story of trans identification in our child doesn't start with loneliness stemming from the pandemic as the stories of many others do. It started about a year prior to the pandemic. I was taking time to deal with some childhood trauma of my own, with the help of a therapist. I dove into my healing and was fully engaged in it. Consequently, my daughter may have felt abandoned by me, for a time, during this process. She had just finished an animation camp and made some friends there who told her about an online drawing group. She was very excited and convinced us to let her have one of our old iPads and join the group. I was nervous about her being online at all. She was only ten, so we monitored her closely by becoming one of her online "friends" in this drawing forum. It seemed to be mostly young girls and seemed harmless, but looking back, I realize we didn't watch closely enough. This was where the ideas about sexuality and transgender identities started. At the time, I didn't realize what kind of actual physical and mental harm these ideas could lead to.

Over the next year, our daughter went through a plethora of identities. She started with aromantic (this apparently means not being attracted to anyone, which made sense since she was only ten), moved on to gay and nonbinary, and then ended up at transgender when she was in fifth grade. At first, I thought these were all harmless and part of exploring who she was, which seemed developmentally appropriate. Interestingly, this was only happening at school, where she had a group of girlfriends who were identifying as one of the many possible gender identities. With girls, these identifications often occur in friend groups, which points to the possibility that there is a social contagion at hand (young teen girls are particularly susceptible to social contagions). It becomes a means of finding one's place of belonging among peers and thus has a very strong pull on girls who struggle with fitting into their peer groups. Our daughter, who had been surrounded mostly by boys her whole life (her brothers and the neighborhood boys she played with), consequently had a hard time navigating female relationships. She also struggled with her place among male peers and in our family, being the youngest of three with two older brothers. I believe she struggled with feelings of not being valued as much as her brothers or boys in general. She never mentioned her new identity at home or to any of her extended family with whom she is close and spent much of her time. Her older brothers, to this day, don't even know it happened.

What we didn't know at the time was that the school she went to, an elementary school, was actively supporting her trans identity without consulting or even informing us. In the classroom, her teacher and thus all the students called her by male pronouns. Nobody asked us what we thought about this or if we had any concerns. We didn't know that adults were reinforcing this identity at school. We weren't consulted or asked for any background information on our child or asked what we thought of our daughter taking on this new identity. It was as if we had no insight into what may be going on with our daughter. The school made the decision to socially transition our daughter completely independent of us, her parents. I would never have imagined they would do this. It was as if we didn't exist! They may have considered this harmless, but it was not.

Schools are always talking about partnerships between parents and teachers. This was the opposite of that. They also were clearly not asked to act *in loco parentis* and should not have done so because I, the actual parent, was available and asking to be involved the whole time. They were willfully and intentionally keeping information from us because they deemed themselves more qualified and more responsible for our daughter's upbringing than us, her parents. They had to make all kinds of assumptions about us in order to draw this conclusion. They would have had to assume that we were not deserving of the information, or that we would not be capable of treating our child with love if we had the information, or that we had no interest in the information, or that maybe we would be abusive or that we would "interfere" in their social development of our child.

I got a call from the school counselor a few months after the school year started informing me that our daughter had confided in a friend that she was suicidal and was self-cutting. (I later found out children encounter suicidal language and self-harm videos when they stumble into trans narratives online and often end up mimicking the same language and behavior.) This took me by surprise as I had seen no evidence of it, but I was concerned, nonetheless. The counselor then convinced me to let my daughter see a "special" therapist from a local hospital that was contracted by the school district and specialized in "these kinds of issues." I met this therapist, and we discussed how my daughter was exploring her sexuality. I expressed that I, as a parent, thought she was too young to explore and understand the meanings of these words (such as aromantic, gay, nonbinary, transgender) but that my husband and I would love her no matter where she landed. Looking back, I realize this therapist didn't agree or disagree with me. She merely nodded. In retrospect, I'm not sure she listened to a word I said.

Our daughter saw this therapist weekly for two and a half months. I asked how things were going in therapy, and she would usually respond by asking me how things were going at home. I said things seemed fine at home. Looking back, I realize that she avoided answering my question. I thought they must not have talked about anything noteworthy, because I assumed this therapist would have told me when I asked. I trusted the therapist would involve me in the decision-making for my young child, since I was her parent and responsible for her.

A couple months later, I got a call from this therapist about our daughter . . . only she didn't refer to her as our daughter. She was using male pronouns and a name that our daughter had chosen, and she informed me that "he" wanted to be with the boys for an overnight school trip. She also told me that "he" wanted to reveal to us that "he" was a "he," and she was going to help "him" present this to us because "he" was very "nervous" to do this on "his" own. She called me on a Tuesday to give us time to "process" this information so our daughter could present it to us on a Friday. She gave us three days to process the idea that our daughter wasn't actually a girl. We had heard nothing of this very important detail until this point, even though I had very pointedly asked the therapist what they were talking about in their sessions several times throughout my daughter's time with this therapist, which was my legal right as a parent of an eleven-year-old child. How could she have failed to mention this very important development? It seems to me that she was purposely withholding that information from me. She was making assumptions based on very limited information, which was not only un-ethical but psychologically damaging to the trust between my daughter and our family. Technically, legally, I had the right to know this information since my daughter was still under the age of thirteen, and she broke the law by not disclosing that information to me.

My first response was, "Wait a minute. This doesn't make any sense. She just hosted a sleepover with six girlfriends and loved it. Why does she need to sleep in the same room with boys at an overnight function? This is starting to feel like a cry for attention to me. I think there's something else going on." I got no response to this observation. I didn't get any response to any of my observations sent to this therapist. It was as if we had no insight into our child's personality, and this person knew something so deep and meaningful from her ten half-hour sessions with our daughter that we had somehow completely missed in all our experiences with her from the moment she was born. Putting our daughter in an overnight school event with boys instead of girls is not something we were ever going to consider. There are so many reasons this would not be a good idea. I wasn't as concerned for her safety (this was fifth grade) as I was about putting her AND the boys in a very awkward situation. It didn't seem like a good idea socially at all, especially for a child who was having some social issues. I had a right to make that decision, and I felt like I was being coerced to agree with something that I didn't think was healthy or safe for my daughter or her classmates.

We never had the meeting where our daughter presented herself as a boy to us with the help of the school therapist. We felt the whole idea was highly inappropriate and that our reactions might cause strife between our child and us. This therapist was not helping our daughter by keeping things secret and not ever consulting us to get insight into what might be happening with our daughter and how we could work together to help her. The self-righteous idea that she knew our child better than we did, so well, in fact, that she was going to help her explain to us such a monumental deep truth about herself, was absolutely ludicrous. As is true with most parents, we know and care about our daughter best. We were there raising her from the time she was born, and we have a much deeper knowledge of our child than a therapist who has met with her for a total of only five hours. It is also ridiculous to believe a preteen child "knows herself" so much better than her parents. This flies in the face of everything known about child development. This therapist was not going to help our family through this period in our lives and reinforce trust and familial cohesion between our daughter and us. She wasn't even going to listen to us. That was clear. She had a script, and she followed it no matter what evidence was in front of her face.

We terminated the relationship with the school therapist, and I started my intense investigation into what it means to be "trans" and what is being done to help kids who identify as such. What I found during this investigation completely turned my world upside down. I consider what this therapist did with our daughter to be medical malpractice. She performed a clinical diagnosis and treatment without consulting us, the parents. That is illegal. I learned that if our daughter was just two years older, thirteen, we would never have been consulted about our daughter sleeping in accommodations with the opposite sex due to new laws and policies in our state and school district. I also learned that it is school district policy to keep trans identifications from parents if the child wishes, no matter the age. I learned that, in our state, there is a "conversion therapy" ban. This brings to mind the idea of "praying the gay away" or shock therapy and chemical castration drugs to "fix" a homosexual and make them heterosexual. These practices are awful, but that's not how that term is being used now. This newer definition disallows normal exploratory therapy when a child identifies as transgender. In many places, it is now illegal for a therapist to investigate why a child feels this way or to question how they came to this conclusion. Therapists can lose their license to practice. In what kind of therapy do we not ask questions about our perceptions? Isn't that the whole basis for any mental health therapy?

I learned what kind of drugs and horrific surgeries were recommended to children and teens who identified as trans to "align" their bodies to their perceptions. These medical "treatments" were meant to fix their feelings of discomfort with their actual sex by changing their bodies with harmful, irreversible drugs and surgeries. I learned that there were thousands of other parents out there who had children that were exploring these types of identities that had similar concerns to mine. I learned that they were scared to share their concerns for fear of losing their children to child protective services or some "glitter family" that offers to take in a child no matter how young to "save them" from an assumed "abusive and hateful" home, which in reality is likely none of those things. I did not know that children are encouraged by others to permanently rupture their connection to their parents—to distrust them, hate them, and leave them. In fact, these things have already happened to other families. I learned that many therapists, doctors, and school professionals were completely disregarding, undermining, and deceiving parents of children who identified as transgender, following a script that assumes the worst of all parents without considering any actual evidence. I was horrified! It felt like there was this system of rule that had been put into place overnight that was functioning to take these life-altering decisions about the health and safety of children away from parents, as if a difference of belief makes a parent unsafe or abusive. I felt an intense need to escape with our daughter to some safe place away from the misguided adults who seemed determined to lead children like mine down a path to being used as a medical experiment.

Because we live in a very liberal area and gender ideology seems to reign, our specific area didn't feel safe to me. I began to realize that asking questions about trans identification was not allowed. If I expressed any concerns, I would be considered a dangerous bigot. I soon learned that similar sentiments were true across our country and around the world. It seemed that there was no safe place to go to and no mental or medical health professionals we could trust.

We wanted to sue this therapist to make sure she didn't harm other families by keeping health information about children from parents. We sought professional legal advice, and we quickly realized that, since we lived in a very liberal area with liberal lawyers and judges, a ruling would very likely not be in our favor. We realized that we were in uncharted territory when we explored the idea of suing this therapist for medical malpractice. We also realized that we could potentially open our family up to scrutiny by the state, so we reconsidered. We closed ranks. We couldn't risk allowing the state to take our child away from us, as has happened to other parents.

We only spoke to close family and friends about what was happening. Even some of them treated us as if we didn't know our child and as if we were ignorant and intolerant. This is still a source of heartbreak. We are not unique in having this kind of a response from people who previously thought we were caring parents and who ignore all of that evidence to adopt the idea that anyone who doesn't immediately accept a child's declaration of a "trans" identity is a bad parent. This ideology has so infected our culture that many people seem to have completely lost their ability to reason when the subject comes up. There is very good reason to question social and medical transition and not any really compelling evidence that these treatments are safe and effective.

Once I had collected myself and felt I was beginning to see what we were up against, I asked the therapist for the notes from her sessions with our daughter. I was legally still allowed to ask for these as our daughter was still considered a minor in our state as a preteen. It took her three months to finally get me the notes that I had asked for several times. She apologized and said, "I'm so sorry. I completely forgot." She blamed the pandemic. When I finally received these notes, I realized the real reason this therapist "forgot" to give them to me. She had apparently decided our daughter was a boy in their first half-hour session together. We had no idea that she was using male pronouns for our daughter the entirety of their time together. This seems like a significant detail she might have mentioned in any one of the several times I asked what they had discussed. Their sessions seemed to consist solely of her teaching our daughter to advocate for herself whenever anyone "misgendered" her, including us, her parents, and her brothers, who were completely unaware any of this was happening. There didn't seem to be any help with some of the real social issues our daughter was having with her friends at school. Later my daughter reflected upon her time with this therapist and said, "Actually, she didn't really help me that much."

We took our daughter out of the public schools because we realized they were not acting in partnership with us as we had previously believed they were. I'm not sure when they decided we were the enemy of our child and that they knew better than we did as parents, but this is how we were effectively treated. This was so shocking to me and felt like such a betrayal as I had spent many years volunteering with this school. I knew many of the teachers and staff. I thought they knew I was a loving and dedicated parent! How could they so quickly change their perception of me?

The pandemic made our choice to pull our daughter out of school much easier than it would have been otherwise. At the beginning of the pandemic, all children were essentially homeschooled. Our daughter didn't have to feel singled out as if she had done something wrong. This was one of our pandemic silver linings. We are continuing to homeschool our daughter, and she is doing very well and is much happier than when she was in the middle of this social transformation at school. All her energy was spent "advocating" for herself whenever she was (mostly quite innocently) "misgendered" by her schoolmates. This identity was very wrapped up in victimhood, and it was the lens through which she viewed everything. It was a negative feedback loop and the mentality she and her friends seemed to be stuck in. Everyone was "against" them. They were "oppressed." They were miserable together and, therefore, not alone. Misery and self-righteous indignation were the price of admission into their social group, and my daughter desperately wanted to be part of a social group.

Not only was the school not our partner, but it was also actively working against our efforts to keep our child safe from harm. The schools are effectively diagnosing and therapeutically treating children when they help them socially transition, and they are not qualified to do this. In our case and that of many other families, they are doing this without the consent or knowledge of parents. Setting aside for a moment the issue of teachers diagnosing and therapeutically treating children, there are a number of things wrong with this approach: (1) it teaches children not to trust their parents; (2) it teaches children that their parents are not supportive of them; and (3) it supports the idea that children should keep secrets with adults who are not their parents. These are the exact same tactics used by predatory groomers. Even if grooming is not the school's intent, our children are learning that this type of predatory behavior is acceptable, which leaves them open to others who may try to take advantage of them in the future.

Social transition is not benign. As Stella O'Malley (a therapist in the United Kingdom who has worked with thousands of families of gender-questioning children) said in episode 40 of her podcast with Sasha Ayad, *Gender: A Wider Lens*, "Social transition is a powerful psychosocial intervention." School personnel are not qualified to socially transition children, much less to do it behind the backs of parents. Schools are seriously damaging the child-parent bond, functionally hindering the ability of parents to protect their children, and leaving them wide open to be preyed upon by others. This culminates in harms being done to children and families.

All of these issues don't even touch upon the reality that most children don't stop at social transition. Many of them will go on to take wrong-sex hormones and have barbaric cosmetic surgeries that have a whole host of harmful health and developmental consequences. A child cannot fully grasp how this will affect their future health and happiness. The social transition alone does enough harm by concretizing an idea that is not based in reality and teaching a child they are not okay as they are.

Our family was mistreated by the school and by this therapist. They broke something in our family that we had to work very hard to repair. There was trust and a closeness that had been damaged. But my newfound lack of trust in schools, government agencies, and professionals may never be repaired. Our life has been fundamentally changed and will never be the same. We will always be wary of any situation that might send our daughter reeling back into this way of thinking. We don't know who we can trust to support us and who will be working against us.

I am actively fighting this ideology in our schools, institutions, and culture. Consequently, I am now in a sea of parents and children suffering at the hands of gender-identity ideology. It's like we are in a never-ending *Twilight Zone* episode where the rest of the world is telling us that all of these harmful treatments are really good for our children, and we are crazy and bigoted to believe otherwise. If we don't agree to allow these harms to be done to our children, they may be taken away from us for their own "safety." I know families this has happened to. I see more and more families being destroyed by this daily. I listen to and read new stories of sons starving themselves to supposedly look more like a girl or of sullen and angry teen girls who hate their bodies because they were sexually assaulted and are trying to escape their bodies. I hear stories of confused autistic children who don't identify with performative sex stereotypes being convinced that that means they aren't the sex they were born with. I hear stories of gay and gender nonconforming children being told they must be the opposite sex. I see all of these kids dealing with the difficulties of puberty and peer relationships and grasping for a life raft, which they believe they've found in trans. While I am watching this all happen with horror, I just have no patience for those with a superior stance that think they are saving our children. The idea that they are protecting these kids isn't even laughable. It's tragic.

I watch these kids who are so confused and just trying to survive puberty (you remember how hard that was?) being told that their parents do not support them if they don't believe these delusions. I just have no patience for an ideology that tells kids to hate and leave their parents, the people who care about them the most. The ones who would protect them. I have no patience for people who really believe there are so many parents out there who hate their kids and are kicking them out of their homes. It just doesn't stand to reason. The thousands of parents I know are not doing this. I have no patience while people sit and celebrate the destruction of children who aren't theirs. These people don't know what they are celebrating. I see the wreckage. I see the families torn apart, not by the parent's doing, but by everyone who supports this ideology. I see the angry, hurt, desperate kids who never seem to feel any better because this is not a solution to their problems. I see the wreckage. I have no patience for people who vilify loving parents who don't buy the idea that their children were born in the wrong body. One that teaches their children to hate themselves and the people who love them the most. I have no patience for people who think children know themselves better than their parents do. What are parents for if not for guiding our children, precisely because our children DO NOT come into this world knowing how to behave and grow into successful adult humans?

I'm in the trenches. I see the wreckage, and it's devastating. I know thousands of families who are torn apart by this. The rest of you, the ones who don't see what's really happening, we know you mean well, but you are not helping when you support these ideas that function to destroy our families and our children. We are begging you to wake up and quit buying into this delusion. You think using different pronouns is kind or, at the very least, harmless, but it is not kind and it is not harmless. We understand that you have been fooled into believing this, but we can tell you from the trenches that it is not helping our children. It is not making them "happy." It's not saving lives. It's destroying families.

You young teachers who are coming out of college and being taught that you are fixing our children, we know you mean well. We know you care, but please realize that we know our children better than you do. It is not your job to psychoanalyze our children. You are not qualified to do so, and you have not been called on to do so. Many of you don't have children yet or, most likely, you haven't lived long enough to be humbled. I can tell you that raising kids will humble you. So will life experiences. I'm in my fifties and I continue to be humbled and to learn, not least of all by this experience. Please listen to those who have more life experience than you do. Age is not a thing to be derided as it usually coincides with the wisdom of humility. As you get older, you will begin to realize how mightily imperfect you are and how much you don't know. I hope that there is nobody there to tear you down and tear your family apart as you go through this process. This ideology captures vulnerable children. I hope you never have a moment where you were distracted and didn't see what was coming for your child, who was misled down a path to potential irreversible harm. This can happen in any home and in any type of family. Please consider what I am saying and realize that when you conspire with our children to hide these new identities from us, you are an active participant in their harm. I know this is not your intention. For those of you who know that there is something damaging about keeping secrets with our children from us but feel shackled by school policies, I empathize with you. I implore you to come forward with your stories, even if it is anonymously. We parents need your help saving our children. We know that is your desire too.

For many reasons, our family was lucky. Our daughter grew to be comfortable with her sex once we removed her from public school, once we took her Internet access away (she now has limited, monitored access), and once she became distanced from her old friend group. She had a falling out with her old friends and never expressed a desire to get back in touch with them. She has made new friends who are not entrenched in gender ideology. She has grown, matured, and blossomed, while her old friends seem to be stuck in the same old negative narratives that were holding our daughter back. We carefully had conversations with her on subjects that were tangentially related to her trans identification without challenging it directly. We found a therapist who treated us as a whole family unit and helped us see where we needed to improve our family dynamics. We let her know that we will love her wholly no matter how she identifies, because ultimately she is a person we know and love and no identity declaration could ever change that. We validated her feelings even though we didn't necessarily agree with her conclusions about what they meant. We spent lots of quality time together with extended family and much of it in nature, away from devices. She no longer desires to be a boy. This change took a little over a year, which is about the amount of time it took her to get into it.

I realize how lucky our family is to have had our daughter come back to herself and us so quickly. I know many families who have been in this battle for their children for many more years. I consider ourselves fortunate not to have been some of the parents at the forefront of this social contagion. We had some warning and examples of what worked and what didn't. I will forever be indebted to the parents who shared their absolutely heart-wrenching stories with me and helped educate me and others in hopes of helping us save our children. Many of them told me things they wished they had done, and a small handful of them told me things they did that helped bring their children back to themselves. I listened to them, and I believe that made a difference. I wait with many of them for the day their children return to them as well. I believe it will happen. I hope for them and their children that they return with the least amount of damage possible, but this attack on our families leaves no one unscathed. It's much like being in a war to save our children, and I think many of us suffer from some level of PTSD and are hypervigilant, always watching for another attack or some type of boomeranging by our children back into this maladaptive coping strategy. I'm starting to see more and more families with children who are desisting. This is encouraging. I believe that it's because more of us are telling our stories, and new families affected by this are catching on sooner, armed with information. Many of us seem to have some level of "survivor's guilt," because there are still so many thousands of families suffering in the grips of this destructive ideology. Maybe that has some small part in why we are still fighting it. Also, we may be fueled by the thought that it still feels like this ideology is an imminent danger to many others, and we don't want anyone else to be harmed by it.

Despite these encouraging developments, however, this is an ongoing medical and psychosocial scandal like none we have seen in our lifetime. What I call the first-wave detransitioners (young people who medically transitioned and realized that they were misled and came back to identifying as their birth sex), those who were at the forefront of this contagion and who are now mostly in their mid-twenties to mid-thirties, had nothing approaching the level of indoctrination our young children are experiencing today in the school systems. I believe this will ultimately be seen as worse than the opioid crisis, which we as a society are still experiencing the ramifications of because pharmaceutical companies and doctors misled the public. This will affect our entire society as we attempt to pick up the pieces of the children and families who were attacked by the hideous lie that our children were born in the wrong bodies. Schools that teach gender ideology and hide social transition from parents are now ground zero for this devastating epidemic.

10

How Our Spirited
Daughter Boarded the Trans Train

Our daughter was unique and spirited from birth. As a young child, she was imaginative and highly intelligent. She loved learning about new things and developing theories about how the world around her worked. She also was extremely girly and loved dressing up, putting on make-up, posing for photographs, and dancing. She never met a stranger and would carry on long conversations with anyone willing to listen to her.

Adults were captivated by her intelligence and ability to carry on a conversation about nearly any subject matter. She was a voracious reader, having read the entire *Harry Potter* series in second grade. She had strong opinions about fairness and right and wrong. While she could relate to adults rather well, she would somewhat regularly get into disagreements with kids her own age over things that she considered wrong or unfair. She could be rather rigid in her thinking, but for the most part, she still had a number of good friends through elementary school.

Much of this changed in middle school. There appeared to be more disagreements with friends in sixth grade, and she seemed to start having trouble fitting in. She became much quieter, declared she was an introvert, and didn't share her thoughts with us like she had just a year earlier. In seventh grade, she told us she was pansexual as she learned more about sexuality and gender. Since she was just twelve years old—and knowing that she knew little about real sexual attraction and that sexuality tends to be more fluid in young females—we encouraged her not to label herself. She also had been very involved in our church and had previously believed in the traditional view of marriage. We reminded her of the church's beliefs on marriage. Soon she started telling us she no longer believed in God and had decided she was an atheist.

During the summer between seventh and eighth grade, she had a lot of unfettered access to the Internet. She spent hours on YouTube. One of her close friends came out as nonbinary, and we started seeing evidence in her writing and drawings that she was becoming more interested in gender issues. At the beginning of eighth grade, she and her female friends became obsessed with the K-pop group BTS. We found that they believed they were actually talking to members of the group and that they had made plans to meet with people who they believed were band members. Multiple girls in her friend group were now identifying as transgender or nonbinary. We confronted her, saying we were going to only support her as a girl. She got very angry with us and would not discuss anything with us regarding gender after this point.

We started researching gender and listened to affirmative advocates that pushed the idea that she would commit suicide if we didn't affirm her gender identity. We wanted a connection with her and were scared she would attempt suicide, so we apologized and told her we would support her to the best of our ability. She soon told us that she was nonbinary instead of trans.

Later in eighth grade, she had a falling out with her friend group and lost all of her friends. She also developed a crush on a girl in her grade but got turned down when she told the girl she liked her. Being a precocious child and an excellent artist, she decided to apply to a specialty high school. It is a school for art and technology that has a rigorous application process. Given her history, we were concerned that if she went to the school, she would encounter gender-affirming teachers and administrators, but we also knew that there would be a lot of students and teachers like her and that she would feel accepted and get an excellent education. Believing that finding her tribe was important, we encouraged her to apply to the school and hoped that, as she matured, she would outgrow her gender confusion. She was one of two students from her middle school who were accepted to this prestigious high school. We were elated for her but, at the same time, anxious about the potentially affirming environment.

In ninth grade, she made friends pretty quickly, and it became obvious that many of her hundred-member class identified as transgender or nonbinary. She developed a romantic relationship with another natal female that identified as trans, but that relationship ended quickly. By the winter of her freshman year, she was identifying as a gay transboy, had claimed a new name, and was using he/him pronouns.

A few short months later, the pandemic hit, and she was home doing virtual school for the next year and a half. We have slowly seen an improvement in our relationship as we have worked hard to reconnect with her, but three years into this journey and she is still identifying as trans. Recently she asked us to allow her to start testosterone. She had completely rewritten her childhood, claiming that she always knew she was a boy but that she felt pressure from us to conform as a girl. It was clear during that conversation that she had been coached online regarding what things to say in order to make us think she had always been this way, so that we might consent to medicalization. She continues to tell us that she is going to transition medically when she turns eighteen and that she thinks her anxiety will improve once she starts "T." At one point during another conversation, she told me that when she turns eighteen she will move out and never talk to me again. She cries and uses emotional blackmail to try to get her way. We haven't caved and pray that she doesn't actually do these things when she is old enough. We sometimes see glimpses of who she used to be and hope that she'll come back to us little by little.

Besides her school, we have run into two other authorities in her life that have undermined our parental authority and connection. We suspect that she has high-functioning autism. We took her to a psychologist that we thought was safe to get a diagnosis. He told us she is likely on the spectrum but never formally diagnosed her. When we tried to push him on this, he said he needed to do a psychological evaluation on her. He did that, and despite the fact that there were multiple questions she never answered, he said she wasn't depressed, anxious, or suicidal. He told me that she just needed to learn how to live as a nonbinary person even though he didn't dig into any of these issues with her for more than an hour. In recent months we have found a nonaffirming therapist that suspects she has generalized anxiety disorder. The other issue we have recently run into is that our governor and state legislature have passed laws and guidance that require schools to allow students to use whatever name, pronoun, bathrooms, and locker rooms they prefer without any documentation or notification to their parents. Schools have also been encouraged to actively hide a trans identification from parents if they believe the parents won't affirm.

We have gone back and forth about whether to use her preferred pronouns and trans name. When we first started researching, we read the information about the risk of suicide and thus tried to follow her lead, but the more we have researched the subject, the more we became convinced we should stand our ground and not affirm. We now use a nickname that is more gender-neutral. It is the name she first requested when she thought she was nonbinary. We mostly try to avoid pronouns, but if forced, we use she/her. She seems sad if we deadname her or call her she. But, even when we were using her desired name and pronouns, she didn't seem any happier.

We are still hopeful that the lies that are being told to our child and to the world in general will come to light soon. There is still time for our daughter to wake up to this cult that she is in. We, like so many other parents, just hope it happens before she is irreversibly damaged.

11

I Sponsored a High School GSA, and Then . . .

In 2018–2019 I sponsored the GSA (Gay–Straight Alliance, today also called the Genders and Sexualities Alliance) in a Midwestern high school. I feel fortunate to have survived my years as a depressed gay teen in the early nineties, and, as a gay parent, I wanted to help.

Predictably, as I'd try to usher the group out after a meeting, they would begin to open up to each other about selecting a college or coming out at home as gay or lesbian. They were a small group of bright and talented students. Many were looking forward to attending a meeting of local high school GSAs at a nearby college as our one allotted field trip.

When we got to that local GSA meeting, I was surprised. I expected the content to be related to sexual orientation. However, upon entering, for the first time, I was given a name tag for my pronouns. And there was only an all-gender bathroom—also a first for me. Students were handed a microphone to announce their name, identity, and pronouns. "I'm Jamie and I'm nonbinary, they/them." Another sponsor, a thirty-ish-year-old straight teacher, leaned over to me. "She's what? What are they talking about?"

I explained, hopefully correctly, as some of the terms I had to later Google. At forty-three I felt old, as if my ten-year hiatus from gay pride parades and bars resulted in me missing key developments. As I looked out at the group of excited students, I thought—what is going on here?

At the end of the next school year, my oldest son announced his trans identity in a text to my wife and me. It was the week of his eighth-grade graduation. We were stunned. We were also terrified of losing our son. While we told him we loved him, we privately had doubts about this new identity. We, of course, accepted and supported our child. However, there had never been any sign of gender issues for him as a child. As his psychologist later stated, "The dots don't connect."

For months after my son's two-word announcement, we heard little regarding gender. My son mentioned an older trans student from Australia with whom he had been playing games online. Our rule had been no strangers, but with the ongoing isolation, I let it go, as uncomfortable as it made me feel.

My son pulled away from his small local friend group. He struggled to do schoolwork and get out of bed. On a visit to the pediatrician, he informed his doctor of his trans identity. She prescribed him anti-depressants and told me to focus on maintaining a strong relationship with him. I never envisioned what a challenge this would be with my sweet son.

Over the next year, my son's hair and nails grew longer and looked unkempt. He shaved his body hair. Occasionally he painted his nails black and wore women's leggings and a sweatshirt to the table. His younger brothers, oblivious, chatted with him about video games.

When I searched online, advice all seemed to point to children knowing their gender. Anyone suggesting otherwise was transphobic. I could not be that. So maybe, I thought, my wife and I, and everyone else who ever met my son, had simply missed some signs.

Just before turning fifteen, my son became more insistent that it was necessary for him, or really us, to make changes, including calling him by a new name. He thoughtfully selected the name we would have chosen had he been born a girl. When we asked questions, trying to build understanding, he stated that he had always felt this way and was uncomfortable with his body.

For us, studying every angle, even when purchasing a new toaster or coffee maker, is a family trait. We asked our son for patience as we researched the issue further, just as we would have done if our son had another serious concern. This time I did not automatically discredit sources.

I spent hundreds of hours reading, watching documentaries, listening to speakers, communicating with other parents of trans-identifying young people, and spending time with our son.

With all this information, our history with our son, and speaking to our son's doctors, we advised him to pump the brakes and to give himself time to explore his identity before making changes that are difficult to walk back—or that are even irreversible. We also shared our own coming out stories with our son—that we were in our early twenties before we were more certain and finally came out to family and then some good friends.

Our son, while very bright, can be impulsive like many teens. And, like many teens, he sometimes does not listen to our advice. So, he approached his school counselor about assisting in changing his name. We, the parents who named him, were never invited to the table in this decision. And so school staff, who knew little about our son, his mental health, our family, and likely even less about trans youth, led the way to my son's social transition at school.

I discovered the name change when I saw a Microsoft Teams message from a teacher: "Hola Anna! I wanted to let you know that I spoke with your counselor. Thank you for letting us know! I am proud of you for communicating your needs and staying true to yourself. I will not be in class tomorrow. The sub should not have many reasons to call out names. Hasta el Viernes!"

This past fall was a period of hell for my family. My son concocted stories of unhappiness during his childhood. He told a story of a suicide attempt that would have been impossible, saying he had been suicidal two years earlier. Only changing his name and transitioning would help him. At eighteen, he repeated with a smug look, he could do what he wanted. Seldom civil, he parroted slogans, including that we should never have had kids. He refused any discussion, saying that talking to us was like talking to a brick. He hid in his room or the bathroom and acted as if he was no longer part of the household.

Several times, in tears, I thought back to a family party just a few years earlier. A friend of the family, who had just come out as a gay man, was attempting to hold a conversation with me. I was frenzied, keeping an eye on the nonswimmers and ensuring the kids with allergies didn't grab the wrong food. Then, he said, "I want what you have." I looked at my extrovert wife chatting away and my three joyful kids. He was right. I had everything. Last fall, I thought it impossible that my family would ever feel that happy again.

At some point, though, during the stressful autumn, a window opened. During an argument, my son asked me why my stance had changed, saying he was hurt by that. I realized that my thinking had progressed from how dare I question my son's identity to wondering, if I was a teen, what path would I have taken? My spouse? Our many athletic butch lesbian friends?

So my son agreed to watch *The Trans Train* with me, to see what I had been learning. He asked why the female detransitioner didn't change her voice back. He insisted she could if she wanted to. Weeks later, we watched the second installment. This time, my son stopped the video every few minutes to discuss. He was disturbed.

Sometime later, my son let us know that he had wanted to change his name back to his real one at school, but he was embarrassed to address this with the school staff. He had been so adamant, so sure . . .

My son now says he changed his name partly to rebel and did not think ahead. Then he told me that he knew that his mothers' holding the line came from love. He avoids talking about his period of being trans, saying he wants to move forward and it was a mistake. He says he just wants to be treated like a regular guy.

My son hasn't attended a GSA meeting in months. I am relieved. Instead of a place of support for gay youth, it has transitioned from a support center for same-sex attracted teens into a place where trans contagion spreads easily and where families who do not immediately affirm sudden trans identification in their children are vilified and deemed abusive.

Many mornings when my son comes down the stairs as I am getting coffee, he gives me a hug. He asks about visiting his grandmother this weekend. My pleasant, sweet, considerate son has returned. I know how fortunate I am. I will never take this for granted.

Recently I was able to ask my son why he had gone down this path. My fifteen-year-old looked at me and said, "Well, it's like this, mom. I'm a kid."

12

$30K a Year—and My Kid Can't Tell the Difference Between a Boy and a Girl

Everything has a price.

Like every American family, our family runs a constant cost/benefit analysis on our lives. There are the small decisions: is it worth the time to drive to Target for the cheaper diapers? Or should I just get the pricier ones at the grocery store? And there are the bigger ones: like, should I live in the suburbs and pay lower taxes but more for car expenses and gas? Or flip that decision?

For our family, one of the toughest decisions was where to send our kids to school. We could send them across the street to the poorly performing public school for free. They'd meet a wide variety of kids and learn some valuable self-advocacy skills, but they would not be academically challenged. For $30k, I could send them to the nearby private school, where they'd benefit from engaged teachers, kids, and families. We'd have to drop the music lessons and fancy trips, but hey—I don't like Disneyland anyway.

So, with some scholarships, sacrifices, and family assistance, we made the choice to send our kids to a fancy private school. The benefits have been great: warm, caring, patient teachers; outstanding academics; beautiful buildings; even a pretty good lunch. But there's been a hidden cost beyond the incredibly painful tuition bills: my kids can't tell the difference between a boy and a girl.

This seems shocking, I know. How can a concept so obvious, so instinctual that nearly every two-year-old on the planet can master it, be an idea that my very expensively educated children don't understand?

Because some teachers don't understand it. Because some administrators don't understand it. And this is where I have to remind myself of something true: half the world is dumber than average.

I know this sounds incredibly snobby. I know this sounds judgmental and awful, but this is true. And this fact helps me take a breath, find some compassion, and slow down.

These teachers are good people. They are kind. They like kids and want the best for children. They believe that education can make the world a better place. And additionally, they were hired for their people skills: they are empathetic, good communicators, patient, and open-minded. Those are exactly the skills my tuition dollars are paying for.

But these teachers are not well-trained critical thinkers. They were not hired for their ability to analyze complex research studies nor to follow the various paths of different complex scenarios. They are not philosophers, ethicists, or religious scholars. They are not lawyers or developmental psychologists. They are not endocrinologists or pediatricians. They are experts at connecting to kids and explaining the types of K–12 content that kids should learn. Thank god for teachers and their talents and skills. Our society needs them. But they are not experts on these other matters. They are just trying to do their jobs.

So when faced with the concept of "gender identity"—the idea that "people have an innate feeling of being female or male," the typical teacher will say, "Sure—that makes sense. I'm female, I know it. That's not a controversial idea."

When faced with the diagnostic definition of "gender dysphoria," the idea that "some people have great distress with their biological sex, and wish they were the opposite sex," these teachers say, "Sure—I know about Jazz Jennings and Caitlyn Jenner. That's a real thing."

When faced with the fact of "disorders of sexual development" (formerly known as intersex conditions), the scientifically observed and natural phenomena of various biological sexual characteristics and markers, teachers say, "Yep—I learned about that once."

And when urged to consider the negative impacts of the difficulty of being an outlier, and the impacts of social isolation and/or ostracism, the teachers say, "Not on my watch. My cousin was gay and poorly treated. I won't let any of my kids be bullied or left out."

So when teachers combine all these ideas and impressions and blend them into their natural "be nice" personalities and "open-minded" natures, they are primed to become believers and advocates of transgender ideology. If Johnny likes skirts and thinks he's really a girl inside, who are we to judge? They were born this way, right?

We really can't blame the teachers. Our society has laid yet another burden of expectation on them. They must educate kids, they must socialize kids, they must address and resolve the emotional and behavioral dysfunctions of these kids. And now they must be responsible for nurturing, protecting, and advocating for the "internal feeling of being female or male" for a kid; otherwise, they'll be held responsible for the kid's ostracism.

This is nuts. These teachers don't stand a chance.

So we can't fight the teachers. We've got to get the administrators and school boards to stop, listen, and think. These people were hired to be critical thinkers, to balance different opinions, and to consider the different consequences of different choices. They still aren't likely to read the studies or think through the ethical or philosophical consequences of different complex scenarios, but they are primed to consider one thing above all: legal threats.

Right now, principals and school boards are hiding behind the guidelines that the World Professional Association for Transgender Health (or WPATH, an activist-led organization), the American Psychological Association, the National Association of School Psychologists, and the National Association of Secondary School Principals have created. These organizations have good intentions, but they are also human and flawed (and remember—half of their members are below average). Even the American Civil Liberties Union (ACLU) seems to have lost its mind on this topic.

I suggest that American parents adopt the "Maya Forstater Approach." This strategy, based on Forstater's highly publicized employment and discrimination case against the Center for Global Development in England, relies on fundamental and constitutional American legal rights: free speech and free religion. I don't care if you haven't been to church ever. This is what you say to your school board: "For scientific, religious, and social reasons, I do not believe that you can change your sex, and I do not want my children to be taught 'gender identity,' the belief that you have a gendered soul, and that your gender soul feelings trump your biology. How is your school protecting my family's religious beliefs and our right to be free from compelled speech?"

Ask your school's principal this question every fall. Send it as a statement to your kids' teachers every fall. Tell them to inform you of any lesson on gender identity before it happens so that your children can have a substitute lesson. Ask them what their policy on requesting pronouns is, so that your child does not feel compelled to use certain speech. Ask them how they balance different opinions on this topic in the community. I can guarantee you they do not see this as a religious issue but as a social justice issue. Say the magic words "freedom of religion/freedom from religion" and "freedom of speech" and see if that works. We've got a long history of protecting underdogs in this country, and right now, the culture glorifies the status of victim. Use this knowledge wisely.

And here's the thing: this is going to cost you. Be ready. Do the cost/benefit analysis. Whether your kids are getting a free public education or an expensive private one, when you ruffle the feathers of the principal, the winds blow. Then again, if you remain silent, your kid may not understand that sex never changes. Be prepared. Everything has a cost.

13

A Pat on the Head

We left our kind, funny, shy, and self-effacing son with you on a late summer evening. His initial impression of university was that everyone else was taking it in stride, having the experience he had been hoping for, and fitting in . . . and that he wasn't. This intimidating start was followed by a relentless march of exhausting days, where each seemed harder than the one before. Eventually, he withdrew. He was tired of being different, tired of being alone. He went online.

And there he found someone who told him that medicalizing to look female would help him, that all he needed was drugs and surgery. That he was really a woman. This was the answer. The reason he felt different. All of this is, in some sense, an old, old story. A young person goes to university, feels alone, and finds some people who say they understand him. In this case, people who would let him join their club if he took drugs, did drastic things to his body. People who told him lies, either out of malice or out of ignorance. It is not the first time in history this has happened.

He told us about his discovery and stated that he immediately needed medical intervention. He added that your university health services quickly offered to provide it. As loving and supportive parents, we got up to speed as fast as we could about what was known about how to help people with his kind of distress and met with your health services to learn why they were encouraging him to start taking life-altering drugs with permanent effects right away.

They should have discussed with us that likely outcomes are not known for these medical treatments, that some people have been badly harmed by them, and that others who are similar to our son have been seen to recover with psychotherapy. They didn't. Instead, the response we got to our concerns was a condescending pat on the head. As if our brains had fallen out the minute our kid had brought this up. As a female professional, I recognized the pat on the head. However, in my profession, facts eventually prevail. In contrast, at your school, facts did not. Instead, your health services people smiled knowingly and gave us a recording alluding, ever so subtly (not), that we'd be better off with a live daughter than a dead son (known to be a false dichotomy, but perhaps not by them). They insinuated that, because we had not enthusiastically thrown ourselves behind our son starting hormones on the spot, we had taken leave of our senses. That we, the ones asking for and showing evidence, were willfully fooling ourselves about his situation, his personality, his developmental stage, the entire arc of his life. That we were denying reality.

Because apparently our son has a magical (but unmeasurable) quality that he self-diagnosed online. And accordingly, your health services believed they had to help him quickly trade away his fertility and healthy body and drastically interfere with his developing (currently distressed!) brain, so that he could grow breasts. And maybe have a knife cut up his sexual organs. They nodded sagely to each other and exchanged satisfied looks when we parents went from bafflement to shock, as we realized that we could not do a thing to get our son appropriate evidence-based care for his distress.

He didn't know one doesn't make drastic life-altering medical decisions in such a way—teenagers don't know these things. Nor did you or his cheerleaders tell him. And he didn't believe us when we tried to explain how serious these interventions are. The interventions are deceptively banal at first: a pill, maybe a patch—and your health services feel so kind, so cozy, so safe! He reasonably but mistakenly believed your school's health providers would know enough to not advise him to do something incredibly risky and unproven. That they would "first, do no harm." We know our son is at the age to turn to his peers and to detach from us, but it was your school, not us, pushing him into danger. And welcoming him into your arms. But I repeat myself.

You are a university. You certainly must know that every nucleated cell in his body reflects that he is male and that if he did change his sex, he would be the first mammal on Earth ever to do so. Has your health services told him this fact remains no matter what he feels or how he modifies his body? You supposedly understand scholarship well enough to teach it, but a key paper used to justify your health services' "affirmative" approach is widely known for misrepresenting the references that it relies on. You're being paid tens of thousands of dollars a year to teach my son how to think critically. So, you tell me, where is the evidence these medical interventions are safe, effective, and necessary? It wasn't that hard for us to discover it's not there (and that much less dangerous exploratory therapy is sometimes effective on its own). Indeed, the U.S. Food and Drug Administration (FDA) hasn't established that the benefits of medical interventions outweigh the risks, so the drugs you prescribed to our son are off-label. The considerable risks and lack of evidence are not a secret.

And surely, as a university, you know that although your students are legal adults, their prefrontal cortex is not yet developed enough to responsibly weigh long-term risk in decision making. Although you proudly intone how much you care for trans-identifying young people, you seem unaware that, for many, trans identification is temporary. No one has any idea how many or which of the 3 percent of college students currently trans-identifying will continue to be so in five or ten years. However, no matter how they identify once they've grown up a bit more or, for some, no matter whether the underlying distress that caused their gender distress is healed, the modifications enabled or offered by your "health" services will be lifelong: the sterilization, the removed or altered breasts or sex organs, the changes to their voices and bodies. A "gift" from their university years, disastrous for some. Their still-developing minds and the wide range of possible paths their gender dysphoria might take are strong reasons for college-aged kids not to rush to medicalize.

There is a rush, however, coming from the Internet and from your signs around campus ("Are You Trans?") and the warm, celebratory, cult-worthy welcome, including from your health services, which even brags about how easy it is for your students to obtain medical intervention. In contrast, they mention nothing about differential diagnoses to try to identify those who have locked on this "solution" by mistake. Not a whisper that for some the wish to transition is an attempt to distance from part of themselves; nothing about those who have recovered with supportive exploratory psychotherapy, many of whom resemble my son. Nor is there any hint of the many detransitioners and their struggles. Do you and your health services know that several countries have recently been carefully scrutinizing medical intervention for young people, and then hitting the brakes? That even American leaders in the World Professional Association for Transgender Health (WPATH) have been sounding the alarm, explicitly warning about the dangers of rushing?

Your health services appear negligently unaware, as they instead enthusiastically "helped" our son chemically castrate himself. (Permanently? No one knows.) But as these unproven drugs are powerful and dangerous, there's more: risks to his bones and his cardiovascular, endocrine, and immune systems, and the drugs have also rapidly attacked his still developing brain, damaging its neuroplasticity, leaching water out of his astrocytes, and shrinking his hippocampus. They likely increased his depression as well, but your health services told us eagerly, eyes aglow, that he could take antidepressants, too. Done. He's a walking pharmaceutical company cash cow now. And he will be, for the rest of his (probably much shorter) life since, in order to be his "true authentic self," he must never stop taking these drugs. We all know that taking drugs to persistently alter your brain and body is the best way to be authentic.

This should have never happened to him. And today, tomorrow, another parent's child will fall in. Another young person, with a full future ahead of them and a healthy body but with a mind in distress (it happens in university, who would have thought?), will go to your dangerously misinformed health services for "help."

Your university is ignorantly and irresponsibly providing lies, poison, and lifetime bodily injury instead of an education. And to parents, pats on the head and Stepford Wives smiles. I have made note that, since the drugs are off-label for treating gender dysphoria, your "health" services, not the drug companies, are legally responsible for the harm done to my son. I am going to do my best to sue you and others like you out of existence in return. Maybe it will stop you from destroying someone else's child. But it won't undo what happened to my son's body, his mind, and his future at your university. While we parents will, of course, continue to lovingly support him in every way we can, I will also do my part to warn every parent, every young person, every college counselor I know of what you have done. I have already started. Before we parents began to organize—before anonymous platforms like Parents with Inconvenient Truths about Trans were available, before organizations like Genspect existed—you profited from our silence, because speaking up risked pushing our very much loved and vulnerable kids even further into their dangerous paths. You have been holding them hostage.

We sent you the most precious being in our lives. We have only one child. And you fed his mental illness, celebrated it, and invited him to further harm. You pushed us aside, pushed facts and reason aside, and shoved him over the cliff. With your brains off, your critical thinking off, following the blind and stupid mob.

14

I Am Not the Same Teacher

Early in the school year, I attended a meeting. I entered the room not knowing that this year, after over a quarter century in education, was to be markedly different for me. That day, I chatted easily with my fellow educators, all of us refreshed from the summer break. Looking back, I vividly remember how sunshine streamed in from the windows, how excited everyone was to meet in person, and how many were dressed in new professional attire. I had no idea at that time that the content of the meeting and events in my family life would leave me contemplating a career change.

On the agenda: equality. The presenters, district administrators, smiled brightly as they explained to us that we must use a student's preferred name when asked; it was no different than using a nickname for a student, they quickly assured us. Parents are not to be informed. That would be outing a student and putting them in harm's way. Failure to do so, the administrator explained while continuing to smile, would be in violation of Title IX. This quick announcement left my mind, as both a teacher and a parent of a gender-questioning teen, reeling with questions.

- If the students had authority to change their names and gender without parental permission, why were we asking for parental permission for field trips?

- Was calling a female student a traditionally male name actually akin to using a nickname?

- Are these interventions something schools should be deciding without parental or expert input?

- Why was announcing a trans identity being treated similarly to announcing a gay identity?

- What if a student, still realizing their sexuality, was confused?

- Wouldn't families eventually get wind of the new name? Would this make it a worse situation for the student?

- What expertise did the presenters have with trans youth? Who wrote the guidelines for trans-identifying youth?

- Why were we only hearing about new guidelines for these particular students and not for any others under the ever-growing LGBTQA+ umbrella, and why now?

- And, "gender-support plans"?

But I am sure the many veteran educators were, like me, both stunned and, in the current polarized climate, afraid of misspeaking and being deemed bigots. And I am sure that we didn't wholly understand the ramifications of what we were being asked to take part in.

The meeting shifted gears and quickly moved on to cultural sensitivity. The same speaker asked a participant to share a story. The educator explained that her second-grade teacher inexplicably could not pronounce Josefina, and that she was dubbed Joan for the rest of her school days. Her old school friends still know her as Joan. There was an audible collective gasp.

I can't imagine not making an effort to pronounce a student's name. At the same time, I was finding a sad irony that we teachers had no observable reaction to being informed that if James told us he is now Sandra, we must immediately oblige. I was wondering, if referring to Josefina as Joan was life-changing for our colleague, how was calling a biological male student a traditionally female name dealt with so flippantly?

And, what would happen if a teacher, all of whom are well versed in adolescent development, questioned the wisdom of this approach? It is likely we might have been escorted out of the building. So because the topic is taboo, discourse is shut down among the very people who have vast experience working with children and adolescents and the power to affirm an identity, even if parents do not believe it is in the child's best interest.

It's possible that this was the day, while I was playing connect the dots in the meeting, that my own son, who had once had such extreme anxiety that he struggled to address adults, contacted school staff to request that he be addressed by a new name and pronouns. This move was against the advice of his doctor, who had known him his entire life, and his parents.

When the pandemic started, so did puberty for my son. Quietly suffering from undiagnosed depression, my tech-savvy son had turned online. In a Discord chat room for coders, he began corresponding with several trans-identifying participants. Both his new online community and teachers found out he was going by his new preferred name before we, his parents, did.

So I had a front-row seat to how schools superseding parental authority plays out. It was ugly. And it was so dangerous. Because we were in the dark regarding the name change at school, we didn't make the connection that my son's sudden behavioral outbursts were caused, in part, because he realized that after going by a new name, he was still deeply depressed and in pain. He had clung to this idea that if he transitioned, it would resolve his anxiety and depression. But he realized it didn't, and that he had made a very public mistake in changing his name. And we were not in the best position to support him because, for a time, we didn't even know.

When he let me know that he no longer considered himself trans and no longer believed in gender stereotypes, it seemed sudden. I never exactly had thought ahead to the day that my son would come to this realization. But I am sure that I envisioned myself as feeling remarkably relieved, as this never had seemed the path for him. Instead, months later, I feel as if the sky is perpetually overcast. I find myself putting one foot in front of the other during my work day. My mind is preoccupied, as if having a small fan running in the corner of my brain at all times, thinking about the youth "transdemic."

This may have led to some positives, such as my own small grassroots effort to speak to others about the sharp increase in trans-identifying youth. So, I now, in small conversations, speak about the unspeakable.

I spoke to an old friend, a gay, liberal librarian, regarding a social media post. A day later, she contacted me for resources. A friend of hers had girls in a homeschool group identifying as trans.

I spoke to an award-winning teacher and highly respected community member who told me that she had had two male students who came out as gay, then trans. Both realized they were gay before pursuing a medical route. She expressed concern that gender nonconforming gay youth may pursue a medical route while not being developmentally able to understand the life-long consequences.

I spoke to teachers who discovered at individualized educational plan (IEP) meetings and conferences that parents had not been informed of the preferred names and pronoun updates of their kids. One went home and watched a Swedish documentary and, disturbed, grabbed me the next day to discuss it.

I spoke to a neighbor with high schoolers who told me of a young man in the community, just out of high school, who was detransitioning but who had already been made sterile.

I talked to another educator who spoke of a student who medically transitioned while in high school. The student attempted suicide not long after graduating.

I spoke to a high school counselor who had five students ask to change their names and pronouns in the first semester of the current school year. And I spoke to her boss, the head counselor, who asked me what social transitioning was.

I am too angry, just yet, to speak to my son's teachers.

I now know that a teacher messaged my son how proud she was of him coming out and living authentically. In her month of becoming acquainted with my son and 125 others, did she know he had never shown signs of gender nonconformity as a child? With her surface knowledge, did she realize what hormone therapy and "gender-affirmation surgery" entails? I have had to wrap my mind around the idea that my son sits each day in a classroom led by someone excited by the idea that he was taking steps toward this.

Months later, another teacher pulled my son into a storage room to probe for details on why he was now going by his birth name again. Why on Earth did she believe this was acceptable? Did it really not occur to her that trans-identifying teens, like others their age, are also prone to act impulsively with little regard to the consequences? Had she never seen a teen try on an identity or belief and cast it back when it didn't fit? Or, did she believe that she knew what was in the best interest of my child, more so than the "bigoted" parents who understood his history and were looking out for his future?

As parents, we are now less concerned about grades, sports, and university admittance. Life is not easy being the former trans kid at school. We now simply hope our son is happy and healthy. We hope he makes a friend again soon.

I am not the same parent, and I am not the same teacher.

At times, the idea of affirming without questioning a student's gender identity results in me feeling nauseous on the way to work. I struggle to sleep at night. I wake up and, riddled with anxiety, I am in physical pain, disillusioned. I have insider knowledge of how the blind affirmation by adults at school plays out in a household and how it harms young people with psychological issues and those who have not yet had the time to discover their sexuality. And I know that the decision to affirm a trans identity is being made in schools by people who are not experts and who may have only known the child for minutes.

Families are slowly waking up and smelling the coffee and realizing what is taking place in the schools. The anger of parents whose children have been introduced to the "genderbread" person or socially transitioned behind their backs in schools has been underestimated. Schools, a major source of affirmation, are fast becoming the next and maybe last battleground in the gender war.

From private conversations, I know I am not alone in wondering how much longer I will last in the classroom. But from wherever I am, I will do my best to spread the word on the flawed guidance for trans-identifying students, including the dangerous circumventing of parental rights, and push to change it.

Parents on Online Influences:
Porn, Anime, and Social Media

15

Brainwashed: Yes, the Internet (and School) Did Make My Kid "Trans"

My teenage son and I recently discussed what led to his belief that he was a transgender girl for a period of two years and why he desisted. My son recorded the following conversation and sent it to me, with the hope that it might help another family. After his experience, he now expresses opposition to the transitioning of youth and is in favor of barring youth from receiving puberty blockers, hormone therapy, or surgery in the name of gender-affirming care.

Me: Tell me about when you first came across the topic of gender identity.

Son: It was really from this one book I read that was from this school reading list.

Me: Was it *Lily and Dunkin* from the Rebecca Caudill List?

Son: Yeah, that was it. After that, I took out other books electronically and was reading about it. I can't remember any of the names off the top of my head. I decided maybe that this is like me and the people in the books seemed so happy after transitioning. I think the main thing was I joined a Discord community. It wasn't even related to being transgender. There just happened to be trans people in there because this has spread so far. Once in a while, we would talk about trans stuff, and it, I don't know, made me more quote-unquote comfortable.

Me: What was the Discord channel for?

Son: It was about Fortnite.

Me: So how would the topic of trans come up in a channel for gamers?

Son: The person who ran it said they were trans. They had a lot of other mental issues too. So they just, not encouraged it, but they talked about it, or other people would even though it wasn't on-topic. After that, I started creating my own personality for myself online, I guess. I was thinking I'm fine with this, maybe this is who I actually am.

Me: You thought it would make you feel better, less depressed. Did it make you feel better?

Son: It was more of a mentality of just a little more, and then I will. I never felt any better from it.

Me: When did you start really thinking that you were trans? When did you tell us?

Son: Eighth grade-ish. At that point, I was really depressed. And going into freshman year, that's when I really started thinking about it. Did I tell you then?

Me: Yes, you sent me a text when you were in eighth grade.

Son: Yes, that was when, around there, I was thinking this is who I am, and I need to tell my parents about it.

Me: Did you feel like anyone in these online communities pushed you in a certain direction?

Son: Not really. It was more of, oh, look at all these people, they are doing it, and you're not the only one. Someone sent me a link to another trans community group.

Me: What was the main platform you used?

Son: Discord. I watched content from some YouTube videos.

Me: At times, it seemed like you were speaking from a script.

Son: It wasn't like I came across a list of what you say to your parents. It was more of a message that your parents wouldn't understand. The stupidest thing I came across was a list of doctors who do things with no questions asked. I thought it was stupid. Imagine thinking that you are smarter than a medical professional! That was toward the end when I was unsubscribing from all these things on YouTube because I was thinking it wasn't me.

Me: When did you start to have doubts about being trans?

Son: When I changed my name at school. I wouldn't answer any questions in class because that is how scared I was of them saying anything about it. I thought, oh, my God, I made the wrong effing move here.

Me: How did you change your name in school?

Son: I went to the counselor quite a few times. She said, "No, if your parents aren't for it, I am not doing that." She discouraged me from coming back, but I did about five times. I really pressured her into it. I lied and said you were coming around. I guess I should be more persistent about other things.

Me: You were insisting on wearing a dress to the dance.

Son: It was more that I was with that group of people—friends from GSA—and I thought, well, look at them, they seem like they are happy, maybe if I keep pushing through, I'll feel better. I see this a lot with people in the trans community, they'll say, "I'll do this one more thing. Then you get to the point where there is no more one more thing. At that point, there is nothing you can do, and they even admit that "it isn't enough for me."

Me: Did you understand why we wouldn't call you another name?

Son: Maybe you did tell me some good reasons, but I was so enraged I didn't even listen to it.

Me: Did you know I spoke to a school administrator and asked them to call you by your birth name?

Son: Yes, she told me, and by that time, I was thinking, thank God! That's why I didn't fight it or anything.

Me: You still were going along with it for a while after.

Son: Yeah . . .

Me: What was the final turning point for you?

Son: At first, you were showing me some of those videos, and at first,

I was tuning it out, thinking it was stupid. Then I realized it was a lot worse than I thought, you know. I don't know if it would have helped had I not been at the breaking point. At that point, I was really torn, and it finally brought me over. If you had shown me it earlier, I wouldn't have believed it—would have thought it was stupid shit. I feel like I am a different person than I was then.

Me: Do you feel the inappropriate content you saw on the Internet was a factor in your trans identification?

Son: Not really, to be honest with you. I feel like more of an issue is that we have so many people pushing it on YouTube, even people who are adults, who should know better. It was like, hey, just know, if you're there, you don't have to doubt yourself, believe in yourself.

Me: Did you get these messages mostly over the Internet or also in person?

Son: Both. When I joined the school GSA . . .

Me: It's okay. I suggested you join. Would the messages be from the GSA sponsor or other group members?

Son: The other group members. She [the sponsor] was really careful with what she said. It was seeing other people there who seemed to be in the same situation as you. I would think, maybe I shouldn't be doubting myself so much.

Me: If we had taken more of a hard line, telling you, "Absolutely not," when you told us you were transgender, do you think it would have made a difference?

Son: That's a good question. I don't think so. I think ideally—and I am not blaming you for not doing this earlier—maybe what a parent would want to do, in a careful way, would be to give them more doubts to think about.

Me: It was really challenging to find information that backed what I thought I was seeing: that a young person who says they are trans might be wrong.

Son: We are not going to shove a kid in a car and say, oh, you're smart enough to drive. Kids just don't have the critical thinking skills.

Me: No matter how smart they are.

Son: Yeah, they don't have the resistance to mob mentality.

Me: Oh yeah, the peer pressure. But for you, it seemed to start on the Internet.

Son: For me, it was trust in older [trans] people saying this on YouTube videos. Because they were older than me, I thought maybe they knew a thing or two. There were YouTubers who talked about only trans and others, that that was who they are, but created other content and mixed in trans every once in a while. Very few people are giving you a list, like, hey, this is what you want to do in this situation. It was more, hey, I'm feeling good now. I did that too. I said I changed my name, and I'm feeling a lot better. Obviously, that was complete b.s.

Me: How does that happen?

Son: I was lying to myself.

Note: For a time, too long actually, I wrote off my intuition that extended time on the Internet could have influenced my son's sudden trans identification. After all, my Google searches told me that just thinking that a transgender identify could be related to Internet use was transphobic. That my child encountered transgender characters during a middle school reading class and had access to multiple books on the topic was a surprise. When he was fifteen, as he took steps to socially transition, I was becoming more concerned that he would pursue a life-changing medical path as soon as he was able. I largely tried to remain calm, but at one point, in utter exasperation, I remember exclaiming to my son, "You're not transgender—you're brainwashed!" It was many months later that it dawned on me that, as a lifelong liberal, I had been brainwashed by trans ideology too.

16

Gender Dysphoria's Undeniable Connection to Pornography

I am a parent of a female child who has rapid-onset gender dysphoria (ROGD). This is a new phenomenon where a child, who was perfectly happy in his or her body until right around puberty, suddenly announces that he or she is the opposite sex. In the case of my daughter, when she developed this condition, she threw away all of her feminine clothes, cut her hair super short, refused to go out in public without a chest binder, and stopped shaving her legs. And, of course, she came up with a new male-sounding name and insisted that everyone use it, along with the associated male pronouns.

With ROGD, from the parent perspective, the change is abrupt and without warning—thus the term "rapid"—but that term is somewhat deceiving. ROGD doesn't quite pop up out of nowhere despite how it might initially appear, nor does the body incongruence of gender dysphoria spring up organically, as the gender ideologues proclaim. It is not something that the ROGD child always felt. And the trans identity is not something that the child determines on her own. Rather, it is carefully manufactured and cultivated on the Internet and in peer groups, like a tended-to plant. The pretty pot is placed out; the dirt is added; the seeds are planted; water is carefully poured; and the pot is placed in the sunshine, so that it can grow stronger and bigger until, eventually, and tragically, the child who was happy in her body is no longer recognizable, and not just by sight. Her personality changes to be sullen, combative, and disengaged. She is no longer jovial or interested in much of anything unless it is related to being trans.

Let me take you on the journey of how my daughter was groomed into being a trans-identifying child at the age of thirteen—and I assure you, my story is not uncommon. I have heard its refrain echoed by many others with ROGD kids. My daughter's story began innocently enough, with a friend joking to her that she always took charge of the games that they came up with at the playground at school. Take-charge girls are like boys, her friend said, and she gave her a male nickname.

That same year, my daughter got her period. She was the first in her friend group to have one, and it was heavy and a nuisance. Her breasts developed. Naturally, she did not like these sudden changes, as most girls initially don't. Most girls in my generation spent a few years wearing baggy clothes to cover up their maturing bodies. These days, that perfectly normal and to-be-expected discomfort is a clear sign of being trans, per the Internet.

Also, in seventh grade, after their sex-ed class at school, my daughter's all-female friend group sat in my backyard discussing what sexual categories they fell into. "I think that I am an L," one announced. "L" stood for lesbian. Another said that she was "agender." My daughter said she was L or pansexual. They also talked about gender. All five girls chose labels other than heterosexual, straight, and what is now referred to as "cis" or, in my daughter's words, "basic," the even more scorned and derogatory term. I was concerned about this new language, so I attended our public school's sponsored sex talk. It was put on by PFLAG, I believe. The presentation was senseless. Gender is fluid, yet immutable. There are forty-six genders, and all kids, regardless of age, should announce pronouns at introduction. I was the only parent interrupting them to question their illogical logic. I was eventually told, essentially, to shut up.

Then, in eighth grade, my daughter stopped being a good student. She became obsessed with an older girl she met, who identified as a boy. My concern grew. I started to go through all of my daughter's devices, old, obsolete iPhones and Kindles. During my initial investigation, I saw some odd texts and TikTok videos but nothing too worrying.

After a night in which my daughter had a panic attack, she started to open up to me about the cause of her pain and anger, and why her behavior had changed so dramatically. She gave me all of her passwords for all of her accounts, even her secret ones. She admitted to having accounts in every possible platform—Discord, Twitter, Pinterest, Instagram, and TikTok—some those I had no idea existed. I spent the next couple of weeks going through each device and every platform. What I saw made me physically ill.

My daughter's crush, the girl who identified as a boy and was three years older than my daughter, had sent her a ten-minute video of herself masturbating with an enormous dildo. Yes, I saw child pornography on the device. That older girl discussed fisting and described in intimate detail female anatomy and orgasms to a group of some six or so thirteen-year-old girls online. This girl admitted to having been sexually abused as a child. She admitted to being obsessed with pedophile cases and serial killers. Now, she was passing that abuse on to my child and other kids. She admitted to meeting random people in the city's park to smoke pot and engage in sexual acts.

The young girl followers treated this older girl as a sage. They hung on every word, asked her for advice, watched her endless stream of Tik-Tok videos, with her drug-induced dances in superhero costumes with bulging packers. They listened to her stories of being on acid and mushrooms. My daughter got interested in the "dark arts," because that is what this older girl liked. My daughter started asking for everything that this older kid liked—a tarantula, a throne, various records, a nose ring—you get the idea.

I now knew why my daughter had become unrecognizable. The history on every device was filled with pornography, and the porn was mostly guy-on-guy. It was violent porn. It was anime porn with rape scenes, pregnant cartoon men being sodomized, gang bangs with cartoon children. There were Internet sites that contained written porn, with beatings, followed by forgiveness and sex.

My daughter had been sucked into the dark web.

She was only thirteen.

There were searches for ball gags, hand-cuffs, whips, and leather outfits. There were surveys to determine what deviant sex acts she would partake in. There were Discord and Instagram chatrooms where girls discussed whether they were bottoms or tops, givers or receivers, abusers or abused. There were discussions of turn-ons with weaponry. There were images of cartoon dogs giving oral sex. My daughter started drawing penises on the walls in her room, her shoes, and her pants.

I accessed my daughter's group chats with young girls from across the country, where they were teaching each other how to disassociate from their bodies so that they would be comfortable posting pictures of themselves naked. Advice that included things like "Since you are really a boy, your girl body really isn't yours, so it's no big thing to sell pictures to stupid men for money." There was a tutorial for how to find a "sugar daddy" and how to set up an Amazon account so he could buy you things. The more seasoned trans-identified girls would say, "Don't worry, you can start off slow, just show your midriff. You can hide your face and show more." "Find a sugar daddy who does not screenshot Snapchat, otherwise you will be all over the Internet," some fourteen-year-old warned. One girl bemoaned how long it took her sugar daddy to climax while he watched her dance.

I dove in deeper. I looked at all of my daughter's followers on TikTok—the followers were male-to-females (MTFs), females-to-males (FTMs), young girls showcasing bouncing breasts, fourteen-year-olds simulating oral sex with their tongues, kids advertising their transness as a way of increasing their followings, and grown men (i.e., predators). I delved into her Twitter followers and found men posting gang bangs with demonstrations of things that I can never unsee. I read the written porn that my daughter had read. It was beyond disgusting.

I started calling random contacts from her phone. Among those who answered were adult men, an anorexic male college student who was taking estrogen, and strangers from other states.

After several tries, I stripped my daughter's phone of all Internet access. I stripped her school iPad of the most egregious sites. I bought a safe and locked up all the phones and devices. I got her a new phone number so that I could block all of the pedophiles and groomers with whom she had been in contact.

I would love to say that was the end of it. But, you see, the plant that grew from the groomers could not be cut down so easily. It kept replanting itself, regrowing as addiction is wont to do. The pull of the porn was so strong that my daughter had friends give her their old phones. She had friends send her screenshots of "food" (her word for written porn). She ran away, stating that I had abused her because I blocked the Internet.

So, you tell me, is my now fifteen-year-old daughter's trans identity organic? Is her transman identity her authentic, true self? Is her self-realization that she really is a boy something that should be celebrated? I know, and you now know, that she was transformed slowly and methodically with intent by those who prey on young vulnerable kids.

This week after finding yet another stowaway phone, my daughter offered to transform back to being a traditional girl—wear bras, grow her hair out, wear stereotypical female clothes, tell everyone to use her female name—in exchange for access to the Internet with limited controls. Is she so addicted to porn that it trumps her alleged "trans identity"? Is she merely offering to bide her time until she is eighteen to transition again? I don't know. I am not sure what we will do, but one thing that I am sure of is that this ROGD group of kids does not come by their cross-sex identities organically or authentically. Someone plants the seed. Someone waters the seed, and someone places it in the sunshine and cultivates it carefully for reasons of their own. And our children are the unwitting victims.

17

Crazy Like a (Trans, Gay) Fox (Girl)

My eighteen-year-old son is getting ready for college, and in his Twitter header he describes himself as a "trans gay foxgirl" who uses "she/they" pronouns.

This is a young man with Asperger syndrome and a profoundly gifted IQ.

This is a child accepted into a mechanical engineering major, into the honors program.

He has beautiful long hair and wears boys' cargo shorts and *Star Wars* or *Dune* T-shirts.

He is a heterosexual male who is attracted to females, but he says he is "very gay" because he thinks he is an anime foxgirl.

He has never had a girlfriend and has trouble connecting deeply with others, though he has a group of equally intelligent, spectrum-ish guy friends who support him in this delusion and call him by his preferred name and pronouns. His younger sister does the same.

We've watched and waited for three years and not much has changed except for what started out as a desire for "she/her" pronouns and a very feminine name has toned down (or up?) to "she/they" pronouns and a gender-neutral preferred name that he will use at college.

During this time, we've seen kids in his high school start puberty blockers, receive cross-sex hormones, and attend voice lessons. Some are very close to getting surgery. A recent male graduate of this high school has had what is euphemistically referred to as top and bottom surgery.

113

The only thing crazier than this is that there seems to be a fair number of highly intelligent autistic boys and young men who have decided not only that they are "transgender" but that they are also, in fact, anime girls. Characters, cartoonish ultra-feminine bunnies or foxes à la Jessica Rabbit. I hear about them in the parent groups I've joined to try to understand this transgender phenomenon that is taking over the lives of many teens. I thought that my kid must be the only one who is this delusional—a fox, but a human girl, who likes other girls, right? But there are others, and I can't help but wonder how many.

I lied—the one thing crazier than that is that if I tell a therapist that my son thinks he's a trans gay foxgirl, they'll likely tell me to make an appointment at the gender clinic. And they will call him by his preferred name!

What will college be like for a "trans gay foxgirl"? I hope it will provide a needed dose of reality, especially since he'll be on a male floor of the dormitory, but college campuses don't really qualify as real world. The watchful waiting continues.

18

Porn and Grooming

I am one of a growing number of parents whose children, after exposure to pornographic content online, experienced a sudden and rapid change in behavior, ultimately culminating in a new transgender identity.

Twelve months ago, I checked my inbox and there, waiting for me, was a link to a Google Doc from my fourteen-year-old son. It began: "I have got something really important to tell you, but it's probably not what you are thinking." He added: "I am not gay, well kind of."

My son went on to tell us that he was transgender and that, for the last three years, we—his parents—actually had a daughter who was a lesbian. In the now infamous Google Doc, he defined "dysphoria" and included a link to a source, "just in case" we wanted to look up more information. He spoke of the pain he was going through and likened it to wearing a mask with razors inside. He expressed his fear that we would not accept him and asked for help. Stunned, we said, "I love you," and, when we saw him, hugged him. We asked for his patience as we looked for help and resources to try to understand what he was going through.

To say that this revelation came as a shock is an understatement—we did not see this particular thing coming. However, we did have an inkling that something was going on. In the time leading up to his pronouncement, we had noticed some significant and out-of-character behavioral changes. A few months before this news, our son had begun brooding and was short-tempered with us and his brother. He was sullen and began sleeping a lot—but we felt that this was the first true sign of puberty kicking in. We got increasingly concerned when he began limiting his food intake and his grades started slipping. He always had erratic scores in school, but he was actually failing a few classes, which was very much unlike him.

When we asked how long he felt this way and where it was coming from, he supplied short, canned-sounding responses, including: "I came across information about being transgender on the Internet, and it looked interesting and just fit." "Being trans explains why I have always felt different and never fit in." When asked why he believed what he believed, he would shrug his shoulders and say, "I just know." I silently kept asking myself, "How does one suddenly 'become' a girl three years ago? Was there a metamorphosis that I missed?" It turns out this is and was representative of the confusing thought processes that we had been encountering so often.

For a month, we were in a fog and did not know what to do. Then, we found writings that included suicidal ideation and drawings made by friends that depicted him as a female. He also started cutting. We removed knives from the house and developed a habit of checking on him in the middle of the night due to fear of him hurting himself more significantly. He made the request for a new name/pronouns and began shaving all of his body hair.

Most disconcerting to me was when he began speaking in a high, monotone voice. He was disconnecting from his body, and the person before us was nothing like the child we had raised. He was becoming something else, and, by all accounts, it was not a healthy situation. We sought out parent support groups and medical professionals. In an attempt to learn about what our child was working through, we found the Wild West that is "transgender medicine" and a dark aspect of the Internet and society that we simply could not fathom; it was so far removed from what we considered to be reality.

After weeks of worsening mental and physical health, I grabbed the school-issued laptop to make sure it was charged and ready for a day of virtual learning. I flipped it open and saw a name I didn't recognize. I never even thought that the school laptop might have anything to do with what was unfolding in our home, assuming (falsely) that it had all the safeguards and site blocking that the school purported to enforce. When I walked into the living room with the laptop and saw his face, I knew instantly that what I would find would not be good. And it wasn't. The laptop was chock-full of evidence from his trip to the dark side of the Internet, where no child should be wandering. I found the pornographic side of Deviant Art, TikTok, YouTube, and Reddit. Late at night, while we slept, my son had been on these sites and was interacting with adults and older teens in many different subgroups.

I looked through the history; I could not help myself, even though it made me sick to do so.

It started out innocently enough. He initially asked simple questions like, "Why am I different from other guys?" "Am I gay?" and "What can I do about hating my body?"

His questions were met with some thoughtful responses, but I was surprised to read comments such as:

"u r trans"

"Have you ever heard of being trans?"

"Maybe ur a girl"

"If u are sad, cutting can sometimes help"

"start skipping meals, you can be thin and look like a girl"

I also noticed that a few users commented and interacted with my child more than others. These people invited him to private chat rooms and then suggested that they video chat because typing was "too much." I continued to sift through the computer and was shocked to learn that one of the online friends was a self-identified adult transwoman who offered to coach him and help him accept who he really was. The "friend" sent what I now know are dysphoria hypnosis recordings to "help him relax and sleep." I listened to this recording, and it included mantras about imagining himself as the woman he was always meant to be and described engaging in sex acts such as fellatio and being penetrated by a man while visualizing himself as a woman. I have yet to listen to the entire track as I was so disturbed by the content and even more disgusted that an adult sent this to my fourteen-year-old kid. This was grooming in action, and my son fell down the rabbit hole.

I panicked, and rather than taking screenshots and reporting this information, like I might have done if I had had my wits about me, I deleted it all. I deleted the account, wiped the history, and cut all Internet access. It all had to go—immediately—for his safety. And I could not cut his connection to these people and this content fast enough.

During this time, we were on an emotional roller coaster. A few days after finding all of the explicit online content, our son had an incident at school. This itself was not unchartered territory for us. Over the years, my son has always had incidents. Such as the time when he slammed a kid down after weeks of the kid repeatedly stealing his shoes and water bottle. The time when he hit another kid in the face with a basketball after being repeatedly called a "faggot." His last day at that school was filled with taunting, with his classmates making fun of the "smart kid." After he got a problem wrong in math class, someone thought it would be funny to have notes about his idiocy follow him to every class.

But this day was different.

At the end of the day, once at home, my child chose to strangle himself. Luckily, it was not well planned, and he passed out and hit his head instead of ending his life. To date, this is the worst day of my life, and I will never forget my terror and fear.

After this event, our son told us that he felt all of the "gender stuff" and self-harm were coming from the things he was dealing with at school, and he begged not to return. We thought about going to the school to discuss what had happened. Then, we reconsidered. In the past, these visits had changed nothing and, in fact, usually made things worse. We are a family for whom anti-bullying campaigns have never helped.

We also thought about letting the school know that its computers had zero protections. My son had accessed all of the adult content on his school laptop. I investigated the steps to report this to the school and discovered that, in many states, this might not go well for parents like us, parents who do not follow the affirmation-only approach (i.e., who do not immediately agree with their child's trans self-diagnosis). One overzealous teacher or administrator could have resulted in a cascade of events that could have ended in us being reported to child protective services. Did you know that there are laws passed in some states that allow a school to hide an alternate gender identification from parents? I also personally know families who have been reported or a parent that has lost custody for this very reason. We are just one family, and we were scared. Hiding our identity and participating in groups using online pseudonyms, we decided to band together with other parents navigating similar paths, and, in the process, we are finding our voice.

After connecting with other parents, we did eventually reach out to local law enforcement to discuss the possibility of trying to track down the online groomers that had targeted our son. Somehow, just as we feared, the conversation became about us as parents, and we were told how "at risk" trans kids are. They indicated concerns about our child's welfare, and there was nothing they could do if my child did not personally come forward.

We brought the concerns to them and now suspicion was being cast on our caring and loving families?! This is what we and other families are encountering. We love our children and are trying to help them become well-functioning adults. We have found that many schools and law enforcement have no idea about what is really going on, and the default is an affirmation, protective approach that views these kids as marginalized and potentially abused. It places any parent pushing against the current narrative in a defensive position.

So, what did we do? We ran from all the services that exist and the people that were supposedly trying to help our son, finding them to be dangerous to our son. Instead, we chose to disconnect from all Internet influence, changed to a new "classical" model school, and found ways to encourage our son to interact in the real world. We listened to books about rhetoric, practiced critical thinking, and worked together to evaluate sources of information. We fed his mental and physical health with physical activity, sunshine, nutritious food, art, and music. We loved him and found a wonderful therapist who let him talk.

Over time, we saw subtle shifts and changes, hints of a smile and glimmers of his previous wit and quirky sense of humor. He never again asked us to use different names or pronouns, and when we asked him about his previous requests, he said that he could care less. He told us that, initially, he was very angry with us but that, eventually, he came to understand that we just wanted him to slow down, take his time, and think about his actions and thoughts.

We discussed porn, and he verbalized that his curiosity had led him there, but that what he saw scared him. He also indicated that he now understood the negative impact it could have on him. Now that he was away from the influence of the Internet, he said that he could really figure out what he thought about gender and sexuality. We had always taught him that thoughts had power and that negative self-talk could harm his psyche. He revealed that, in never feeling like he fit in, he had tried to put himself into a more restrictive box. A box that really did not work for him. Today he is still working through things, but he is healthy, happy, enjoying his music, and interacting with the world.

The World Professional Association for Transgender Health (WPATH) is telling us to shut up and let the professionals discuss transgender medicine in journals behind a paywall. Trans activists call us transphobic; trans allies say we are harming our children. The media says affirming and celebrating a trans identity is suicide prevention. I disagree! In our experience, the more our child attached to the trans identity, the less functional and more self-destructive he became. We are the parents of a formally trans-identifying kid—what more of a stakeholder could we be than that? Where would we be if we had not disconnected our child from the influences and influencers on the Internet? Where would we be if we had rushed to the gender clinic and followed the advice of affirming professionals? What if we had approached the school?

I am a parent, and I will continue to fight against the medicalization of young developing bodies and minds. I will help others uncover the disturbing influence of online porn and destructive subreddits where predators find and target young kids, encouraging them to disconnect from their physical body. There's nothing that WPATH can do to stop me, and the thousands of other parents that are now, at last, questioning the harmful trans narrative.

19

A Clusterfeck of Internet Indoctrination and Doctor Failures

I am a fifty-four-year-old working mom of a fifteen-year-old gifted girl—my only child, she was fourteen at the time of her trans self-identification. Our story is a textbook story of rapid-onset gender dysphoria (ROGD) in almost all aspects. The only real difference is in my daughter's cluster of mental and endocrine diagnoses that went undiscovered until she was fourteen, after she had already fallen into the trans trap. The toll the trans bomb has taken on my child and our family has been tremendous.

As a child, my daughter was mellow, radiant, well-behaved, articulate, and caring toward animals and friends. She was an avid hiker, went on nature trips often, and was surrounded by books, culture, and meaningful interactions with relatives, peers, and our circle of adult friends. All teachers wrote, "A pleasure to have in class," except for the math teachers, who always wrote, "Makes careless mistakes; does not complete work." She never exhibited significant autistic behaviors, although she was obsessed with plush animals and had various other hyper-fixations (fashion, book series about cats and dragons, and nail polish and products).

And she loved the ocean . . . Oh, how she spent hours in the water, floating and playing with the waves . . . (The ocean is supposedly extremely soothing for kids with attention-deficit/hyperactivity disorder.

I knew none of this then.) I taught her how to look a person in the eyes when speaking with them. Since birth and into her puberty, my daughter was 1000% consistently stereotypical feminine in presentation and in her tastes. She wanted long hair and fine lingerie and was into arts, fashion, and crafts. Since second grade, she had had two close, genuine friends—a girl and a boy. She was invited to birthdays and sleepovers all the time. We hosted parties for Halloween and at the end of the school year, as well as for all her birthdays.

In seventh grade, she came out as a lesbian. The house got proudly decorated with rainbow flags, and I supported, affirmed, and loved her, as always. She fell in unrequited love with a female classmate who identified as a trans boy and who was also the ring leader of their friendship circle of five gender-nonconforming girls. Then, in eighth grade, she revealed that she was not a lesbian after all but that she was instead pansexual and queer. And in ninth grade, she declared that she was trans, despite her zero masculine interests, behavior, or presentation.

I did not know until later, but all throughout middle-school, my daughter suffered from undiagnosed autism spectrum disorder (ASD) and ADHD–inattentive disorder (ADD). For fourteen years, she had flown under the radar, undiagnosed, even though she had had a seasoned, well-respected pediatrician in his sixties since her birth, and we never missed an exam. In seventh grade, she saw a therapist for more than six months at an institute that specializes in girls' psychology, and yet, her therapist didn't suspect autism or ADD. This, in hindsight, is unsurprising. Girls often go undiagnosed because they learn to "mask" their autism traits.

Throughout middle school, while suffering from these undiagnosed conditions, my daughter was mercilessly bullied and called names, including "ugly," "dyke," and "fat." During the Covid-19 lockdown, the chaos, confusion, and trauma of having school on Zoom made things even worse for her. She started binge eating, and I helplessly observed her crashing self-esteem and worsening anxiety and depression. In August 2020, she experienced a mental breakdown, right after the trans announcement.

My daughter used to be a straight-A student, a writing prodigy in a gifted magnet class. Now, suddenly, ninth grade on Zoom was insurmountable. Additionally, the social situation that went along with the new virtual school was untenable for my daughter. After the collapse of the school and daily routine, these teens were spending twelve-plus hours daily on their phones—on TikTok, Instagram, and Discord. The online classes were a joke for these ADD girls. They had ample time and opportunity to watch videos of transgender activists, look at male nudes and vile porn, and encounter nonsensical gender garbage on social media.

Within four months into the lockdown, after endless hours of texting on Discord and sharing trans propaganda on their "LGBT server," the friends began converting each other to trans. After the original ring leader (a teen girl with ADHD–combined, autism, and a host of other mental diagnoses) announced that "he" was trans, another teen joined in as well. This teen also had ADD, in addition to severe family trauma, including early sexualization, an alcoholic mother, and a delinquent father. My daughter then hopped on the trans train too, quickly followed by another girl, this one with divorced parents where the mother had an "evil boyfriend." Basically the entire peer group was now trans, just like that. Out of the five girls, four were trans-identified, using male names and pronouns, with one saying she was "bi" but continuing to use her birth name. Of all the ruinous fallouts of the lockdown, the trans-indoctrination of teens via social media is inarguably the most catastrophic.

In my view, the four close friends of my teen who continue identifying as "trans gay men" are lesbians, or gender nonconforming. Not one has ever said, "I was born in the wrong body." I see their loneliness and need to fit in. They all buy cosmetics, Hello Kitty, "cute" Asian knick-knacks from the Asian boutiques (plush animals, purses), do crafts and cosplay (either a furry or female costume, always inspired by anime), and giggle in high-pitched feminine voices. Often they talk about real-life guys, schoolmates of theirs. The overall effect is disconcerting and chilling. These girls have lost their grip on reality.

Meanwhile, after my daughter's mental breakdown, we panicked and began going to doctors. First, we met with a psychologist, but the psych tests were not going to be available for ten weeks. As our daughter was getting more catatonic and unhinged with each passing day, we sought an immediately available psychiatrist. We were so lucky to find a great one who was able to render a diagnosis—autism (intelligent, high-functioning), ADHD–inattentive disorder, binge eating disorder, anxiety, and depression. Before prescribing medications, the psychiatrist wanted a physical exam, so we made an appointment with our pediatrician. The pediatrician, in turn, diagnosed her with "explosive weight gain," PCOS (polycystic ovary syndrome), insulin resistance (hyperinsulinemia), hyperandrogenism (very elevated free testosterone in teen girls), secondary amenorrhea, and prediabetes (from snacking on sweet foods to cope with the trauma of the lockdown, online school, AND A LACK OF DIAGNOSTIC CLARITY).

From a healthy, radiant, communicative, mellow, outdoorsy, affectionate child, our daughter turned into an obese zombie teen with nine new diagnoses, lying on the floor all day long with the phone in her hand, catatonic, occasionally attacking me like a vicious dog (for not buying her a binder immediately), and unable to care for herself. She was afraid to go outside the house, citing "anxiety." Only after her psychiatrist demanded that she go on thirty-minute daily walks did she begin to get out of the house.

This clusterfeck of illnesses that went undiagnosed before October 2020 set the stage for her falling into the trans cult. Back in January 2017 (age eleven), we were referred to a pediatric endocrinologist who was supposedly a top children's diabetic specialist. At this point, my daughter was moderately overweight. He did not suspect PCOS and did not test for it. He diagnosed her with prediabetes, but did not give her Metformin. He asked her, in front of both me and my husband, "Are you going to be three hundred pounds when you grow up?" Those were his exact words. An interesting approach to use on a teen girl, much less an autistic one. At the time, we didn't know that our child was autistic, with rejection sensitivity dysphoria. Turns out this question traumatized her profoundly. The doctor's advice was, "Eat better," not suspecting ADD and not acknowledging that people with ADD use food to cope, to soothe their noisy, chaotic brains.

We implemented healthy changes in her diet, but her weight gain did not improve. We were growing frustrated and started seeing another pediatrician, an experienced woman in a major clinic, who also did blood labs and also gave her a simple lecture to "eat better." Neither she nor the next pediatrician and top nutritionist for diabetics suspected PCOS, which, in hindsight, was so obvious given her fat around the belly. No one ever questioned her genuine "wolf hunger," which stemmed from insulin resistance and spiking insulin, a typical symptom of PCOS. No one raised the clinical suspicion that maybe our daughter was autistic and/or ADD, that maybe she was using food to cope, as she was grappling with big questions like, "Why am I different from my friends?" "Am I a lesbian?" "Why am I gaining weight so fast?" "Why do I feel disconnected from my body?" "Why do I hate exercising and am so uncoordinated?" Our large team of pediatricians and our endocrinologist, therapist, and even a personal fitness trainer never looked at the big picture until the lockdown and trans declaration brought her to a catastrophe.

My greatest regret is that, when I became a mother, I did not also complete a medical degree. Just so I'd have the knowledge to cope with all this and help my daughter. I thought we surrounded our child with the best, most seasoned medical professionals. I thought we were conscientious, consistent, loving parents who prioritized the health and well-being of our child. How was I supposed to know that she was autistic, with ADD and PCOS? How could I know that this would lead her to self-harm through trans ideology?

To the unholy list of medical providers who failed to see the big picture of these interconnected diagnoses, I must also add her affirming therapist. The therapist was a lesbian in her seventies who, in hindsight, caused profound damage by affirming my child's trans delusion. The therapist casually discussed nonsensical terms such as "gender congruity," without delving deeply into past traumas. I trusted her experience, wisdom, and depth of understanding of lesbians, which I thought my daughter was at the time. To be honest, though, now I am not positive my daughter is a lesbian. Maybe she will be a very late bloomer, like me and her dad, due to autism. The pressure for kids and teens to label themselves very early is ruinous. Autistics mature emotionally much later.

The therapist knew full well that my daughter had prediabetes. At the time, she was a hundred pounds overweight (this has been successfully managed since), and her liver enzymes and cholesterol were abnormal. The therapist also knew all her mental diagnoses. The therapist suggested things such as, and I quote, "Try calling your parents' insurance to see if you are eligible for testosterone." ("T" causes liver cancer and liver failure in women, alongside uterine atrophy.) "Yes, T will bring you gender congruity." I am still trying to understand, was the therapist trying to provoke my daughter, to see her reaction, or was she serious? The level of unprofessionalism to the tune of $250 per session was staggering.

I was emphatic with the therapist about the fact that my daughter had never before exhibited interest in being the opposite sex. None of my questions were answered, such as, "Is it no longer okay to be a lesbian? And if so, why?" "The ninth-grade art teacher told me that 25 percent of her female art students use male names and pronouns—what is the explosion in trans all about?" When I asked the therapist, "Please discuss with my child curtailing her hours on social media," she replied, "She is using social media to nurse her broken heart and to distract herself. It's okay to be on her phone all day . . ." As though she wanted my teen to consume more and more trans propaganda online.

I did ask her in writing the following questions: "Could this epidemic of girls self-identifying as 'trans' be a revolt by teen girls toward the extreme sexualization and victimization of women? Toward the total fetishization of the 'Barbie doll look' and the elevation of it as the only possible model for femininity? Toward the constant bullying and degrading attitudes toward teen girls who don't look like Barbie dolls? Toward the pervasive, profound, and unchanging misogyny that girls experience at every step, personally, professionally, spiritually?"

I also asked, "Could this be teenage rebellion against overprotective parents? Teenage revenge against a neurotic, snarky father and over-whelmed-with-work-stress and deadlines mother? Because, sure as hell, our daughter does not have the first idea of what a transsexual person is, and this is all imitation and parroting."

The therapist never gave me answers to these questions. She called my daughter "he."

We discontinued working with this therapist in May 2021.

* * *

In June 2021, my daughter and I fled the city she'd lived in her whole life. She left her home, her school, her friends who got her into this, and her pediatrician, clinic, and therapist. I left behind my professional community, my home, and my husband of eighteen years. We moved to a small farming community where my daughter had a summer job being a farmhand and helping with animals. This experience has been intensely healing and centering. She started tenth grade in a tiny school for local families. I am extremely fortunate to work remotely on the computer. Over the last fifteen months, my objective has been to put her on a path of healing: first, pulling her out of the black hole of mental crisis, then setting up tutors for her to not flunk ninth grade, then managing her PCOS and weight loss, then organizing the big move to the mountains and her summer job, and now helping her navigate tenth grade and keeping her on the path of healing. The only doctor from 2020 we are still seeing is her wonderful psychiatrist.

We have left everyone and everything behind in the quest to save my daughter. My daughter and I still do thirty-minute daily walks together. I see glimmers of hope and healing. She and I remain close and have an open, authentic relationship. She has not desisted yet. I take it one day at a time. The future is unknown.

20

An Internet-Fueled Crisis

How many female teens with rapid-onset gender dysphoria (ROGD) have ever experienced orgasm? I don't know the answer, of course, but I do know that, despite being in her late teens, my own trans-identifying kid has never even kissed anyone, boy or girl. She mistrusts her body, likely because she hasn't yet become acquainted with it. Yet she's suddenly sure that she wants to undergo radical sex-change surgery, which, along with a host of other irreversible somatic changes wrought by cross-sex hormones, will destroy her chances of ever experiencing sexual fulfillment while massively reducing the dating pool of potential partners of either sex.

This generation, thanks to lockdown, the Internet, and parental fears of "stranger danger," stages its teen rebellion indoors. My own generation's learning curve was a messier business, involving flesh and blood interactions—underage drinking, clumsy snogging and fumbling in the back row of the cinema, smoking weed together on the school field, going to gigs and nightclubs, sneaking back into the house at 3 a.m. We parents of trans-identifying kids ought to feel relieved then. After all, we know that our loved ones are "safe" in their bedrooms and not about to announce an unwanted pregnancy or a substance addiction.

Our kids are beating a retreat from adulthood and puberty—the uncompromising femaleness of breasts, periods, body hair. And is it any surprise? Regression to the safer space of childhood all while making the ultimate *épater les bourgeois*/fuck you statement to your parents, you get the best of both worlds—to stay forever young while exercising the ultimate choice over your future incarnation, the nuke in the arsenal of teenage shock tactics. And how to resist such temptation? A Hansel and Gretel–style cornucopia of candy-striped flags, buttons, and paraphernalia in baby pinks and blues, the stylized anime universe, a more sophisticated take on the dressing-up box in cosplay, the lure of the glitter family, the love bombing and acceptance—all in all, a ready-made community for the shy and confused.

Sexuality and identity are distinct from one another, but how distinct? After all, the trans movement, supposedly having nothing to do with sexuality, has piggy-backed onto the LGB movement, which has everything to do with it. Can you have a defined sense of your identity without first understanding your sexuality? And can you know much about your sexuality without actually testing it out with a partner? Many of the kids in question are underage, so no one would want to encourage such premature experimentation. But the "born in the wrong body" narrative refines and justifies the more widespread body hatred among girls reaching the terrifying precipice of puberty. Young transitioners are reacting to what Ariel Levy termed the "pornification of mainstream culture" with the shockingly, and in many cases, literalized fantasy of inhabiting another, more acceptable body—a male body—made possible thanks to the efforts of Big Pharma and the trans lobby.

Internalized misogyny and internalized homophobia are well-known triggers for young women seeking to transition. The majority of trans youth, whether male or female, if allowed to explore their dysphoria without medical intervention, go on to desist. Of these desisters, most come out as gay or lesbian and go on to live fulfilled adult lives. Under such circumstances, the rush to affirm itself can be read as a kind of conversion therapy, i.e., "transing the gay away." So is it a push to suggest that, for many, the identity question at the heart of transition could be reframed as a crisis of sexuality?

To go back to the earlier point about the puerile presentation of a trans lifestyle—the manga, the saturated graphics, etc.—the cynicism is evident. It's aimed at very young kids, tweens and younger, yet its appeal stretches to older teens who seek refuge from their burgeoning sexuality. At the very same time that they stage their grown-up revolt against the oppressive cis-world, they long for a simpler time when their alarmingly obvious sexed body and the real ravages of dysphoria did not shape their lives—they're nostalgic for Never Never Land, the rewind-button fairy-tale childhood that the newfound trans-utopia seems to promise.

My daughter becomes justifiably outraged at the merest whiff of pedophilia attaching itself to various royals and celebrities, yet she's unwittingly been groomed online by a bunch of autogynephilic (AGP) fetishists, alongside the usual trans-male influencers, into thinking she will never be happy unless she undergoes "top surgery," that childishly euphemistic term in a growing lexicon of authoritarian newspeak. She's autistic and she's bisexual, like so many other ROGD-presenting girls her age. She claims to be okay with her sexuality, but at this point, it's a theoretical proposition, given that she's never actually had a girlfriend or boyfriend. I suspect, though, that she is really not all that "okay" with her sexuality; that she's running away from it with the encouragement of YouTube and a group of virtual "friends" on social media; and, most of all, that she would rather annihilate her sexed body than come to terms with it, first by herself and later on with a loving partner of her choice.

21

A Death Cult with Anime and Unicorns

Six months ago, my daughter, who is sixteen and identifies as trans but has not yet socially transitioned, took a massive paracetamol overdose. It was sheer coincidence, or perhaps a mum's intuition, that I checked in on her at 1 a.m. that morning—usually I would have been asleep at that time. We rushed to the hospital where we spent three days. It was touch and go, but she survived, and I cannot even begin to contemplate the alternative scenario.

Since then, the promised weekly sessions from the Child and Adolescent Mental Health Service (CAMHS) have not been forthcoming. Instead, I did lots of research and found only one psychotherapy practice in the whole country (we're in the United Kingdom) that has not explicitly been captured by the affirmative model. Ambiguities in the government's proposed anti-conversion bill for LGBT people, which has now been overturned for trans people but upheld for LGB people, would have left scope for this clinic, which just offers no-frills, standard psychotherapy, to be branded transphobic. So now, mercifully, my daughter is able to explore her feelings about her dysphoria in a nonjudgmental and supportive environment and will hopefully stave off, and even divert, the seemingly inevitable pathway to irreversibly damaging medical transition.

My daughter is autistic. She suffered early trauma when I was hospitalized, on more than one occasion, with suicidal psychosis. I am schizophrenic and, when delusional, believed that everyone in the entire world wanted me to kill myself. We are very close, and as a single-parent family, her own world was turned upside-down when she had to leave our family home and go to stay with my sister. I'm not a psychotherapist myself, so I can only speculate that seeing her mum, the closest woman to her, in such a frightening and disempowered situation, might have impacted her conception of her own gender identity, along with putting ideas into her mind that suicide is a viable option when in mental distress. Add social contagion to the mix, beginning with a penchant for anime, as in so many cases, and the powerful obsessions kids on the spectrum can develop about a whole range of subjects, from *My Little Pony* to unicorns and double mastectomies, and the conditions were ripe for rapid-onset gender dysphoria (ROGD).

As far as I'm concerned, my daughter has joined a death cult. The figures surrounding suicidality and trans are deliberately obfuscated—for example, the charity and advocacy organization Mermaids, which "supports gender-diverse kids," cites the distorted and inflated survey stats on child suicidality provided by "LGBT+ mental health charity" PACE in order to argue for early medical intervention (blockers and hormones). My daughter has cited these same statistics on several occasions. Thanks in part to this "study," she firmly believes that as a trans person, whether she goes ahead with transition or not (this is still a question in her mind), the chances of her taking her own life are much higher than for other people. This is, frankly, terrifying. Beliefs can be made manifest. Suicidality, like trans ideology itself, is contagious.

Suicide is romanticized in the collective psyche, especially among alternative, marginalized communities. Marilyn Monroe, Kurt Cobain, and countless other cultural icons are mythologized decades after their deaths, their untimely and tragic demises glamorized in the popular imagination. Émile Durkheim demonstrated, back in the nineteenth century, that cultural factors could influence this otherwise most personal of decisions. Teenagers, especially, are drawn to romanticize suicide. I did it myself, as a young Goth back in the day—like my daughter, I sat in a darkened room and self-harmed while listening to my favorite moody tracks—in fact, the parallels between Goth and trans are striking in so many ways, the main difference being that, unlike my daughter, the most serious bodily modification I was considering undergoing at that tender age was a homemade tattoo, but that's a story for another time.

If, as is so often argued, the trans population has always been significant in numbers but historical oppression meant that trans people could not come forward or seek medical transition, why were there not proportionally high suicide rates across history that reflect the currently touted suicide stats?

Yesterday, my daughter came home and initiated a chat about hormones and surgery. I held my usual line—she can be as gender nonconforming as she likes, but I won't support her harming her body. She seemed satisfied by this answer, although she disagreed with it at first. Then she went off to play with her teddies, dressing one fluffy dinosaur up as Che Guevara. She's a young sixteen and needs help to do lots of things that other kids her age have done independently for years. Following her devastating attempt last year, I took advice from an affirming psychotherapist. I was, of course, wracked with guilt. Had my nonaffirming stance led to this? I relented on the issue of respiratory-restricting binders. I asked my daughter about preferred pronouns, which she was unsure about. And then, once things had calmed down, I trusted my gut. I found a more compassionate therapist and realized this: my daughter wants me to keep her safe.

Parents on Gender Ideology

22

Why Our Smart Kids Think They're Trans: The Idiotic Reasons They've Given Us That Come Straight from the Gender Cult

Are you under the impression that trans kids just know who they are and that transition is how they become their true selves?

As parents of these trans-identified teens you read about on the news, we beg to differ. You see, our kids are smart, many of them extremely smart. In some ways, they are wise beyond their years. We love them more than anything and would and do put our lives on the line for them. At the same time, in many ways (and we say this in the most loving possible way as their parents), they are total idiots—just like we all were at their age. They are teens, and, by definition, they are immature, moody, mercurial, lacking in judgment, rebellious, sarcastic, and impulsive.

In other words, our kids are just regular kids . . . except for the fact that they have been swept up in a socially contagious gender cult. They don't know what they are asking for, they don't think through consequences, and they should not be allowed to self-diagnose a condition that involves body modification through life-altering drugs and surgery.

We, the parents of Parents with Inconvenient Truths about Trans (PITT), communicate with our kids—and our kids feel comfortable talking to us as their trusted parents and caretakers. And, what you might not know, is that what our kids have told us highlights their total cluelessness and lack of understanding of cause and effect, choice and consequence. They have no real comprehension of what they can expect from "transition" and, instead, view it as an instant cure for their transient teenage angst, other existing disorders, woes, friendship difficulties, and love lives. Whatever transition may be, it certainly is not any of that.

So, before you start with the *blah, blah,* we're just transphobic parents and trans-exclusionary radical feminists (TERFs), take a look at this representative sampling of why the kids of PITT parents think they are trans—in their own words—and why, in their own words, they believe that "transition" is the cure.

Maybe after reading this, like us, you'll think twice about injecting children and young people with wrong-sex hormones and puberty blockers, chemically sterilizing them, and enabling surgeries to lop off their healthy body parts.

I *know* I'm trans because . . .

- I like rom-coms and lesbian porn. (male, 15)

- I felt euphoric when I put girl clothes on my Animal Crossing avatar. (male, 13)

- I felt uncomfortable with my appearance, and when I searched online, Reddit suggested a trans subreddit that I read. Then it all made perfect sense—I'm trans! (male, 15)

- A social worker I talked to at school said I was trans. I hadn't really thought about it before she brought it up, but it seems right to me. (male, 17)

- I don't know how to explain why I feel trans, but it's sort of like when you get a bad haircut that you know isn't right for you. (male, 14)

- I know in my brain, and I know my brain. (male, 15)

- I'm a girl because I like long hair, clothes for girls, hair clips, and makeup. (male, 13)

- I like soft things and I am sensitive and kind and soft-spoken. (male, 21, with a known sensory-processing disorder)

- I just feel like it. (female, 13)

- I don't want to be anyone's arm candy, and I don't like my boobs now that I have them. (female, 21)

- Because I have gender dysphoria. Also, taking testosterone will allow me to have a muscular physique while working out less. (female, 15, with a known eating disorder—exercise bulimia)

- I don't know . . . I just feel like a boy. (female, 13)

- Because I prefer he/him pronouns and I have a boy brain. I feel like a boy. What does it mean to have a boy brain? I don't know; I just do. What does it feel like to be a boy? It feels like what I feel like. (female, 12)

- I prefer more masculine clothes and male pronouns, although I'm not opposed to feminine things and wearing dresses. I hate my breasts and my period, and how my body changed during puberty. (family, 17)

Gender transition is the answer for me because . . .

- I've had crushes on girls and boys, but transition will make me sure if I like girls or boys. (male, 13)

- It just will. (female, 21)

- Then I wouldn't have to go through puberty. Male puberty would be too stressful for me. (male, 12)

- Once I'm on hormones, I can wear loud colors. (male, 14)

- I had a crush on a hot guy and I'm a guy. Reddit said when I'm a girl, the object of my desire will like me back. (male, 15)

Our kids have really thought this through with some pretty sound logic, huh?

Still think our kids are trans? Better prove it before you interfere with our teens.

23

An Ideological Threat to My Daughter, My Family, and Women's Healthcare

"We will be examining our gendered naming conventions, including the Women's Clinics and Mother Baby Clinics, in order to be inclusive of those who do not identify as women." As the Executive Medical Director for Women's Services of my organization, the email landed like a punch to the gut.

I am an obstetrician-gynecologist (OBGYN) and leader in my organization, where we take great pride in the respectful, high-quality care we provide patients. We are especially proud of our partnership with community organizations in our efforts toward reducing disparities in birth outcomes. Our efforts toward inclusivity include sensitivity to different family configurations and the use of preferred pronouns with our patients. But now—will we no longer be identified as caring for women or mothers?

My sensitivity to issues involving transgender individuals started as these issues began to seep into the media. I wondered: Why are people fussing over what bathroom is used? Don't they have something more important to think about? If a child's path to self-acceptance is through transition to the other gender, why would we object? After all, it's a rare situation.

This all changed when the gender storm hit my family. My daughter was bright and social with adults from an early age. She had always been a typical girl. Her friends were virtually all girls. She begged for Cinder-

140

ella dresses and preferred to wear purple and pink. She ignored her older brother's books and toys, instead preferring crafty activities. She never asked to wear his hand-me-downs. In early high school, she started going by a gender-neutral name. I laughed when I started receiving emails addressed to the mother of "[gender-neutral name]." I assumed it was just another one of my independent daughter's quirky pranks. This was followed by her hair getting shorter and shorter, finally culminating in a shaved head. I know now that is a typical foreshadowing of what was to come, but, at the time, I was naïve. It simply never occurred to me that this was anything beyond a teenager trying on different styles. A year into the pandemic, her mental health deteriorated. She would fly into rages easily and became intolerant of any request or slightly negative comment. It became more difficult for her to attend online classes, and she began missing commitments. Finally came the statement: "Mom, I am a boy."

My first response was a deep sigh as I braced myself for a shared struggle to figure this out. I took responsibility for communicating this news with my family. I reiterated my support for my daughter. Despite my initial affirming response, her anger at me only grew. My husband and I met with an online support group for families of trans-identified kids. There we heard similar stories of previously gender-conforming girls whose declining mental health was not reversed when they began testosterone. One family of a five-year-old natal male shared, "We are a gender-expansive family. We asked our child if they are a boy or a girl. She said a girl, and we are here to learn how to support her." This announcement was met with accolades from the group. My husband and I got off the call and turned to each other. What on Earth is happening? Are they really willing to engage in this social experiment with their child?

The fourteen months since then have been a whirlwind of learning and crisis. I have since immersed myself in understanding the literature as it relates to the care of gender dysphoric children and young adults. I now know that the science doesn't support transition as a path to well-being. I recognize the steps of my daughter's journey into the cult of transgender ideology. I see how her middle-school body dysmorphia and conflicted relationship with her dad set her up for this. While I spent those years watching for signs of an eating disorder, I now see that

I should have been on the lookout for the "new anorexia," gender dysphoria. As things became even stormier at home during these months after her announcement, my daughter moved out and into the home of a friend. She has since graduated from high school, started college, dropped out of college, and spent three weeks in a psychiatric facility. I have periodically raged at her, raged at the world, and always raged at myself.

My grief has been dominated by a deep fear for her future. The *60 Minutes* segment featuring detransitioners was aired in the same month she shared her news with me. The tragedy of the detransitioners' regret has always been front and center for me. I grieve the loss of the beautiful young woman with a passion for singing that my daughter used to be, now replaced by this unkempt, angry, gravelly voiced stranger. Grief has often been mixed with self-hatred. Why didn't I catch this sooner? How did I not protect her from the harm that put her at risk? What kind of a woman am I that my daughter would want to be a man? My grief has been tinged with a deep sense of betrayal. How can you just quit the team?

Through all the turmoil and my great despair, I have had great support. My husband is a rock. My family has wrapped their arms around me and are bravely, persistently positive to my daughter.

And I have taken tremendous refuge in work. As I berate myself for my apparent failure parenting a daughter, I take comfort that I am contributing to an organization that provides for women. I take joy in the work, knowing that we support women as they grow into young adults, as some of them become mothers, and as they grow older. Many times, in the depths of my anguish over my daughter's well-being and our damaged relationship, I have been pulled into a position of equanimity by the sense of accomplishment and good that has been done as part of the woman's health team I work with.

The afternoon the email arrived, I had left the office for a haircut. As I waited in the lobby, I quickly checked my phone for any needs that had arisen in the past hour, and my heart started pounding as I digested the message. When my hairdresser called me back and I laid my head back into the sink, the shock of the email washed over me. Tears crept out of the corners of my eyes and mixed with the soapy water. By the time I returned to my inbox, several colleagues had responded to the email with messages of support for the effort. I felt alienated from the team with whom I work so closely. I spent the evening in a new state of grief—not only has trans ideology taken my daughter, but now it is threatening my vocation and sense of self as a provider of women's healthcare.

Subsequently, the team acquiesced to my plea that the needs of women to have sex-specific medical care should not be subjugated to the needs of men, even when those "men" have female reproductive parts. We are setting aside renaming our services for now and are instead considering sensitivity training to ensure our staff is well prepared to accommodate trans men in our care settings. I was able to influence the direction for two reasons only: (1) I have a position of power and (2) my colleagues know the situation my daughter is in and are trying to treat me gently. But I have only kicked the can down the road. Either I will ultimately decide I am not the right leader for the organization at this moment in time or, hopefully, others will see the pendulum has swung too far and attitudes will settle into a more moderate position. For the sake of the women we serve, I desperately wish for the latter.

24

Testifying and Repenting: A New Cult

Nobody intends to join a cult. One day, you realize you are in one, and then you panic—because now you have to make a choice. Leaving means you are going to have to give up your entire life. You could lose your friends, your support system, and sometimes your family. Everything you knew about the world and how life works is now questionable. Staying means you live every day in a lie, pretending to believe when you know that you don't, and slowly you start to go crazy. You want to re-enter normal society, but as you do, you realize how much of yourself was given up while you were immersed inside.

I was raised in a community that many people, including myself, would classify as a cult. I remember the sense of community. I remember feeling sure of my purpose in life, safe in the knowledge that there was a road map to happiness. I remember sitting around the campfire in the woods as a teenage girl, surrounded by other girls, singing songs and testifying to the truthfulness of our prophet, who we knew spoke directly to God. One girl would speak, and then another, and another. As the night got darker, every girl was filled with the spirit of the Lord, all of us weeping and gasping for air as we felt the burning of the Holy Spirit lift us up. I would have died, gladly, if I had been asked to during one of these sessions.

The entire congregation would meet in church on Sunday for hours at a time. Adults would stand in front of the congregation, grown men and women, testifying with tears streaming down their faces. They knew the Church was God's Church. They would tell stories, which proved what they were feeling was God's Witness. All good feelings were the Holy Spirit. All bad feelings were Satan, leading men astray, away from the Truth.

We raised a lot of money for various causes, all of which were funneled through the organization's coffers. Archeological digs, books, various classes, all of which were purported to be academic pursuits that proved we were right and showed that The World was too stiff-necked and arrogant to admit it and join us. There were very educated and important people in our ranks: PhDs, medical doctors, lawyers, politicians, CEOs, and movie stars. We used them as even more proof that we were on the right path, straight up to the Kingdom of Heaven.

And then, one day, I realized I was in a cult. And I left. It took years to recover. I lost friends, family—my entire life was uprooted. I learned a lot in leaving. Now I knew that my feelings were not an indication of what was real. Now I knew definitively that I could be manipulated. In reaction, I learned how to evaluate evidence. I learned that educated people were not always right. I learned that there are people who are willing to prey on the lonely, and the confused, and those of us that have a deep need to connect with something bigger than ourselves. I learned that people can believe something to the core of their being and build a life on it and, in the end, turn out to be wrong.

For the past year, I have watched with horror as my own child has descended into a new cult, and I am powerless to stop it. The more I push back, the more he holds on, which is an act that I recognize. One-fifth of his grade at his high school now identifies as "trans," and the school has responded by printing up a new policy on inclusion and teaching a course called "Trans 101" for the parents. It is taught by a local trans resource center, which is connected to the gender clinic at the nearby university. My son has several peers who have started hormones this year, and those of us who have balked have been branded as right-wing, abusive parents. There is a support group at school and a secret Discord server for the kids run by adult activists in our community. Separating the new converts from their skeptical families is also a tactic I recognize. We are trying to lean in with love, but how do we compete with a promise of glitter and no consequences?

This new cult has swept the Western world with its promises of a

happy life—a better self—if people would only follow the simple pre-
cepts and tenets of the new morality. Gender is the description of who
you are, and people need to modify their bodies to match their feelings.
Feelings are how you decide how to sculpt yourself, and there is a new set
of terminology to describe them. Euphoria means you have found your
correct gender, and there is a step-by-step guide to salvation. Dysphoria
means you are living in falsehood and are on a certain pathway to misery
and self-harm, a hell of your own making. The prophets have medicine
you can purchase. They have surgeries you can undergo and emerge as a
new, better version of your true self. They have articles of faith you can
memorize and recite when you are feeling low or use as weapons against
the nonbelievers. They have sins to which you can confess and repent—
new sins that have been constructed to support the gender doctrines:
misgendering, dead-naming, ignoring pronouns, referring to a biological
binary, saying the word "woman." The list is ever-growing, and it provides a sense of superiority to those on the inside.

"Educate yourself" is the constant refrain of the devout, as they
count the angels dancing on the head of their gender pin. The apostates
are evil and deserve to suffer, and believers have the right to force them
into atonement. The saints can do no wrong and are guaranteed a spot in
heaven, no matter what acts they might perform. Questioning any part
of the scriptures they believe makes you an anti, a transphobe, a TERF, a
demon full of the spirit of contention, a cis-het. The apostles live online,
preaching the Good Word on Twitter, and Reddit, and Youtube, and
every other social media platform, collecting converts and smiting the
sinners.

I don't understand it, but I see it very clearly. The United States has
always exported its new religions to the rest of the world. Our culture
seems to have a deep need for a new type of spirituality, a joining of
traditional religious fervor with the hope of exploring new territory and
worshiping individuality. It has happened many times before. But why
are the liberal politicians supporting this new theocracy? Why are the
medical doctors paving a pathway that can only lead to more suffering?
Why are mental health experts jumping on the train that clearly has
"social contagion" written on the manifest?

When I joined conventional society as an adult, I thought I had
left this type of thinking behind. But here it is again—a religion that

I have to believe or I will be shunned by my own child, my peers, and my colleagues. I am afraid of what I see forming all around me because I already lived this life . . . and I know how it ends. It ends in suffering and a wasted life, a malformed sense of self, a world of opportunities left untried. But you cannot logic Believers out of a cult. They do not want to hear why their new knowledge is illogical. They do not want to see evidence of the grift of the leaders and their acolytes. The more you reason with them, the more the ideology entices, burrowing in and taking deeper root. Persecution makes a Testimony burn brighter, to recap a phrase I heard many times from the pulpit.

I don't know how to protect my child, or yours, when it seems the entire world has gone mad and joined a religion that no one can clearly articulate, let alone understand. There are only feelings to support this ideology, which I learned is not a way to find Truth. There is no magic medicine. There is no such thing as "gender" in the way it is preached today. And I will continue to believe this until I see hard evidence otherwise. We are all people—complicated and emotional, seeking meaning and connection. We are men and women because our bodies are coded to support the existence of human life in two different ways. One does not have more value than the other—they are complements to each other—and it has nothing to do with what we wear, what we like, or who we love. We cannot change our sex, and it is our biology that determines it, not our feelings. Anyone who tells you otherwise is trying to sell you a lie, to manipulate you. But until we remove the blinders constructed by the gender cult, which has seemingly overwhelmed rational forces in our society, adherents to the faith, like my son, will never see through to the truth beyond.

25

I Was a True Believer

I was a true believer.

I was a social justice organizer and facilitator before social justice overtook the world. I was at the forefront, introducing the concept of intersectionality to progressive organizations and having people share their pronouns. My friends and I felt we were the cool kids, the vanguard of revolutionary work to change the world, to achieve what people in the social justice movement call "collective liberation." I was deeply committed to the work of creating another world that was possible.

Within this context, I came out as a lesbian and identified as queer. And then I fell in love, entered a committed relationship with my spouse, and gave birth to our first son. Two years later, my partner gave birth to our second son. Having children and experiencing the absolutely life-changing love and devotion to them was a game changer for me. And it was when, to paraphrase the subtitle of Helen Joyce's book *Trans*, ideology began to meet reality.

I immediately began to feel the tensions inside of me between what I felt intuitively and instinctively as a mother and what I "should" be doing as a white antiracist social justice parent. Because of my own experiences of perceived victimhood with my own parents' rejection of my sexuality, I wanted to make sure I would honor my children's "authentic selves." I was primed to look for any clues that might suggest they could be transgender.

We raised both our sons as gender neutral as possible, with gender-neutral clothes, toys, and language. While we did use he/him pronouns and others in their life called them boys, we did not call them boys, or even tell them that they were boys. We made all language gender neutral. In everyday reading of books or descriptions of people in our lives, we did not say "man" or "woman"; we said "people." We thought we were doing the right and best thing, both for them and for the world.

At an early age, we noticed that our first son was a bit different. He was highly sensitive and was extremely gifted. By about the age of three, he started to orient more toward the females in his life than the males. Since he did not have the language, he would say, "I like the mamas." Some of this difference we started to attribute to possibly being transgender. Instead of orienting him to the reality of his biological sex by telling him he was a boy, we wanted him to tell us if he felt he was a boy or a girl. As true believers, we thought that he could be transgender and that we were to "follow his lead" to determine his true identity.

At the same time that this ideology was shaping my view of my son, I was also taking a very deep dive into attachment and child development. This opened my eyes to understanding the nature of attachment as hierarchical and the fact that parents, not children, are meant to be in the lead. I began to struggle with the conflict between putting my child in the lead on gender and my deepening knowledge of my responsibility to lead and orient my child. Sadly, my commitment to ideology had the upper hand.

At around the age of four, my son began to ask me if he was a boy or a girl. Instead of telling him he was a boy, I told him he could choose. I didn't use those words—I thought I could be more sophisticated than that. I told him, "When babies are born with a penis, they are called boys, and when babies are born with a vagina, they are called girls. But some babies who are born with a penis can be girls, and some babies born with a vagina can be boys. It all depends on what you feel deep inside." He continued to ask me what he was, and I continued to repeat these lines. I resolved my inner conflict by "leading" my son with this framework— you can be born with a penis, but still be a girl inside. I thought I was doing the right thing for him and for the world.

His question, and my response to it, would come back to haunt me for years and continues to haunt me now. What I know now is that I was "leading"—I was leading my innocent, sensitive child down a path of lies that were a direct on-ramp to psychological damage and life-long irreversible medical intervention. All in the name of love, acceptance, and liberation.

About six months after my son began to ask me if he was a boy or a girl, he told my spouse that he was a girl and wanted to be called "sister" and "she/her." I received a text message about this at work. On the way home that night, I resolved I would have to put all my own feelings away and support my transgender child. And that is what I did.

With this one declaration, after months of refusing to tell our son he was a boy, we changed his entire world. We told him he could be a girl. He jumped up and down on the bed, happy, saying, "I'm a girl, I'm a girl!" (What a relief it must have been to him to actually have an identity to hold on to!). We, not him, initiated changing his name. We socially transitioned him and enforced this transition with his younger brother, who was only two years old at the time and who could barely pronounce his older brother's real name.

When I look back at this, it is almost too much to write about. The grief and the shock of what we did is so deep, so wide, so sharp and penetrating. How could a mother do this to her child? To her children? I truly believed that what I was doing was pure, right, and good, only to later realize with horror what it could have led to for my child. This horror still shakes me to my core.

Once we made the decision to socially transition our son, we received resounding praise and affirmation from most of our peers. One of my friends who had also socially transitioned her young child assured me that social transition was a healthy, neutral way of allowing children to "explore" their gender identity before puberty, when decisions would need to be made about puberty blockers and hormones. We sought out support groups for parents of transgender children where we went to find out if we had "done the right thing." After all, our son showed no signs of actual gender dysphoria—was he actually transgender? At these support groups, we were told what good parents we were. How kids on the autism spectrum (which he likely is) simply "know" they are transgender earlier than other kids.

At one of the support groups we attended, we were also told that transgender identity takes a few years to develop in children. They told us that during this period, it is very important to protect the child's transgender identity, and therefore, you must eliminate contact with any family or friends who do not support this identity or go along with it. Yes, the gender therapist running this parent support group said this, and at the time, I believed her. Looking back, I now see this in a shockingly different light: this was an intentional process of concretizing transgender identity in children as young as three—the age of the youngest child in this group. When identity is concretized at that young age, children will grow up actually believing they are the opposite sex. How could medicalization not follow?

The therapist also employed the same script that many adolescents use on their parents, helping parents of transgender children script letters to grandparents, aunts, and uncles to declare a child's transgender identity and make conditions of engagement clear—you must use the name and pronouns, and embrace the new identity, or you will not have contact with the child.

After about a year of social transition for our older son, our younger son, who was only three years old, began to say he was a girl. This came as a complete shock to us. None of the things that made our older son "different" were true for our younger son. He was more of a stereotypical boy and did not show the same affinity for feminine things or females that his older brother did. We began to look more deeply at attachment again and realized that the drive for "sameness" is a primal attachment drive. We felt that this assertion of being a girl was very likely a desire to be like his older sibling, in order to feel connected to him. This assertion of being a girl became more insistent when both brothers went to school part-time, because the school program they were in included sharing their pronouns. Why could the older sibling be a "she" when the younger sibling could not? Our younger son became more and more insistent, and we became more and more distressed. The ideology was crashing with reality and shaking what had felt like solid ground. If our younger son was driven by attachment to want to be a girl, could our older son have been driven by the same thing? An attachment drive to be the same as me?

We made an appointment to see the gender therapist whom we had met at the support group in order to discuss our younger son. We truly believed that she would be able to help us sort out whether or not he was actually transgender, to pick apart the nuances of what could be going on for him as the younger brother to a transgender older "sister"—and as the only "he" in a family of "shes." To our shock, the therapist immediately began to refer to him as "she," stating that whatever pronouns a young child wants to use are the pronouns she will use to refer to them. She patronizingly assured us that it might take us more time to adjust, since parents have a hard time with this sort of thing. She expressed that it was transphobic to believe there was anything wrong with our younger son wanting to be like his older transgender sibling. When I pushed back and asserted that I was not yet convinced our younger son was transgender, she told me that if I did not change his pronouns and honor his identity, he could develop an attachment disorder.

We were unconvinced, but again, we wanted to do what was right for our son and for the world. We decided to tell him he could be a girl, and that night at dinner, we told him that we would call him "she/her." Right after dinner, I went to play an imaginary game with him, and I wanted to be affirming. I put a big, warm smile on my face and said, "Hi, my girl!" At this, my younger son stopped, looked at me, and said, "No, mama. Don't call me that." His reaction was so clear it made me stop. It pierced me to my core. I did not turn back after that.

For the next two years my partner and I dug deeper, agonized, and continued digging. Everything we thought we knew or believed that had led us to socially transition our older son began to unravel. I continued to study the attachment-based developmental approach and learned more about autism and hypersensitivity. We decided not to socially transition our younger son. We began to see clearly not only that our younger son was not transgender but also that our older son was likely not either. We knew we had to do something but struggled to figure out how. All I wanted was to go back in time, to undo what we had done. But I was still bound within the ideology. On the one hand, I felt clearer and clearer that my older son was not transgender and that we were responsible for leading him down that path by mistake. On the other hand, I worried that if he was actually transgender, I would do great damage to him by reversing the social transition. This period of time was deeply agonizing and was marked by incredible despair.

Somehow, my partner and I came to clarity that the deeper truth for our son was that he was not actually a transgender girl, but rather a highly sensitive, likely autistic boy who was born into this world without a skin and for whom the structure of certainty the girl identity provided him was a type of protection, or defense. It also provided him a way of attaching to me through sameness, a primal need for his sense of security in the world. We decided that since we were the ones who led him on this path, we were the ones that needed to lead him off of it.

A year ago, just before his eighth birthday, we did just that. And while the initial change was hard, incredibly hard, the most immediate and tangible emotion we felt from our son was relief. Actual relief. In the days following my first conversation with him about going back to his birth name and pronouns, a conversation in which I told him that males cannot be females and that we were wrong to tell him he could choose to be a girl, he was at first very mad at me, then sad. Then the next day, I felt my son rest. I felt him release a burden, lay this adult burden down, that he, as a child, was never meant to carry. He felt incredible relief. He came to rest.

Since that time, we have been healing. He has been healing. It was not easy, but my son is happy and thriving. We have watched him come to a deeper peace with himself as a boy, and he is blossoming and growing. For now, he is safe, and as each day passes, he grows into himself more. As for our younger son, he is also happy, thriving, and healing. Once his older brother became his older brother again, he happily and almost immediately settled into his identity as a boy—a further validation of our insight into the primal attachment drives that were underneath his pursuit of sameness for so long.

I fear for the future, the future for a sensitive, feminine, socially awkward boy who has spent his early childhood years actually thinking he was a girl. I fear what our culture, our institutions, his peers, and the Internet will tell him. I fear the power of the state, which seems hell-bent on destroying the parent-child relationship. No matter what the future holds, I will never ever stop fighting to protect my sons.

I am no longer a true believer.

This experience for me has felt like leaving a cult, a cult that would have me sacrifice my child to the gods of gender ideology in the name of social justice and collective liberation. I have left this cult, and I am never turning back.

Once one brick was pulled out of the wall holding up this belief system, the rest of the bricks tumbled. Now I sort through the rubble, and I seek to slowly and carefully rebuild. Rebuild my values, my view of reality, my belief system, my relationship with myself and my children, and my understanding of the world. Whatever may emerge, the protection of my children will be the compass for every step on the road ahead.

26

This Debate Is Too Important for Political Divides: As a Liberal, I Think the Right Is Right

For two years I could not look away from the governor of Florida's response to the global pandemic. It felt like I was watching a train wreck in slow motion. I knew I shouldn't read his tweets about how we didn't need to wear masks, but I couldn't look away, rubbernecking from several states up north. When the vaccine finally came out, I was so relieved, and I immediately signed on to get vaccinated, and later boosted. My family members in Florida did not; while some fell ill, some did not. They merely went about their lives, unmasked, ignoring this global health crisis, arguing that they knew what was best. I continued to listen to their governor with alarm, disagreeing with almost all he said.

And now here I am, in a state of cognitive political dissonance. This same governor, who angers me in so many ways, is now one of the few voices standing up against gender ideology. The new Florida law will prevent teachers from discussing gender and sexuality with children between kindergarten and third grade. That's kids roughly between the ages of five and eight. Should gender and sex be a focus while children are learning to read, to add, and to finger paint? I think not. Was it a topic of discussion before? Not in my memory, and not in my parents' memory, and we are all teachers. And yet, this law has become so controversial, quickly denounced by naïve liberals and teenagers concerned about protecting their trans peers. By cynically referring to it as the "Don't Say Gay" law, Democrats brilliantly managed to simplify people's thinking

155

about an important issue and to short-circuit the possibility of any reasonable discussion on the matter for their own political ends.

A new law such as this one almost always stems from currents in the socio-political sphere. Our country is in the throes of a new state of panic about our children, whose mental health has been plummeting since the beginning of the pandemic. We are looking everywhere to place the blame. Since it cannot be our own fault, it must be the public schools. This kind of argument used to drive me crazy. Nancy Reagan's overly simplistic and alarmist "Just Say No" anti-drug campaign led to the founding of over five thousand Just Say No clubs in schools; the campaign targeted racially and economically oppressed groups and resulted in a war on drugs that continues to disproportionately incarcerate BIPOC individuals. Newt Gingrich's idea of rewarding girls who graduate high school as virgins puts the burden of sexuality on girls, as do most abstinence-based education programs whose hidden curriculum is based on gender stereotypes about chaste girls who serve as gatekeepers for frenzied male sexuality. These programs, like many others, receive massive funding from the government; the United States has spent over a billion dollars on abstinence-only programs.

Today's concerns are slightly different, but the undercurrents are similar. Critical race theory (CRT) has conservatives again in a tizzy, worried their children will feel ashamed for their whiteness and guilty for the sins of their forebears. Parents are often at the forefront of these culture wars—for example, in protesting the teaching of CRT in schools—but their concerns have often been blown out of proportion. The Heritage Foundation blames CRT for the Black Lives Matter protests, diversity training, woke college campuses, and yes, the rise of LGBTQ+ clubs in schools.

This is where things get interesting for me.

As you might have guessed by now, my social views have always placed me left of center. I chose to live in a college town. I sent my kids to public schools. I supported the ACLU, Planned Parenthood, and gay marriage. I have happy adult friends who are trans and gay friends who are amazing parents. I believe that our country was built on the backs of people of color and that it's time we recognize that many of our country's laws reflect a white supremacist culture.

Despite these "liberal" beliefs, I now find myself aligned with the

Republicans when it comes to parenting.

When my daughter was twelve, and she told me she wanted a binder, I asked her to tell me more. She said she hated her new breasts and had "dysphoria"—her words. This was not the vocabulary of my twelve-year-old. Her Internet search history revealed the usual suspects of groomers and trans "influencers" on Reddit, Discord, and YouTube. She joined the GSA at school. She persisted in her beliefs, cutting her hair short, wearing "boy clothes," progressing from having a boyfriend to identifying as nonbinary to having a trans identity. Like so many parents, I got an advanced degree in trans ideology and now spend most of my free time reading, writing letters, and talking with others to explain what is actually going on here.

To most liberals, "supporting trans kids" is just another way to stand up for oppressed minority groups. It is a reflexive act for many people. This is why "Don't Say Gay" works so well on us liberals. We don't want to oppress anyone, especially not children. But supporting children is not akin to brainwashing children with gender unicorns and confusing them with choices their young brains are unable to comprehend. Kids under the age of eight live out fantasies as if they are real; they believe fairies visit their gardens and think they will become a superhero if they put on a spiderman costume. We have crossed a line by introducing this kind of magical thinking about gender to our children, and teachers, therapists, healthcare providers, pharmaceutical companies, and surgeons are now all entwined in collective, excruciating chaos.

Ironically for me, this activism of the left has come to resemble that of the conservative groups I once shunned. Using extreme rhetoric and fear-mongering, they, too, have managed to infiltrate the federal government and public schools. When the government put out an executive order last year preventing and combating discrimination on the basis of gender identity or sexual orientation, I did not applaud as I might have before. And when I learned that the ACLU outlines how you can start a GSA in your school, I stopped sending them a check. I also learned that there are now more than four thousand GSA clubs in public middle and high schools, a strategy reminiscent of the days of Just Say No. And finally, when I learned that my beloved Planned Parenthood—whom I have supported in a myriad of ways for over thirty years—was doling out cross-sex hormones to teens after a single visit, I spoke to my feminist friends about withdrawing their support as well. We now fight for abortion rights through NARAL.

I write this piece in an attempt to muddy the political waters. This cannot be another "us-versus-them" ideological political fight. We have already done this to public health and to our planet's health. For our children's health, we need to come together, regardless of where our politics lie. Children are not political tools. They should be protected from ideologies that fly in the face of biology, especially ones that manipulate their developing brains and fragile mental health. Especially ones that set them on an irreversible path to permanently changing their bodies, bodies they should be taught to love and to accept and to respect.

27

The Argument for Transitioning Children Is Based on Faith in Gender Ideology —Not on Facts or Scientific Evidence

At the age of thirteen, my daughter, following some stressful social changes in her life and a large amount of time spent on the Internet, joined a wave of teens that feel discomfort with their sex or gender role and believe they are "trans." As part of this identity and her conclusion that she is really a boy, she believes she needs to "transition" to find happiness. This phenomenon in teenagers who had no childhood gender distress has been dubbed "rapid-onset gender dysphoria" (ROGD).

Inherent to the gender ideology that my daughter has adopted is a belief that early, unquestioned gender transition is warranted for pretty much anyone who declares that they are *actually* the opposite of the sex of their biological body. And the current prevailing view in the United States and many other countries around the world is that if I want to be a good parent, I must support my daughter's gender identity and treat her gender dysphoria by affirming it (i.e., agreeing that she is male), allowing social transition (i.e., allowing her to pretend to be a male at school and home and to use a male name and pronouns), and encouraging her to medically transition (i.e., having her take puberty blockers, inject testosterone, undergo surgery to amputate her breasts, etc.) as soon as possible to allow her to be her true self.

This is a big problem for me. I don't believe that there is such a thing as a gender identity, I don't think the best treatment for gender dysphoria is chemical and surgical alteration of the body, and I don't think anyone becomes their true self by modifying their body. I am also horrified by the mental and physical side effects and long-term risks of all that transition entails. In essence, I question all of the tenets of gender ideology.

As a lawyer, I tend to boil things down to pro and con arguments, researching the facts and then debating the merits of each argument. I use logic as my guiding principle, and I do my own research.

What my research has revealed is that there is no scientific basis for the claim that "affirming" a young person's new gender identity and giving them synthetic hormones and surgeries to remove and alter body parts actually benefits those affected by this condition or feeling. No research demonstrates that these treatments decrease the suicide rate—which is supposedly extremely high among those with gender dysphoria—and no research says that better mental health results from these treatments.

My own daughter echoes common themes of gender ideology, but when I asked her what it meant to feel "male" when she is biologically female, I was met with a blank stare. Like most ROGD kids, she had no answer and said it was too difficult a question for her to answer. (I've spoken to many parents with ROGD kids over the last two years who report the exact same experience.) I explained that I was not going to encourage her to medically alter her body and risk her health because of a feeling that could not be explained. Since then, I have read and listened to everything I can get my hands on, both by advocates of gender ideology and by its critics, and I have never once seen or heard a definition for "male" or "female" in terms of gender identity.

Given the lack of science and evidence, what is the argument for medically risky treatments and telling vulnerable young people (including young children) that they are the opposite sex just because they think they are? There must be a pretty strong argument in favor of what I will call "early transition" as the preferred form of treatment for young people complaining of gender dysphoria. Otherwise, it would not be the new standard of care by medical institutions, and it would not be promoted in schools and in the media, right?

After thinking about this for over two years now and reading and listening to everything I could find on the topic, I have come to an understanding of what the arguments are in favor of early transition. I have also come to my own conclusions about the lack of merit to such arguments, and I have heard from many professionals (both therapists and at least one endocrinologist) who agree with me.

From what I can tell, the best argument for early transition is that these treatments are both psychologically and medically necessary to avoid misery and suicide. The two components to gender ideology used to justify recommending these risky treatments that permanently alter young people's bodies (in sharp contrast to rules regarding things like tattoos, alcohol consumption, or cigarette smoking, all of which are prohibited until an individual reaches a threshold age, ranging from eighteen to twenty-one) are gender identity and gender dysphoria.

Arguments in Favor of Early Transition as the Preferred Form of Treatment for Young People Complaining of Gender Dysphoria

1. *Gender identity is innate and immutable.* Gender identity is a thought or feeling that exists within all of us, although we are not all aware of it. Gender identity is the sense of one's "gender," which is either "male," "female," both, or neither (or, some would argue, one or more other genders). Gender identity has nothing to do with masculinity or femininity. Gender identity has nothing to do with sexual attraction. Stereotypical behaviors or preferences are simply not part of gender identity. Thus, by way of example, a twelve-year-old girl (someone with a female body) who feels that she is male has a male gender identity. It doesn't matter if she is feminine, gender-conforming, and never had body issues until puberty started. Her sense of her male identity is what matters. Gender identity can be realized by us at any point in life, and, once realized, never changes (or at least it's very unlikely to change). Nobody, regardless of age or circumstance, is ever confused about their gender identity, as it is an internal knowledge that is beyond challenge. Because of the relative stability and reliability of gender identity, it can be the basis for serious actions.

2. *Gender identity mismatches cause distress.* If the gender identity, which is separate from biological sex, does not match the biological sex of

the individual, this causes gender dysphoria—the distressing feeling that one's gender identity does not match one's biological sex. In the example above, the twelve-year-old girl who realizes her gender identity is male has a mismatch between her gender identity and her biological sex. This invariably causes her great distress. Gender dysphoria is not a psychological ailment but is instead a normal response to the mismatch. Although some have called the huge increase in the number of people complaining of gender dysphoria a social contagion, in actuality, it is the result of more readily available information and a more welcoming climate that allows people the freedom to express their gender dysphoria today, whereas in the past they did not feel comfortable doing so, or didn't know how to label their discomfort, and were thus forced to suffer in silence. Presumably, many of these people committed suicide.

3. *Gender distress must be remedied.* Gender dysphoria likely will drive the person to suicide if left unchecked, or, in the best case scenario, will lead to a life of complete misery. Because of this, the distress is unsustainable as a state of being and must be remedied as soon as possible. To hesitate is to court disaster.

4. *Gender distress can only be remedied by transition.* Because gender identity is innate and unchanging, and mismatches with the body cause unlivable distress, it is harmful to attempt to convince or assist the person with gender dysphoria to accept biological reality. Any attempt to help the person to come to terms with their biological sex is really an attempt to change the gender identity, and any such attempt to change the gender identity is improper conversion therapy, similar to attempts to force gay people to be attracted to the opposite sex. Notably, gender identity is one's "true" sex and is more important than one's biological sex because one's thoughts and feelings are all that matter. Since it is inappropriate to take a psychological approach to treating gender distress, everyone must uniformly treat the affected person as though they are the opposite sex to protect their fragile mental state, and the person's body must also be modified as much as possible to make the body appear as the opposite sex. This means that society is obligated to affirm a young person by using pronouns and a name that matches their gender identity, and that it

is wholly necessary to administer dangerous chemicals and perform risky surgeries on a young person who suffers from gender distress, even if this means sterilizing them. To do otherwise will lead to the young person's suicide.

Arguments Against Early Transition as the Preferred Form of Treatment for Young People Complaining of Gender Dysphoria

1. *Gender identity is undefinable; its existence cannot be demonstrated.* Gender identity rests on the assumption that "male" and "female" have definitions independent of biology and of socially created stereotypes. What does it mean to be "male" or "female?" One could speculate that biological boys and men feel different than biological girls and women, but in what ways, and are any of those ways not related to their bodies? Surely, every female or male experiences being a female or male differently, so there are billions of ways to feel like a girl, a woman, a boy, or a man. Thus, the idea that one can feel "male" or "female," separate and apart from biology and from stereotypical male or female preferences and behaviors, is nonsensical.

2. *The concept of gender identity is overreliant on gender stereotypes.* If the feeling of being male or female is really related to social expectations of masculinity or femininity (essentially stereotypes), so that the feeling that one is in the wrong body is really just a fear of being gender nonconforming (e.g., many men who go through painful medical procedures to make themselves appear like women do so because this is the only way they feel comfortable expressing their feminine side), this is a cultural issue, not a biological/medical issue. Transition is inappropriately risky to remedy social distaste with cultural stereotype nonconformity in attire, social roles, and personality. It is ironic that society calls itself accepting and progressive for encouraging people to medically alter their bodies and create the false appearance that they are biologically the opposite sex when society could instead simply accept gender nonconforming behavior.

3. *If gender identity does not exist, separate and apart from both biology and stereotypes, there is no reason that early transition is necessary to prevent a mismatch between gender identity and biological sex.* If gender iden-

tity is not real, then gender dysphoria is not a normal response to a mismatch between gender identity and biology but is instead a psychological ailment in which one is uncomfortable with one's body. There is no precedent in medicine for medically altering a healthy body as a treatment for a psychological disorder.

4. *Even assuming that gender identity is a real thing, something that is separate from biology, there is no compelling argument that it needs to match biological reality.* Why can't someone have a male gender identity and be in a female body, and why can't someone have a female gender identity and be in a male body? Can't society simply be more accepting of people whose gender identity is different than the sex of their body? If the mismatch is not inherently a bad thing, then gender dysphoria is not a normal response to a mismatch between gender identity and biology but is instead a psychological ailment in which one is uncomfortable with the mismatch. Again, there is no precedent in medicine for medically altering a healthy body as a treatment for a psychological disorder.

5. *There is substantial evidence that gender identity (if it exists at all) is NOT stable and that early intervention actually causes medical transition where it would likely have been unnecessary.* Detransitioners and desisters are emerging in droves. These are individuals who held a trans gender identity at one time but now do not. Desisters changed their minds about trans before medical transition. Detransitioners are those who medically transitioned and then reverted back to identifying as their natal sex. This indicates that gender identity, if it exists at all, is not stable. Further, it is common knowledge that children and adolescents are exploring their identities and changing their preferences and opinions constantly. Even as adults, we still change our minds, although the stability of one's "identity" increases over time. It is known that the brain is not fully mature until around the age of twenty-five. Given this basic knowledge about humans, it is irrational to make permanent, irreversible changes—that come with negative health risks—to the body of a thirteen-year-old child based solely on their feelings. It is similarly irrational to socially transition a four-year-old based on that child's self-described feeling of being "male" or "female," terms which, as I have already stated, are

devoid of meaning when it comes to gender identity. To do so with a young child is tantamount to gaslighting—in this case, making the child think that his or her current fanciful thinking is stable, unchanging reality. Studies reliably show that around 80 percent of all children who complain of gender dysphoria ultimately outgrow it if left alone to mature naturally. By contrast, around 96 percent of children put on puberty blockers go on to synthetic wrong-sex hormones. It would seem that early intervention is actually causing children to medically transition when they otherwise would have gone on to be comfortable in their healthy bodies. Thus, there is every reason not to apply early transition. This would be jumping the gun and actively interfering with, and likely even preventing, a favorable natural outcome.

6. *If unremedied gender dysphoria will likely drive a person to suicide, and if the increase in the percentage of people suffering from gender dysphoria was always about the same, where are the astronomical numbers of suicides by the silently suffering from gender dysphoria in the past?* There should literally be many thousands of such suicides. Yet, from everything I have read and heard on the subject, I have not seen a single indication that such a mass extinction of the historic dysphorics exists. Conversely, despite the claim that those who do not receive affirmation and transition interventions will surely kill themselves, the few studies on this topic have not shown a decrease in suicide rates for those who are given the recommended transition treatments.

7. *Gender dysphoria complaints are not rapidly rising due to increased modern acceptance of trans; instead, they are on the rise due to the emergence of the gender-identity belief system and the phenomenon of social contagion, as well as to ongoing homophobia and rampant sexism.* Telling people that they have a gender identity, that they need to determine what it is, and that it's possible that it doesn't match their body fosters confusion, particularly in gender-stereotype nonconforming young people, and people with issues of body dissociation. If a young person does not feel particularly female in a stereotypical way, or has nonstereotypical interests and/or same-sex attraction but has a female body, that person may conclude that they have a male gender identity and must be "transgender." After learning that it is possible

to be born "in the wrong body," someone who is gender nonstereo-typical might easily reach this conclusion. The impacted individual may obsess over the mismatch between their nebulous gender identity and their body . . . actually creating gender dysphoria. Add on normal teenage angst and social struggles, and it is not surprising to see a huge increase in gender dysphoria. Since many of the young people with gender dysphoria today are on the autism spectrum or suffer from anxiety or other mental health issues, this explanation becomes even more plausible. For very young children, gender non-conformity is most often cited as evidence that a child is trans. As in, if a boy child likes girl fashion, or dolls. Or, a girl prefers short hair and toy trucks. This is clearly a form of homophobia on the part of the parents, who push their child to become the opposite sex because they happen to have non-gender-stereotypical interests. Once the child declares that they are the opposite sex, if the parent gaslights the child, there is little hope for the child to accept themselves as they are—a gender nonconforming boy or girl. Strangely, our society encourages the creation of trans-identified children.

Conclusion

I have examined the pros and cons of early transition, and I have concluded that there is no basis for a rush to pump young people full of powerful drugs and narrow their vision of themselves. The arguments in favor of early transition have an excessive burden on belief and faith and are not based on evidence. I hope anyone reading this will weigh the pros and cons and make their own choice.

Parents on the Betrayal
of the Medical System

28

Think My Kid Is Trans? You'd Better Prove It

Here's how it goes now. You're in a family therapy session and the psychologist looks at you somberly and says, "What you need to do now is accept that this is not your son, it's your daughter. This may be hard, but after mourning for your son, in time you will accept your daughter and all will be well!"

You burst into tears, hug your child, and say, of course I will love you no matter what. You accept the inevitable and schedule a trip to the gender clinic and another therapy session.

THIS IS RIDICULOUS.

We need to stop and we need to stop now.

Extraordinary claims require extraordinary proof.

If you are going to tell me that my boy—observed at birth, with no disorders of sexual development—is a girl, you'd better be able to prove it. And not just sort of prove it—prove it beyond the shadow of a doubt, with extraordinary, overwhelming evidence, test results, and statistically significant, indisputable studies.

If you told me my kid had cancer, I'd look over the test results, pore over the research, join a study, and seek a second opinion. If my son needed knee surgery, I would explore all the pros and cons and think about the lifelong impacts and alternative options before moving forward in any direction. But I'm supposed to accept, without question, the idea that my male child is a girl and needs to alter his body to make it match some invisible internal identity?

No. That is crazy and it's time to call out all medical professionals on this. I will not accept it without proof. Not just that this is the diagnosis for the condition my kid has (if any), but also that "transition" is the appropriate treatment for it, that alternative treatments have been considered and ruled out, and that differential diagnosis has been conducted.

But you won't come up with any proof because there isn't any. This is all made up, religious, ideological nonsense and deep down we all know it. If you had proof you wouldn't need to threaten me that my child will kill himself if I don't go along. Real science doesn't need to rely on threats and intimidation. And don't you dare medicalize or operate on my child based on your theories and concepts of gender fluidity, which have zero basis in biological fact.

Tell me that there is such a thing as transgender and you can define it? Prove it.

You tell me my kid has this condition (or state of being) of transgender? Prove it.

Tell me my kid needs new pronouns or he will kill himself? Prove it.

Tell my kid needs cross-sex hormones to be happy? Prove it.

Tell me there is no alternative diagnosis for my child? Prove it.

Tell me that no alternative non-medical, non-body-modifying, non-endocrine-disorder-inducing treatments are available? Prove it.

Tell me my kid needs to be castrated to be his true self? Prove it.

I dare you.

Oh, and if you can, THEN we're still going to have to have a chat about your proof that the proposed "treatment," which we know will make my child a medical patient for life is (A) going to work to resolve his problems for the rest of his life and (B) going to be safe for his body and not introduce additional life-threatening risks.

You'd better believe I'm going to make you prove that too before you get your hands on my child.

All you other parents out there—what level of proof are you going to ask for before you allow your child puberty blockers, cross-sex hormones, and surgeries? Are you ready to just take someone's word for it? Or, like me, are you going to ask them to prove it?

29

Parents Deserve Real Answers

What a difference six months make.

Some kids are born in the wrong bodies. Since gender identity is fixed by the age of three, kids can and do tell their parents their real gender, which is sometimes different than their natal sex. Good parents listen. These kids get to go to gender clinics where they are carefully treated by a team of professionals who are there to protect them. The kids socially transition. They change their names, and they get to dress like the other gender. When it comes time for puberty, this is a stressful and traumatizing time, because they are now confronted with the sexual characteristics of the "wrong body." We block puberty, and then, when it's medically appropriate, we give them the "right" gender hormones so they can go through the "right" puberty. Later, they can have surgery that can make their bodies "right" at last, and they live happily ever after.

Some parents don't listen. In bad families, kids are repressed, trapped, and unable to be their true selves. Their parents enforce old gender tropes. Dolls and cooking sets for girls, trucks for boys. Pink and blue. These kids are forced to follow gender stereotypes for their birth gender. The resultant unbearable dysphoria and mental anguish from being forced to live in the wrong body can last for any number of years. Some teens and young adults without access to appropriate treatment for their natural condition kill themselves. Some live out their whole lives in anguish. Some, after years of repression, finally get the help they need. With the support of the community, they are accepted as they are, get medical treatment, and finally transition to their rightful gender, and they also live happily ever after.

All of the above is what this fairly liberal Jewish mom believed until only a few months ago. I bought into that narrative wholesale, like many other well-meaning people, thinking, "What's the harm?". . . until it came into my home.

One night this summer, my young teen son revealed he was "trans."

My husband and I sat down with him right away to learn more about this strange new creature that had just appeared to us. He gave the following evidence: he did not feel comfortable in his body and, about a month prior, had realized that this was because he was not a boy. He knew that he was trans because when he put girl clothes on his video game avatar, he felt "euphoria." He had had crushes on girls, but he recently wasn't so sure about his preference since he may have had a crush on a boy. He didn't like his shoulders or his voice. He felt different.

My husband and I held his hands and told him how all his feelings sounded like regular old puberty, where nothing about your body feels right, and you are starting to develop your sexual identity. We told him that people like to pretend in games. That feeling a thrill or arousal at using a female avatar in a game is not what being a girl feels like. We love you no matter what, we said. Later, in bed, we talked about how confusing puberty was for us, about our early crushes, about my husband's late development where he wondered if he was gay because he didn't really like girls (or anyone) yet. We told ourselves it was just how kids express themselves these days. It's no big deal.

Because it seemed like the thing to do, we brought our child to a psychologist. We had talked with her in advance, and she said that our son certainly didn't fit the mold of transgender and that she'd be glad to speak with him. She spoke with our son for thirty minutes. In our meeting with her that followed, she said that she agreed with our son's self-diagnosis and that it would be a ten-year process to transition him from "boy" to "girl." No doctors would see him until he was sixteen, but then he could start blockers and hormones, and later he could complete transition through surgery. Eventually, his parents would come to accept that he was our daughter, but first, he had to understand that we would be hurt and distressed and would have to mourn the loss of our son. She asked him when he planned to tell his grandparents.

Just like that, my son was a girl because he said so—and a therapist agreed after thirty minutes. This was strange to me in so many ways. My kid was not feminine. He never expressed an interest in "girl things" and he had no friends who were girls. He was happy, not in distress. I pored through my memory. Since kids "know" their gender by three, how had I so repressed him that he never told me? As a feminist, I had wanted to raise my son to respect women and to be a sensitive, good man who believed in gender-role equality. I had given him cooking play sets, presented dolls, and dressed him in gender-neutral clothing. He wasn't interested. He wanted trucks; he reveled in dirt and frogs. He climbed trees, ran around naked, had superhero sword fights with his brother. He ate with his hands and put spiders in my bed. Contrary to my understanding of how this all works, my son had no signs of distress or dysphoria, neither in childhood nor now.

I went online and learned, to my surprise, that you can become transgender at any age. According to the Internet authorities, it's biological, not mental, but sometimes you don't really know who you are until you're a little older. But once you articulate the feeling, it's a permanent thing. Not everyone feels distress. The treatment for everyone in this state is transition, again according to the online "experts." I read all sorts of reports from parents who were also initially confused because their kids didn't fit the mold. But they trusted that their kids knew who they were, and after an initial period of angst and crying, they helped their kids to transition. Now their new, restructured families were doing great!

This was all news to me. I didn't know it could happen that way. I wondered if my kid had always been that way. How did I miss that? How can I be sure now? I scoured the Internet for research showing how transgender was an immutable biological trait, but all I found was a bunch of tiny, flawed studies, including false and misleading statistics about suicide, and a whole lot of propaganda.

I started to make a table of facts and studies to understand the various positions and what we "knew." Try as I might, I could not find any definitive "facts," only ideas and concepts and a lot of emotion.

I was told that parents have to make one of two choices:

1. Accept your child's gender feelings, unreservedly and without question. In today's world that means the following: accept their new

"gender" as immutable, change their name and pronouns, dress them in stereotypical clothes for their "right" gender, and convert them to the opposite gender as soon as possible, up to and including cutting off healthy body parts. You need to accept that this is the right thing to do because it is how they are wired; their bodies must change because their minds cannot.

2. Be a transphobe, reject your child, and push them toward suicide, since living in the wrong body is an intolerable state. Subject them to mental therapy for an innate biological condition. Deny their very humanity.

Yet, I had a bunch of questions that I wanted answers to before my family set off on this life-changing path:

1. How do we know this is "hard-wired"—biological and not mental? Is this like hair color, or more like anorexia?

2. If it is hard-wired, why does it sometimes develop later in life, like it did with my teen?

3. Why is it "conversion" therapy to help kids see if they can be comfortable in their own bodies (which has no social or medical consequences) as an alternative to "transition" to another gender (which has social and medical consequences)?

4. Why do some people report that therapy helps, and they come to identify with their birth gender?

5. If kids can be sure of what they are at a young age, why do most kids grow out of feeling gender dysphoric?

6. If it is possible to know that you are a different gender, why do many kids only articulate this after taking an online quiz or hanging out on egg_irl on Reddit?

7. Is self-identification appropriate in authorizing medical treatment for children or young adults? If so, why is only gender dysphoria handled this way and not anorexia?

8. Why are gender "feelings" immutable and factual, but other ideas of inner self are not and are considered forms of mental dysphoria?

9. If there's no way to know, definitively, that transgender is a biological condition, why is medical treatment appropriate?

10. What is the evidence that "transition" is the "cure"? What about the process works and why?

11. Is the treatment safe? Why isn't it FDA approved if so?

12. Is the "cure" permanent?

After combing the Internet, I was baffled—why weren't we asking these questions? Was I the only one in this boat?

Six months later, I was entirely disillusioned. And I had learned why we aren't asking these questions. All those happy rainbow stories, those glitter families—they are cover-ups. One-sided stories were designed to show a black-and-white version of reality that is simply false. At best, the noise on the Internet is ignorant, if well-meaning. But in most cases, it is self-preserving, money-making propaganda that we are all adopting wholesale under the guise of social justice. It's not harmless, and it is not about social justice. We are confusing an entire generation, and it's having a real, irreparable, harmful effect on way more people than you realize. I'm now one of them.

We can't ask these real and valid questions about gender dysphoria today because other parents, doctors, and therapists DIDN'T ask them before they prescribed puberty blockers and cross-sex hormones to kids and young adults. And now, they cannot face asking these questions because, if they were wrong—and transgender is a mental condition, not a biological one—they just gave our kids experimental hormones and allowed surgery on their healthy bodies to treat a mental illness. The doctors would be liable. The therapists would be liable. The activists would have to admit that they might have a mental illness and that they are not a new gender. The pharmaceutical companies and gender identity clinics would be on the hook, sued out of existence, and deprived of their revenue stream.

Without the ability to question, no one can truly know one way or another. Even though there is a lot of evidence that the current approach is not sound, maybe they are right and gender identity is biological. But we cannot attempt to discover what's true or real because the costs of being wrong are too high for the stakeholders that have already bought in. For a great explanation of how good, smart people can fall into this trap, see Carol Tavris and Elliot Aronson's excellent book, *Mistakes Were Made (but Not by Me)*.

We know that most kids outgrow a trans identity by their late teens. That there is strong evidence that what we call trans behavior in kids often turns out to not be about gender identity at all, but rather is related to same-sex attraction or a mental health issue like trauma, OCD, or any number of other things. We know that a great many people come to regret transition. We're starting to hear the heartbreaking stories of young adults who fell onto the medical pathway for transgender as confused teens. After life-changing procedures, a few years later, they now feel that there were no adults in the room (for example, see Keira Bell's case), yet they are being told that their experience is not valid and that they do not deserve our help.

I've since found that there is a parent community made up of many caring moms and dads that want to ask these questions. There are also medical professionals, therapists, ethicists, politicians, and philosophers who are horrified by the ethical implications of medicalizing gender identity, and many—if not most—of them are afraid to speak out because of the inevitable and likely career-ending backlash. There are LGB groups that feel marginalized, that don't understand what gender identity and transgender have to do with sexual orientation and why they are lumped together. Most of this is being discussed in secret because it's taboo to ask the questions, to lift the veil on what I now consider to be a mass deception of the public.

The parents' stories are all like mine. Their teenage boys and girls announced they were trans out of the blue. (And don't tell us we missed the signs—we are parents—we pay attention to our kids.) These kids were never, for the most part, gender nonconforming. They were gifted loners that didn't really fit in. Many, like mine, had had extensive grooming on the Internet prior to their revelations and had fallen into the reality-bending void of porn, virtual-reality gaming, and adult-only chatrooms after engineering their way around our well-considered parental controls and screen-time limitations. The parents come from across the religious, social, political, and economic spectrum. Universally, we are told that if we don't accept our kids' new self-identifications wholesale, we're horrible people, horrible parents, and transphobic bigots.

Well, name-calling and thought suppression like this should be a sign to all of us to dig deeper, especially if we're being asked to sign up for a lifetime of expensive and untested medical care.

Do we KNOW that gender-identity conflict is a mental illness? No, we do not. But we also don't know that it isn't.

And we're not allowed to ask.

Just because others may have made life-changing decisions based on bad or nonexistent facts doesn't mean that we have to. Just because others signed the consent forms saying they understood that the risks were unknown and unstudied doesn't mean we will. We shouldn't be shunned by society or threatened with the loss of our kids if we don't blindly follow.

We are good parents, not bad ones, for asking questions and trying to understand the facts before jumping on the bandwagon that encourages our children to receive medical treatment for something invisible and theoretical. We are good parents to question dogma before we tell our kids and young adults that their natural bodies are "wrong." It is not evil to think that maybe our children's human potential and happiness are not solely defined by their gender identity but by their appetite for self-improvement, personal evolution, and internal growth, and that gender obsession will hold them back from reaching their potential. That happiness can come from within, not without. From internal, not external acceptance.

Before you tell us what our children need, before you judge us, we want a real discussion. We want real answers.

30

Doctors, Stop Gaslighting Our Gender-Confused Children

Doctors, stop gaslighting parents about their gender-confused children! We know our kids, and it turns out, you don't always know what you're doing when it comes to gender-ideology interventions.

My son was a happy-go-lucky kid in every way, until high school. Then, suddenly, he became self-conscious and insecure about himself and started discussing this with a friend who felt the same way. They both decided together that being trans was the answer.

When I found out how he was feeling, I strongly suspected my son was questioning his gender because he's on the autistic spectrum and has ADHD. So, at his pediatrician's suggestion, we took our son to a gender doctor, thinking a specialist would know how to handle the situation. But sadly, we were sorely mistaken. Instead of probing and assessing the context, the gender doctor doubled down on my son's insecurities. He validated my son's unhealthy, distressing thoughts and reinforced the idea that my son would commit suicide if we did not support this trans identity. To me, this felt like emotional blackmail.

This was a turning point for my son, in a negative way, because what doctors say to children makes a difference, and my son was raised to trust the experts. When, after extensive online research, my son clamored for puberty blockers because that seemed like the way to become a girl, his pediatrician advised him that he was too old for puberty blockers, and my son dropped it, trusting his doctor. When my son refused to leave the house during Covid-19 and spent a year indoors, my husband called the trusted pediatrician. He told my son he needed exercise to stay healthy, and, again trusting his doctor, he began to exercise. When my son purposely lost twenty pounds during his gender distress, his pediatrician stepped in and told him that he was thirty pounds underweight and that this could cause him a host of health problems. Once again, my son listened. He started eating again and has since gained thirty pounds. All of this advice helped to keep my son safe and healthy, and he was better off for it.

I used to think it was great that my son trusted his doctors. But, it really backfired when he encountered the gender doctor. Far from keeping my son safe and healthy, AFTER the session with the gender doctor, my son's mental health declined precipitously. He started having gender dysphoria and depression, which he had never had before. This is a result of iatrogenic harm—illness caused by medical examination or treatment. It's very clear to me that if the gender doctor had simply said that feelings of body disconnect and insecurity are common in adolescence and you'll grow more comfortable in your body, everything would have been different.

Although I, too, am inclined to trust medical professionals, my gut knew that something was off with the gender doctor's affirmation approach to my son's gender confusion. I knew my son, and I had observed him changing his identity numerous times throughout his short life. How would the doctor know more about my son after speaking to him for thirty minutes? It's not like teens never make up stories to get what they want. If heroin, which leads to feelings of contentment and euphoria, was suddenly available to all teens, if they said they had a feeling that they needed heroin, would this be treated the same way? Of course not. But somehow, medical treatment based on a vague and nebulous feeling is accepted and even mandated in the field of gender.

My husband and I now had to decide how to walk back the gender doctor's trans reinforcement. This doctor harmed my son with words that took my breath away, and these words had tremendous weight on my son. It's been very difficult to overcome what the so-called expert said, but we've been doing it with success. We are improving our relationship with our son; he knows we love him and care about his future. We are giving him the space to grow up and to accept his healthy, natural body the way it is, without medical intervention. My son is no longer gender dysphoric or depressed and is happy and making goals for himself, although he still sees himself as trans. We feel secure in the knowledge that we are doing the right thing, because we know that children who are convinced they are trans change their mind 61 to 98 percent of the time.

On the other hand, my son's friend, the one who developed his trans identity at the same time as my son, is now on hormones. Unlike me, his parents believed their doctor unquestioningly. He is now on a path to be a medical patient for life, and there is mounting evidence that his mental health, as well as his physical health, will suffer due to this path he, his parents, and doctors have chosen for him.

Parents, don't let doctors emotionally blackmail you. Get informed. Your kid is fine in his or her body and does not need hormones or puberty blockers to find happiness. Your kid will grow out of their gender questioning period. Look at the detransitioners before you believe a doctor who does not know your child and only benefits from them transitioning.

Don't let doctors convince you that a child knows themselves better. How can this be true—they are children! How can a child who is too young to vote, rent a car, or drink alcohol be capable of informed consent to sterilize themselves and lose their sexual function?

Our lives have been completely changed by one fresh-out-of-med-school doctor telling us, in front of our son, that if we don't support him by doing this dangerous experimental treatment, he will commit suicide. Had the doctor decided to use "watchful waiting," which was the standard protocol of doctors for many years, our lives would not have been upended. Doctors are supposed to safeguard children, not push their ideology on them.

Doctors, don't you think it's odd that every kid that comes into your office has the same identical online-sourced script about why they think they are trans? Do you really think it's a random coincidence that all these kids are coming to this conclusion simultaneously, as my son and his friend did? Or are you choosing to look the other way? I think it is more what Upton Sinclair said: "It is difficult to get a man to understand something, when his salary depends on his not understanding it."

Doctors, stop gaslighting our children and us parents.

31

Parental Disempowerment
by the Gender Industry

The first time I heard my daughter's masculine voice, I threw up.

I was caught off-guard, alone in the house (I thought), picking burrs off the dog.

"Hello, hello? Hello, is anybody home?!"

I knew my son was not home. And his fifteen-year-old voice was deeper than this voice. Was it him? Was he in distress?

My eighteen-year-old trans-identified daughter had left home five months before, claiming we had "kicked her out." She moved in with another family who prided themselves, in their "woke" church community, on taking in the poor, homeless trans kid. She had proudly started testosterone injections three months ago. I had not realized that these injections could cause such rapid change.

I had no idea what doses she was getting, mind you. Since she was fifteen, I was completely excluded from giving input or receiving any feedback or even guidance about her healthcare decisions. The doctors had colluded with her and excluded me, her mom, in the name of "privacy," making it clear that her health is none of my business. Though, of course, I was still expected to drive her to appointments, buy her breast binders, and pay for therapists. I never questioned her evolving identity, whether gendered or otherwise, but I did question the medicalizing of it.

She would say to me: "Mom, your problem is that you are a scientist, and you know too much, and you read too much! You need to go meet with some other kids' parents who let them transition. Maybe then you would let me do this."

When I was young, people talked about lobotomies and thalidomide. My copy of *Our Bodies, Ourselves* talked about diethylstilbestrol (DES) and the Dalkon Shield. I knew that people had been unsafe at the hands of doctors and pharmaceutical companies for decades. I could also see North America buckling at the knees from an opioid crisis that had expanded and infected communities in every corner of North America, thanks to Big Pharma's appeal to treat pain with their newer, more improved opioids. "Pain is the fifth vital sign. Doctors need to treat it more aggressively. Let the patient decide how much they need. When they have real pain; it's not addictive." These were the marketing mantras that doctors now reveal they were given. Now, in my community and in the whole country, I am watching doctors buy into a new mantra: "medical affirmation" is the only treatment approach for all these kids.

As a mother, I had not worried about the safety of my child before trans; I was not an overattentive parent. I often forgot to take her for check-ups or to get her vaccines. She, on the other hand, was cautious, anxious, and a bit of a hypochondriac, sometimes obsessing over the workings of her body. It was common to hear things like, "Mom, I have a thing in my throat. Is this normal? Do I need to see the doctor? Mom, I ate yogurt and three peaches this morning before I ate the Froot Loops. Am I eating healthy?"

My little girl's father had an unpredictable presence in her life. He lived in another city and contacted her by phone only once or twice a year. When he did speak with her, he tried to lure her into living with him because he knew it would upset me. He offered her pets, treats, a new house, a trip to Disneyland. These conversations would accelerate if she went to see him for a few days at Christmas. She would come home in tears, crying that she felt sorry for him and guilty, although she did not really want to go live with him. It made her anxious, especially at night. She stopped going to sleep unless I was within twenty feet of her. She told me she was never going to grow up and move out, that she was going to live with me forever. She became increasingly insecure as she struggled through middle school.

Only her father had ever made me feel unsafe about my relationship with her. And even then, I knew the bond between her and me was immutable and solid. Nothing could loosen it. So I focused on reassuring her that she was good, that she was a healthy eater, that the thing in her throat was just a tonsil stone. She was with me; we were a safe dyad.

But there I was, in my living room, realizing all at once that the croaking sound of a pubescent, twelve-year-old boy that was emanating from our doorway was my daughter. And that our dyad had been permanently broken by other adults who I felt should know better, who should be reading the scientific evidence that says that doing this to children is not safe, is not settled.

What hit me was not a sudden wave of transphobia or even shock at the change itself; the sound of her voice made me feel threatened. It reminded me that, beyond the normal teenage modus operandi of rebellion and doing things to herself against my advice, I was no longer allowed to protect her and that there were health professionals out there willing to harm her in the name of "gender affirmation," the newest political football.

The first time I realized that our dyad was in trouble and that "professionals" would exclude me completely from trying to protect her was the day I walked into a psychiatrist's office with her at fifteen. Her anxieties about bedtime and about her body had started to generalize as she reached menarche, and her pleas for "treatment" of her "gender dysphoria" had worn me down. She had begged me, for months, to see a doctor to "treat" her with "T." I still felt confident that we would walk out of that office intact—I knew the psychiatrist as a competent professional in our community. Surely they would reassure my daughter and me that this was something she had learned about and glamourized through social media—that this trans identity was a phase of development that would evolve and resolve on its own. Or perhaps it was a new manifestation of her profound anxiety. But after thirty minutes in that office, I was welcomed to the "gender journey," where my daughter sat smugly as the psychiatrist spoke down to me, skirting pronouns by saying: "Well, you're 'the' mother; it will take a while for you to adjust."

When we left that office that early summer afternoon, my cheeks burned. I drove away flushed, speechless, nauseated by this sudden disempowerment. My daughter tried not to stare at me as I drove. I believe she was almost as surprised as I was by this new acquisition of power she had just been given. But she was pleased with the outcome; her "transgender path" had now been cleared for her. And by a perfect stranger.

Now, she was back at home again. The drop in her voice—which I also knew immediately was permanent—signaled that all the years of parental love and devotion I had given to this child had now been tossed onto a familial pyre by (supposedly) well-meaning but inexperienced and incompetent clinicians. In fact, I am not convinced they are all so well-meaning. I often wonder whether this is just a new way to be paternalistic while the old ways are frowned upon as politically backward. How ironic.

This team of "wellness providers" offering "gender-affirming care" had no idea who she is or was. None of them knew her growing up. None of them knows or has ever asked her about her absent father or tried to analyze her vulnerabilities or even attempted to fully assess the roots of her anxiety or the extent of her body obsessions. Nope. They were and continue to be bent on their singular mission of "affirmation." In fact, as far as they knew, her most traumatic life events consisted of being misgendered, verbally violated, and "abused" by her own mother.

Affirmation used to be a benign, gentle word that made me think of things people stick on their mirrors and repeat to themselves every morning for positivity and self-confidence. Now everything linked to the term "affirmative care" just makes me nauseous. Which welled up into a force that pushed its way from my throat that afternoon when I heard my daughter's voice.

She called out again. I answered with my son's name and a question mark, thinking it was him, home early. She said, "It's just me!"

"Oh," was my response. "Oh!" was my realization.

She slipped past me and up the stairs as if she had never left the house five months earlier. I ran to the nearby bathroom and retched. As a scientist and as her mother, I realized that my daughter and her female voice were gone.

This is neither transphobia nor bigotry. I know, I work, and I socialize with transgender adults. I understand and have seen the barriers they have faced. But children and teenagers suddenly announcing to the world that they need to permanently damage their bodies with the help of doctors, medicine, and surgery is not the world of gender medicine that I have known. And, anxious children being alienated from the care of their parents in the name of "affirmation medicine" feels like yet another attempt for marketers to ply a new demographic with their wares, which will be needed for my daughter's lifetime. All the while, this unsafe industry is supported and promoted by a "woke" new world of postmodern intellectual domination, which has now taken over my home and my life and left me to vomit quietly, alone, into the void left by my lost, confused child.

32

A Letter to My Son's Affirmative Therapist

Dear X,

I see that J is getting worse and worse despite the depression medication and all the therapy sessions with you. He complains of having a lot of anxiety—plus, as you know, he is still on sick leave. The really concerning thing is that when he started the sessions with you, he was fine—he had two jobs and was working on his PhD—and now he is barely surviving and has given up everything.

I don't mind you telling him that I wrote to you. Frankly, I'm convinced that this whole "trans thing" is nothing more than a maladaptive coping mechanism to deal with his previously diagnosed depression, and I'm very concerned that you keep pushing him in a direction that seems to be hurting him even more. It is terrible to think that this perfectly healthy boy has come across such unscrupulous health professionals. My son suffers from depression, which is not unusual in the midst of the current global pandemic that, as has been amply documented, has greatly affected the mental health of young people. Now an endocrinologist (whom I am in the process of denouncing even if it is the last thing I do in this life) and you, a psychologist convinced that people can be "born in the wrong body," instead of treating his mental conditions, push him to change anatomy to conform to gender stereotypes. Neither of you is the least bit curious to explore the traumas that can make a healthy person feel that they can't be happy without physically hurting themselves.

186

I know my son much better than you do. I have known him for twenty-four years, almost a quarter century. I gave birth to him and cared for him. I know he is not a woman and never has been. I don't doubt that he had dysphoria, because what is depression but superlative dysphoria, and isn't depersonalization ultimately a symptom of depression? And this idea, is it to leave his boy persona with all his sorrows behind and become someone new who can start from scratch, applauded by his friends and the sick society we live in as a hero? I don't know if that's it, I don't know if he's gay and having a hard time coming to terms with it, if he's traumatized by his feminist friends' view that all men are predators, if he's watched too much porn, or if he just felt so lonely that he needed to create a partner with his own body. These are all questions that you, as a psychologist, should be curious enough to help clear up, rather than pushing him further and further into irreparable physical and psychological damage to himself.

I do know that my son had a very traumatic childhood, that his parents' divorce affected him a lot, that he has missed his father a lot and probably me too. I know that he has suffered a lot in life and has felt very lonely at times. His girlfriend left him before the pandemic, and he had a severe depression diagnosed and untreated. And then came a pandemic that cut short his plans to travel and go back to school when he was just starting to get back on his feet. It's no surprise that it was then that he came up with this totally sudden and unexplained idea that he was a woman. What was a surprise, though, is that it took him five minutes to get wrong-sex hormones from the endocrinologist and to find himself an "affirmative therapist" to agree with his self-diagnosis and to push him further into it. If someday he regrets getting on this train you are pushing him on, as is happening to so many already, he will certainly blame you for not questioning his sudden transition and not having the interest to find out what was really wrong with him.

I recommend that you read the detransitioners forum on Reddit, which already has more than 24,000 members and is growing at a rate of a hundred per week. So sad and eye-opening to read these stories. And also read the new studies that are coming out about the reality of suicide and medical transition and the physical and psychological damage involved, as well as Genspect's statistics on the truth behind gender "facts" and "science."

I know my son is an adult, but he is a vulnerable adult with a previously diagnosed mental illness that you were well aware of when you treated him. Let this serve as a notice that I believe that with your therapy, you are harming my son, as shown by the progressive worsening he is suffering. You are not complying with the protocol that recommends not transitioning people who suffer from other prior mental illnesses in the case of my son, and I believe sooner rather than later, you will answer for your unethical practices.

Sincerely,

J's Mom

33

The Madness of "Gender Specialists"

This is my story. I am a professional woman, and I dedicated my life to the study and practice of medicine. For twenty-five years I practiced general psychiatry. I gave birth late in life. I had two children—a son and a daughter. My son and firstborn died suddenly when he was only five years old from a tragic accident. My daughter was only two at the time. At that tender age, she experienced a significant change in the affect and behavior of both of her grieving parents, but especially in me, her mother, who had to return to work but had been her stay-at-home caregiving mother until that point.

When she was six years old, my daughter's best friend lost her own mother in a traffic accident. The distraught widowed father could not be relied upon to sustain his daughter's relationship with my daughter, and both of the girls suffered as a result. The following year, I, too, was involved in a serious auto accident and almost lost my life. I mention these incidents because these were some events that traumatized my young daughter—my only remaining child. They surely shaped her childhood and her view of the world, but were never a focus for therapy, as far as I know.

My daughter seemed perfectly normal throughout her childhood and into her middle school years. She chose her own clothes and toys for the most part, and there was nothing unusual about her choices. She did pick a few friends that I didn't care for, but I never prevented her from socializing with these children. Nevertheless, by the end of junior high, it was clear that my daughter needed a change of venue. She was unhappy and had not really found her peer group, and seemed to be floundering academically as well. We took the fairly drastic step of buying another house in a different city a short drive away so that our daughter would qualify for matriculation at a local art school with a drama program.

Even though I was more informed than many other parents in my situation, I was not prepared when my daughter, in her junior year of high school, informed me that she considered herself to be partly a boy. I laughed it off rather casually. I told her the females who were in touch with the male parts of themselves were the lucky ones, able to access an inner Animus. I had no objection to her wearing boys' clothes once or twice a week to school. She was playing with characterization and costumery at the time and seem to be thriving in her high school milieu.

Little did I know the extent to which pornography, fan fiction, images on sites like DeviantArt, and various social media websites were influencing my child in insidious and dangerous ways. At the beginning of her senior year, she announced to her teachers that she was now identifying as a boy. She chose another name, with a more gender-neutral sound, and sought permission to use the boys' bathrooms and locker rooms. The principal, who met with us (her parents), informed us that he had no choice but to honor her wishes, thanks to Obama's new interpretation of Title IX, allowing so-called "gender identity" to trump biological sex.

During my daughter's senior year of high school, I took her to see a friend and colleague of mine, someone who had known my daughter all her life. This woman was a gynecologist, and I thought of her as a family friend as well. She informed me at the very first visit that she would be likely to place my daughter on Lupron, a hormone blocker, and that she would not be discussing my daughter's treatment with me, now or in the future. Under the law, my daughter had a right to privacy, and as her physician, the doctor had a duty to maintain it.

For ten months, my seventeen-year-old daughter took Lupron injections once a month, administered under the direction of this gynecologist. This Lupron was described to me as safe and fully reversible, a kind of "pause" button to allow my child time to consider her decision. In reality, it is like stepping onto a runaway train, as it is the first step in a long chain of events that leads along a predictable pathway. I believe that the gynecologist prescribed the Lupron under false pretenses, almost as a kind of placebo, because at seventeen, my daughter was already through her puberty, and prescribing cross-sex hormones to a child would have triggered an assessment by a panel in a city two hours away. Finally, on the eve of her eighteenth birthday, she referred my daughter to a local clinic with a "gender specialist" who would take over the case from now on. It is my distinct impression that the gynecologist was happy to wash her hands of any responsibility for my daughter's future.

One Monday, my child met with this "gender specialist," a marriage-and-family counselor, who told her she could be on testosterone by the end of the week—by that Friday. As a psychiatrist and a former employee of this very clinic, I could not take this news without some pushback and discussed my strategy for doing so with friends. I walked in on Wednesday to confront this therapist. I brought in a written summary of what I considered the pertinent events of my daughter's life, which I knew would be added to her medical record. I asked about the differential diagnosis and the counseling she would receive prior to beginning something as drastic as cross-sex hormones.

Of course, neither was forthcoming. The therapist attempted to shut me down by once again invoking the patient-therapist relationship and Health Insurance Portability and Accountability Act (HIPAA) rules. I reminded her that I was the person paying for my daughter's medical coverage, and I was prepared to take her off my policy if it meant I could prevent her from being placed on cross-sex hormones. I believe that from that point forward, the therapist cast me in the role of villain and unsupportive, possibly even abusive, mother. My daughter's father, whom I had divorced the year after our daughter graduated, has taken a backseat in all of this. He disapproves of her calling herself a boy but is happy to date women who do so. For the most part, he keeps his disapproval to himself.

My daughter is now twenty-four years old and only recently began using testosterone. Her medical coverage is no longer tied to my own, and, as she proudly states, I thus cannot stop her. She has at least four current friends who are also young women on testosterone and who currently "identify" as "men." Because some of them are in intimate relationships with each other, they purport to be gay men, having gay male relationships. Lesbian is no longer a fashionable word in her circle; instead, they are gay trans-identified males. Queer is another word popular in my kid's crowd. But the accent on masculinity is no coincidence. Needless to say, this seems surreal to me.

My daughter and I have a strained relationship. We no longer live in the same city. We talk about superficial things. I don't want to call her my son or refer to her as a boy, and that annoys her. She won't allow any substantial discussion about gender issues, medical issues, mental health issues, sexual issues, and so on. I feel shut out by her, but at the same time, I am afraid for her. I do not think her choices are healthy. Nor do I expect her cohort of friends to all remain on testosterone indefinitely; one or more of them is likely to desist in the next few years. I hope and pray that my daughter will be one of the lucky ones, someone who figures out what a lie she has been sold before it is too late—before she has ruined her fertility and has her organs removed. But, in any event, her entire generation will pay a heavy price for this madness that has gripped our young, enabled as it has been by the medical and mental health professions.

34

Why I Can't Reveal My Son's Therapist's Name

My son has a great therapist. That sets us apart from, I think, the great majority of parents. Mental healthcare for children is difficult to get, and it's even more difficult to get mental healthcare that doesn't just check the box or blunder about, but that actually helps a child. My son's therapist, someone my son has been seeing regularly for years to help him work through a long list of problems, including anxiety, depression, and autism, is a great therapist. But I can't tell you his name.

He's asked us not to tell anybody his name. He's asked us not to tell anybody where he works. He's done this because he could lose his job, even his career, for providing great and helpful therapy for our son.

You see, the problem is that when we brought our son to this therapist (after fleeing another therapist who we felt had behaved inappropriately with my son), our son was suffering from gender dysphoria. He had told us he felt like he was really a girl inside. The other therapist berated us for not taking him immediately to the clinic where they specialize in transgender medicalization of children. She told him that he should sneak out of the house (where she had told us he was to be kept on close watch for suicide) and go to meetings with trans people.

We didn't think our son was really a woman inside. We knew he was a boy, which he now also knows he is (yes, it was a long and difficult road, but the road can go back to reality). And we asked the new therapist if he could treat our son—who was upset and obsessed by transgenderism—for his other problems and leave the gender stuff alone for the time being. That's all we asked—we didn't say, "Please talk him out of this." We just said, "Please treat him for his anxiety, his depression, his hallucinations, his breakdowns. And put the gender stuff off for later." And this kind, good man did.

In time, as my son's mental crisis subsided, the belief that he was really a woman subsided with it. That belief wasn't a solution; it was an escape, and it was a false escape at that. How could discomfort with his body, his growing, pubertal, hairy man's body, be made better by the sort of eternal fixation on one's body that medical transition entails? He might have traded one set of problems for an even larger set if we—and his therapist—hadn't been able to help him work through them.

And that, in our state, may be illegal. It may be illegal in your state too. If I told you my son's therapist's name after telling you this, it's possible he could face legal charges under our state's law against "conversion therapy."

How did this happen? "Conversion therapy" for homosexuals was a thing back in the bad old fifties, but nobody reputable has really been doing it for a generation, just a scattering of religious fanatics. Yet, somehow, despite this being a horror story from the days of lobotomies and insane asylums, it has seemed urgent enough to have legislation and executive orders written that have outlawed it in half of the United States. Why right now, when the last citation of gay conversion therapy in psychological literature is decades old? We had already gotten to the point of legalizing gay marriage before these bills started popping up all over.

It's not really about homosexuality, that's why. The people pushing for these bans aren't gay, they're trans-identified men and their supporters, and they aren't doing this to help boys grow up gay. Instead, the legislation may prevent boys from growing up gay.

The language in these bills is almost identical. After California's S.B. 1172 got passed in 2012, the trans lobby caught on and got busy. California's bill says this:

> "Sexual orientation change efforts" means any practices by mental health providers that seek to change an individual's sexual orientation. This includes efforts to change behaviors or gender expressions, or to eliminate or reduce sexual or romantic attractions or feelings toward individuals of the same sex.

Almost every bill after that, starting with New Jersey the following year, changed the language to include "gender identity" alongside "sexual orientation." A.B. 3371 says the following:

> As used in this section, "sexual orientation change efforts" means the practice of seeking to change a person's sexual orientation, including, but not limited to, efforts to change behaviors, gender identity, or gender expressions.

And there it is: "gender identity" is legally in the same category as "sexual orientation." The fact that the great majority of children who feel like they're the other sex will change their minds after puberty is papered over and tied up with red tape. The fact that transitioning a child changes his gender expression earns its own exception:

> except that sexual orientation change efforts shall not include counseling for a person seeking to transition from one gender to another . . .

It's spelled out there clearly: it is permitted to tell a kid he is the other sex and transition him. It is not allowed to tell him he isn't. One type of intervention is legal, another type is prohibited, and anything in between is iffy. In other words, it's illegal to give therapy to a child who believes they should be the other sex, unless that therapy confirms that belief.

After New Jersey, similar bills or executive orders, with almost identical language, were passed in the following states: Oregon (2015); Illinois (2016); Vermont (2016); Connecticut (2017); Nevada (2017); New Mexico (2017); Rhode Island (2018); Delaware (2018); New Hampshire (2018); Maryland (2018); Washington (2018); Hawaii (2018, revised 2019); Colorado (2019); Maine (2019); New York (2019); Massachusetts (2019); North Carolina (2019); Utah (2020); Virginia (2020); North Dakota (2021); Michigan (2021); Minnesota (2021); and Wisconsin (2021). Only in Illinois is the bill limited to sexual orientation.

The practice of therapy for kids with gender issues became a legal minefield at that point, as a therapist who followed what had been the standard of "watchful waiting" could be accused of "sexual orientation change efforts" if a child went into therapy believing he was the opposite gender and came out no longer believing that . . . as most children confused about their gender do, even without therapy.

In all of these states, it is hazardous for the therapist to accept a child with gender issues. I live in one of these states. My son is still a child, yet all these laws were passed in his lifetime, and they compromised his ability, and the ability of other children, to get adequate mental healthcare.

My son's therapist says that working with kids with gender issues is a legal minefield. His personal policy is to never bring up gender but to work on other issues (which are always there). If a kid brings up gender, this therapist will not argue or question, just nod and move on to something else. If a kid doesn't want to work on any issues but only wants to talk about gender, he will pass that kid on to someone else. Most therapists are even more hands-off: they won't even take kids with gender issues.

My son's therapist says there are three types of kids therapists always try to get off their hands:

1. Kids who are harming themselves or others in concrete ways;

2. A kid with plans for suicide;

3. Kids with gender issues.

Any one of these kids can cause no end of legal complications for the therapist. We are lucky that this therapist agreed to work with our son, and if I must keep his name secret forever, I will.

In states with such laws, kids with gender issues may be shut out from one therapist after another until they end up at a "gender therapist." There is no real qualification for a "gender therapist": it's just a therapist who is enthusiastic about trans ideology and transitioning children. This means there's a population of children who need help and can't get it, or can only get one type of help—a type that causes harm.

Most boys who believe they are girls will grow out of that belief after puberty. This has been demonstrated in study after study. Most of these boys will also, after puberty, come to recognize that they are homosexual or bisexual. Boys can learn to cope with gender dysphoria as they can with other sources of discomfort. But if these boys are passed down the line like hot potatoes until they get to the gender clinic, they might not just never learn to cope; they may also never be able to express their sexuality. The first line of medical treatment for these boys at the gender clinic is the same medication used to castrate Alan Turing for the then crime of homosexuality.

This is the horrible contradiction this sly legislation has wrought. Inserted into bills that purport to end the mistreatment of homosexuals is language that mandates the mistreatment of homosexuals.

Telling confused boys who will most likely end up gay that their discomfort with gender roles means they are trans is itself a form of conversion therapy. It's used as such in Iran—where gay men are given the option of death or trans surgery—and it's being used as such in the West as well. If a boy goes into therapy believing he's a girl and comes out knowing he's a boy, the therapist could lose his career. But if a gay boy goes into therapy and comes out believing he's a straight girl, the therapist has done what the law says he should. Remember: "sexual orientation change efforts shall not include counseling for a person seeking to transition from one gender to another . . ." Per the law, there's one way out. The Mullahs would approve.

How much of the next generation of gay boys will be castrated because of these laws? How many children will never develop functional sexual organs because of this ideology? How many good therapists will refuse your son because he says he has gender issues?

My son's therapist has told us not to say his name to anybody because of this legal minefield. Although he's merely helped a boy through the most difficult years of his life, he could get crucified for it. I will respect his wishes and privacy, but what a shame and what a loss. How many others could he help? How many other children and families could benefit from open-minded, ethical therapists like him?

Parents on Family, Love, and Loss

35

My New Identity, Not By Choice

My daughter is a young adult, a very intelligent one at that, with a science-based college education. She tells me now that she is transgender. And my heart, my mind, and every fiber in my body scream, "NO!" because I know that she has been dragged into a cult, a cultural mania, however you choose to think of it. Never in a million years did I ever think I would be mother to a "transgender" person. This new identity, chosen for me, has turned my world upside down. What am I now? What I am is confused, bewildered, lost, and depressed—beyond that, I really can't say.

My daughter was not born in the wrong body, a mythical concept that I do not subscribe to. If transgender is based on conformance to feminine or masculine stereotypes, there were never any signs of that— no requests to wear boys' clothing or asking Santa to bring toys like her brothers. There were, however, requests to wear dresses exclusively, starting at the age of three. There were begged-for trips to the American Girl store to add to her extensive collection of beloved dolls. There were dance classes and recitals, a bedroom with a fairy motif and bed canopy, playdates only with girls, manicures and pedicures, hair appointments, shopping . . . the list goes on and on. There was no body distress, no gender dysphoria. There were serious boyfriends, each relationship spanning several years. There were glimpses of questioning when it came to sexuality, but gender—never.

Now, my days are spent wondering if and when the hormones will start. If the "top surgery" will be done as well as the hysterectomy. I'm expected to cheer throughout the social transitioning, the grand pronouncement of new pronouns, the breast binding. There is no room for me in her self-centered world. There is nothing left of an identity that (I didn't even realize) was core to my very being as my daughter's mother. My daughter is choosing to disappear herself, to erase her past, and to shut out herself and, in the process, our mother-daughter bond, so precious, so carefully constructed and nurtured over her short lifetime. The distance between us now is palpable. It was not my choice, but hers. She has thrown away not only a part of herself, but a part of me.

My love is undiminished and will always be. But my heart and soul have been damaged and torn. I didn't ask for this . . . but in choosing a new identity for herself, she has changed me too—and I have to live with it.

36

Reflections on Time in the World of Trans

Like other parents of a teen caught in the steel grip of gender ideology, my life has been turned upside down. People not familiar with this issue would be stunned by how much time this tragedy can eat up in a day. I can't speak for every parent stuck in this living nightmare, but I'm betting there are similarities among us.

First, there's the inordinate amount of time we spend scrutinizing our kids. We replay our interactions, laser-focused on whether we've seen any shift in direction, any sign that they're inching closer to, or further from, the major decisions that will have grave permanent impacts on their young lives—impacts they are too immature, too naïve, too anxious and afraid to understand. This focus requires a level of intensity that leaves little room for other things, like our jobs or our spouses or our partners or our friends or, oftentimes, our other children. We are too busy processing what they chose to wear or not wear, looking for subtle changes in mood, examining and reexamining what they've said, hoping to find openings, places where we can hold them just a little longer before they jump back on their single-minded track.

Then there are the usual calls and emails to clinicians, begging for a meeting. Or an explanation. There's the futile search for an available therapist who won't give our kids that extra shove off the gender cliff.

We squeeze in a few moments to look for classes and lessons to fill up our kids' time and brains, distracting them from the poisonous rumination normally overtaking it—classes and lessons that our kids very likely won't (but just possibly might!) be willing to participate in.

There's the writing or journaling, documenting this grim, grief-filled slog, either for posterity or for some far-off, mythical criminal prosecution for medical negligence.

There's the time spent trailing our kids on social media, looking for interlopers and enablers.

And then there's the ultimate time sink, reading and researching, keeping up with any developments, honing our newfound expertise in deciphering the intricacies of scientific studies, reviewing expert testimonies, dissecting the legalese behind the ever-expanding legislation set on eroding our ability to protect our children from their own bad judgment.

On top of all of that, there are the blessed support groups, desperately needed to remind ourselves that we are seeing things as they are, even when those around us aren't seeing them at all. Reassuring us that we haven't been transported (for lack of a better word) to some parallel Orwellian universe where the obvious has become unmentionable, and where realities are deemed fantasies, and where fantasies are deemed true and noble and brave. Where caring for your child has become abuse.

There isn't much of it, but in my spare time, I obsessively check my phone and computer for anything relevant. I read one support group's Facebook posts, I check another group's Team posts, I check Discord, I subject myself to Twitter. Then I catch up on the podcasts. And I check my email. Like constantly.

Some of this is just the normalized bad habits associated with living a digital life plus the need for the hit of neural reward juice I get when something good hits my inbox, but a larger part is likely the same reason other parents of a child (or children) who has latched onto a new gender identity spend their days like I do. I am desperately looking for a sign of hope. Word that the *New York Times* or the *Washington Post*, or maybe Rachel Maddow—anyone to balance out Fox News and the *Daily Caller*—has "broken" some hot "hidden" story about how the medical community has followed up their complete failure of the opioid epidemic with the cosmic-level betrayal of vulnerable, confused children by rescuing them from reality and leading them on the path to sterilization and mutilation.

Or that SOMEONE has figured out a way to reach our unreachable kids, to get through to them that they're perfect just the way they are, that we love them fiercely, that we would walk barefoot over glass shards to get them real help if only they'd accept it, and that there's no magic potion that will turn them into more than a cosmetic facsimile of something they are not and will never be.

Or that there has been a great truth-telling online by all of the posers and groomers and the young people who were looking for validation that they hadn't made a terrible mistake by encouraging others to follow in their footsteps.

That, finally, the dam was breaking and that our kids were coming back home to us. Maybe terribly, tragically, irrevocably damaged, and maybe needing tremendous support to make things as right as they could be, but home. Finally home.

37

Reflections on Pain
and Things That Break Our Hearts

This morning Facebook reminded me that I once had a handsome son with a smile that would light up a room. The picture was taken five years ago. Staring at me on the screen was a dark and handsome tall boy with a dazzling smile. He is standing at the beach in his swim trunks, wearing a blue rash guard and holding a boogie board. I remembered that moment and that vacation, the last one we took as a family. He had just come out of the water, and he smiled as I snapped that picture.

It stabbed me like a knife in the heart knowing that he looks nothing like that picture now. Three years ago, my son stumbled into Internet groups that told him that the reason why he didn't fit in socially was not due to his autism, but because he was really a woman, not a man. My son now thinks that he's a woman and is taking hormones to try to achieve an impossible dream, that he can be a woman, fed by his own delusion and a world that tells him daily that he can be one.

I took a snapshot of the Facebook memory, with my phone's camera, and added it to the ever-growing collection of my son's pictures from those memories that I'm keeping in the camera roll. I will never forget the dark-haired boy with the magnetic smile.

I remembered that it's Sunday, and I was excited to go to church. As a Christian, when I go to church, the music, prayers, and preaching comfort my soul. The people there are like my family. They have walked with us through many challenging situations for the last thirty years. I enjoy seeing these dear friends and socializing with them weekly.

As soon as I stepped into the church, my heart was stabbed again. There, standing by his parents, was my son's former best friend who was home visiting from college. Like my own son, he was a nerdy kid, but he is now maturing into a handsome and delightful man. Then his other former best friend, tall and handsome, came in. His parents, our dear best friends of years, were sitting next to me. My mind flashed back to when the three musketeers would sit together in church and then come to our home to play video games with other boys from church.

My heart broke into a million pieces, and the sadness overtook me. Today, the music bounced off the walls and didn't comfort me. As the music played and tears rolled down my eyes, my heart screamed to God, "Why my son? Why our family? Why does he have to be the messed-up one who wants to eradicate his identity and who is killing any chance to be a functional man one day? Why do my best friends have their SONS and I don't have mine? Why? Why? Why?"

The tears kept rolling down. Today church was for lamenting, not encouragement. It felt right to do just that.

I feel so sad today. Church is usually so comforting for me, but today it was one more reminder of our abnormal, fractured family, our prodigal child, our loss, emptiness, heartbreak, and sorrow. I walked out as soon as church was over. I didn't say hi to the college kids who used to spend Sunday afternoons at our home playing video games with my son. I didn't want to face the awkwardness or see the puzzlement that they feel about their former friend (because he has cut off contact with them) as they exchanged polite pleasantries with me. I saw them talking to each other, knowing that they will get together and hang out, but my son won't be there because he has rewritten history past and present about who he is. I fled before I saw my son's boss from his work, with the sad blue eyes looking at me with such sorrow. I fled because I didn't want people to say, "How are you?" What do you say when your heart is bleeding from sorrow and no one can really understand what that feels like?

I love my supportive church community. They love us so well. Those who know, their hearts are broken for us. But there's a special kind of sadness that comes with people knowing. Our own sadness, reflected in the eyes of people who are not in our situation, is like a mirror that I avoid looking into. I am fortunate to be in a church that makes room for lamenting and grieving. I am blessed to have the support and love of people who weep with me and hurt with me. So, why do I cringe from the looks of sadness in other people's eyes? Maybe because it reminds me that, at church, my family alone is living in the middle of our lives being broken by a cult, that we have a broken child who is systematically breaking his own body down because he's looking for a cure for his broken heart and that we are surrounded by a society that tells him he will fix himself by breaking himself down.

So what do people with broken hearts do? They find other people whose hearts are broken for the same or similar reasons. I have found this tribe of parents who understands the grief and sorrow of having a child who wants to change who he or she was born to be. The same thief that stole my son has stolen their children too. I don't shy away or cringe when I see the pain in their eyes. Somehow the reflection of pain in their eyes and the distorted faces from sorrow heal my pain because we share the same burden across many backs. They carry my burden of grief for the loss of my child, and I carry theirs. Somehow we lighten each other's burden of pain. I'm able to comfort them, and they comfort me. We are in this war together. We are the wounded from this gender war that has snatched our sons and daughters from our families. We grieve together, but we also fight together. We cry today, but tomorrow we fight.

We will keep fighting until this war against our children and your children is won. Because I have found that fighting is also medicine for my broken heart.

38

Mourning the Living

As I lay alone on my back in Room 23, waiting for the lidocaine gel to do its job, I heard myself say, aloud, "You asked for this . . ." I know that, as a woman of a certain age, one cannot live on coffee, wine, leftovers, and no water. I never drink enough water. And, yes, I did ask for it. In fact, I prayed for it. My body is bleeding somewhere, and the doctor is trying to figure it out. I confessed the poor self-care to her at our consultation, but I didn't tell her that I had been praying to get sick with something, possibly terminal, for months.

Now, here I was, waiting for her to check inside my body to see if the power of prayer applies to nonbelievers. For the record, I also simultaneously prayed for famine, war, and civil unrest, but I am certainly not taking credit for the pandemic or the violent Summer of 2020. Why, you might wonder, would a healthy, happily married, middle-aged mother of two teenagers and a dog, with an enviable life, pray for terminal illness?

Well, my world changed forever about two years ago when my smart, beautiful, self-confident, extraordinary girl crashed and burned in the next room and was "saved" by a transgender identity. Yes, my girl, with no history of issues with being a girl, suddenly decided that her whole life had been a lie, a secret, and that she "had always known but was too afraid to say anything."

After the initial recovery from such a slap in the face that I would have missed something so obvious to her, I took to the Internet and found a lot of websites that congratulated me on my kid finding her "true self." I found a lot of "would you rather have a dead daughter or a living son?" rhetoric. I read stories about child protective services removing children from "unsafe" homes that did not affirm their child's new identity.

I quickly realized that I would not be able to investigate this using my real name, since those that did before me had lost jobs and had their lives ruined for trying to talk about it. I created an anonymous email account and began looking for rational voices. I joined Twitter, which is, sadly, the only place I found valuable information. The left-wing media, my sole news source for my entire life, was refusing to address this. I found an *Atlantic* article by Jesse Singal. I wrote to him, and he responded with empathy but offered no answers. I wrote to Lisa Damour, expert on all things teenage girl and renowned author of *Under Pressure* and *Untangled*. She never replied. I wrote to James Caspian of Bath Spa University, and he wrote a thoughtful reply and mentioned that he had been seeing this sort of thing in girls and boys since 2013. Dr. Eric Vilain directed me to 4thWaveNow, which was a wealth of information and confirmation that I was approaching this the right way.

I found Lisa Littman's paper. Then it made sense. If my daughter hadn't sounded EXACTLY like the anecdotal descriptions in the paper (a depressed and anxious young teen who spent too much time online and had just fallen hard for another kid identifying as a boy), I might have gone against my better judgment and succumbed, like so many parents do. Taken down pictures of her in the hallway. Called her a boy. Given her a binder for her fourteenth birthday. Celebrated her rebirth on social media. I didn't do any of that.

I did let her get a haircut. I did buy her some men's shirts.

Maybe that was a mistake, but I felt that she needed to be able to explore this gender business a little bit. Forbidding it only leads to an increased desire. When she played the suicide card, we took her to a psychiatrist. When she threatened to harm herself to get out of a girl's soccer game, I told her I would have to take her to the psych ward if she made good on that threat. We went to gender therapists, met with specialists, consulted with cult experts. My husband called twenty psychologists, most of whom told us that she was unlikely to change her mind. I attributed this to the recent passage of a bill in my state that forbade discussion of gender identity with minors.

My husband really wanted to go "full Hungarian" (a phrase that came out of a support group for parents like us, where one mother, a Hungarian woman, didn't give into anything and actively badgered her kid until she desisted). Based on all the people we had met with, that was unlikely to work and would very likely strain our relationship with her. Things kept ramping up, and I became overwhelmed with managing my spouse and my younger child and pretending everything was normal to our friends, despite the obvious and sudden change in our daughter's appearance.

We became closet activists. We put up billboards, wrote letters, sent emails, mass-mailed *Irreversible Damage* to doctors, schools, and psychologists, and met with lawyers, senators, and representatives. We organized protests and talked to our close friends. Then I started praying. For something HUGE to happen to shake it all up. To stop the momentum so we could breathe. You see, I can put this away for moments, even days at a time, and experience joy and appreciate my wonderful kids. My husband, on the other hand, eats, sleeps, and breathes the terror of this experience. He never puts it away. I am grateful that he is on the same page, as so many of my new friends in this gender club have no support, but it is taking a toll on our relationship in ways that may never be repaired. I'm worried he might die from the stress. He went to his doctor, and when he explained the source of the stress, the doctor made a light-hearted joke: "Ah, well, so, now you have a son!" It is all we talk about. Living in a state of urgency is profoundly unhealthy and unsustainable.

So, I prayed.

Maybe, if I got really sick and everyone had to contemplate death and the value of life, health, etc., maybe my kid might see that trying to become someone else is not the solution. Maybe I could, on my deathbed, make her promise not to do anything medical, ever. If that would end this constant state of stress and worry that we inhabit, I am all in.

The worry we feel about her is the same worry we feel about someone we love who might die. I tried to explain this to her, but I don't know how it landed. I am not trying to be dramatic or play the victim card. I am just expressing what this experience feels like firsthand for all of those people who have no idea. It feels like she is edging closer to death every day that her eighteenth birthday draws nearer. Death by testosterone. Death by double mastectomy. Death by self-annihilation. It is unbearable to think about the future.

It turns out that my prayers were ignored. I am not sick with anything but worry. So, I am not meant to die as a martyr in the Gender War. I am meant to stay and fight. For my kid. That is what I will do.

39

Kills Me Every Time

Years ago, I was sick with a serious disease. Let's call it cancer. People were uniformly kind in their concern, but their attempts to say just the right thing could be misguided and sometimes downright comical. Some folks got it right—a look in the eye, a squeeze of the hand, an "I'm sending good thoughts your way." That's really what I needed. But others got it terribly wrong. Among those were stories of their friends or family members who had had the same cancer as me and died or their description of the litany of horrible side effects I could expect from chemo or, my favorite, "You're going to need a miracle to beat this." Really? Because I was kind of hoping that modern medicine would cure me. And, thankfully, it did. So now I can look back and laugh, especially since I know they did mean well.

Today I find myself a member of another sad community—parents of trans-identified kids. Mine is twenty-three. A daughter. On testosterone for four years. Now I have to contend with another collection of people's reactions to (what I consider) a very unhappy turn of events. The comments run the gamut from the ridiculous to the sublime. A sampling:

1. *Would you mind if she was gay?* Me: Do you mean am I a homophobic bigot? Well, no. As a matter of fact, I wouldn't mind at all if she was a lesbian. I hear they are a disappearing breed. I honestly don't care how she presents herself to the world or who she sleeps with as long

as she doesn't have to commit to lifelong medication with debilitating consequences to do so. But thanks for asking!

2. *She signed an informed consent, right? So, she knew what she was getting into?* Me: You'd think so, but not really. She signed the informed consent when she was at university. She was nineteen years old, in the throes of depression and anxiety and caught up in this social contagion. I don't think she was in the right state of mind to get out of bed, let alone understand and agree to all that transitioning entails. What nineteen-year-old, in the best of mental health, can comprehend lifelong medication, possibly resulting in a hysterectomy and infertility? Did she really understand the dental complications? Or the baldness? Who thinks this is possible for a teenager?

3. *You're not going to believe this, but my neighbor's cousin's daughter just came out as trans!* Me: Yes. Yes, I am going to believe it. I told you it was a social contagion. Clearly, you didn't believe me.

4. *So, like Caitlyn Jenner?* Me: Nope. Not at all like Caitlyn Jenner, who was a mature adult when she made this decision. I wish her all the best.

5. *How is [my daughter's trans name] doing?* Me: I take a deep breath, smile, and reply, "Fine, thank you for asking." But inside, I'm thinking, if your kid was anorexic, I would not ask if they had achieved their target weight yet. But you know nothing about this topic other than what you read in the mainstream media, so I'll let it slide.

6. *How is [my daughter's birth name] doing? She must have graduated by now, right?* Me: Clearly, this person has no idea what is going on, and I envy their innocence on the topic. Not wanting to introduce tragedy to a friendly exchange, I give my standard elevator pitch. "She left college and is taking some time off to 'discover herself.' You know how kids can be." They usually respond with a chuckle and an "Oh, do I!" and we go our separate ways.

But the worst and by far the hardest reaction to deal with is when they say nothing. When they don't ask about her by any name but ask about every other member of the family. Because then, I know they know. And they know that I know they know. And they feel terrible for my family and don't know what to say. Then it feels like she really is gone. Like I never had a daughter. Like she didn't exist. Like she's dead. And that kills me every time.

40

The Abyss

How does it feel to watch my child embrace gender ideology?

It's like I am watching my daughter jump into the abyss. She is falling in slow motion, having purposely leaped past me into a gaping hole with no bottom in sight. I am holding out my hand to catch her as she falls past, but she refuses to take it. I have tried before to grab her and pull her out of the darkness before she fell too far, but she pushed me away, which made her fall a little faster toward the bottom. Seeing this and trying to learn from my errors, I stopped trying to grab her. Now I just leave my hand dangling where she can see it, where she can easily grasp it and be pulled to safety, should she want to. I've tried other things too. I've left a few ropes hanging into the pit that she can grab on to (the seeds planted in her brain), if she so chooses. I live in hope that she will take my hand, or latch on to one of those ropes I left hanging, and then, tied to reality, she can carefully climb up the wall on her own before hitting the bottom. Or maybe she will pick up the pieces of rope and supplies I've nailed to the wall for her and create her own rope or ladder that she can use to climb up.

If she falls until she hits the bottom, she will likely sustain severe injuries. I've seen this happen to others. I know some who have fallen into this same abyss and recovered completely from the fall. Others I've seen make their way out of the abyss still struggle with their injuries, but they will ultimately survive. It's unclear how many of the survivors will thrive. It surely depends on how quickly they fell, and how they fell (what body parts were injured in the fall and how severely)—and how determined they are to recover from their self-inflicted descent.

I have also heard of others who fell to the ground and chose to remain where they fell. The way they tell it, they don't feel the injuries; they actually feel better than before, they say. Maybe that means there are some who will always feel okay and will totally survive the injuries, and make a life for themselves at the bottom, never feeling the need to crawl out of the abyss. Will my daughter be one of them? Will she be one of the ones who crawl back up and eventually lead a great life? Will she hit the bottom, suffer injuries, crawl out, and learn to live with her injuries but never be quite the same? Will she grab my hand, a rope (mine or her own), or scale the wall rock-climber style before she hits the bottom, thus avoiding any injuries? Right now, I simply don't know the answers. And that's why the wait here, with my hand dangling in wait, is so devastating.

I'm angry that there are many parts of society encouraging my daughter and myriad other young people to take this leap of faith into the abyss, cheering them on, saying that to jump is the best thing—the only thing—they can do if they simply "feel like it." These cheerleaders don't caution these young people about the dangers (in fact, they likely are unaware of the dangers themselves). They don't tell those they egg on of the potential injuries, of the fact that many don't survive, or survive but are left hurt and debilitated. They tell these young people that if they feel like jumping into the abyss (i.e., if it seems attractive to them), they must. Our children (who, in a great many cases, are somehow "different" —autistic, ADHD, gay or lesbian, etc.—and may have suffered trauma) are told that their anxiety about being teenagers means they must jump into the abyss or they literally can never be happy and never be their "true selves," as if jumping into the abyss is somehow braver and more authentic than trying to avoid falling into the abyss.

Those who never have the urge, or easily resist the urge, to jump into the abyss are dismissed as "cis," which is supposed to mean people who have no struggles. They could not possibly understand the tortured souls who are born with the need to jump into the darkness.

Of course, the reality is that we all struggle. Some of us just don't buy into the idea that jumping into the abyss would be helpful. We try and deal with our struggles in other ways and are not attracted to the obvious dangers of the abyss. Most of us, particularly if we are over a certain age, realize that jumping into the abyss won't bring us happiness, and we also are in touch with our mortality and don't take our healthy bodies for granted. Thus, we would never encourage anyone to risk their healthy body in a futile search for unearned happiness.

These societal messages about jumping into the abyss are dangerous and inaccurate and create a cult-like environment for our children. In fact, if any of our children question these messages, they are ostracized, criticized, and laughed away. And parents who counter these messages are called out as ignorant, narrow-minded, hateful fools just because we advise caution, just because we advise being mindful of your precious body and your health. We don't really understand why it would be a good idea to jump into the abyss when there is no evidence whatsoever that it is necessary or even helpful for anyone in the long run, and the risk of injury is so damn obvious. Again, even if some people survive the fall and the inevitable injuries and manage to thrive, who is to say that those people would not have also been able to thrive without the injuries and risks of jumping into the abyss? The claim that some people were born with the requirement that they jump into the abyss to ever be happy sounds very much like a cult to me.

We need to put up guardrails around the abyss, and warning signs, indicating the dangers. We need to create a minimum age for those who choose to jump, regulate the line of adult jumpers, and make sure each adult jumper is ready to go and aware of the dangers before they take the leap. And we need to close the gate when a teenager attempts to jump into the abyss.

To be a parent of a teenager who has bought into this ideology is to see the danger of the abyss, to see no guardrails around it, and to see signs for it everywhere—in schools, on mainstream media, in doctors' offices, in governmental offices—that, instead of warning of the dangers of jumping into the abyss, actually encourage young people, and all people, to jump into the abyss. It's difficult to watch edited videos of those who jumped that look like vacation videos—that don't even contain the types of warnings that are given during every medication ad on TV. Instead, jumping into the abyss is sold as the most fun ride ever, with the lie that only a small handful of people ever regret hitting bottom, and even then, the jump was good for them despite the injuries from which they still suffer. How many young people will have to be hurt before the rest of the world sees what, to me, is clear as day?

41

Behind the Curtain:
The Reality of Gender Transition in a Family

I have heard it repeatedly said, ad nauseam: "As long as they are happy and being their true self . . ." This is what well-intentioned friends and acquaintances say when I drop the trans bomb in their laps—that my son, suddenly, out of nowhere, at the age of twenty-four, announced he is a woman and not a man. That was almost three years ago, and life has been, well . . . a journey is the best way to describe it. I am writing the story of this journey down for one reason only: so others can understand the depth and breadth of how transition affects a family. I do not want your sympathy. I only want the same compassion you allow those undergoing a transition. Or parents who have lost a child.

Our story is basically the same as the stories of other parents whose child transitions, whether it started when the child was eight, eighteen, or twenty-eight, whether the child is male or female. Whether you immediately affirmed, questioned, or were critical of the decision. Whether you held their hand when they came out of their double mastectomy surgery or whether you cried all day wondering from two thousand miles away if they survived their facial feminization surgery. I know this firsthand because I am involved with parent support groups and hear these stories. I hear about the mental and emotional gymnastics parents perform to support their children while also trying to protect and defend them.

As a parent, you are damned if you do and damned if you don't. If you supported medical transition and your child years later detransitions, they say, "Why didn't you say something? Why didn't you stop me?" And when you express concern about medicalization and the dangers of rushing into treatment, you are told you are transphobic, unloving, evil, emotionally abusive, and hateful—words often proceeded by months or years of estrangement. We have been told by medical professionals, pro-affirmation websites, and society that if we do not completely support our children's decision to transition, then they will commit suicide. Just think about that for a moment. It is navigating a minefield.

What no one tells you is that the son we have adored for almost twenty-five years no longer exists. And his removal from our shared family history and lives is self-inflicted. He has erased himself. We cannot talk about him in the past unless we want to be accused of deadnaming and misgendering. We cannot reminisce about family vacations, the sports he played, the things he said or did. But I had a son, not a daughter. Speaking his new name and gender is an affront to us. It feels like a punch in the gut every time I hear it.

I was asked just the other day how I view our situation. Have we lost a son and gained a daughter, or have we lost a son and gained a stranger? It was a very insightful question from an acquaintance that does not have a child caught in this nightmare. Here is my answer: We have lost a son for whom we cannot publicly mourn. Our family has lost a brother, cousin, nephew, grandson, and friend. This new "girl" is nothing like the person we used to know. Along with his identity change, his character and personality have changed. His actions and words are so unfamiliar to us that it is like having a stranger in the family.

There is a huge misconception about what transitioning is all about, at least for those of legal age. Transition isn't a fairytale where everyone lives happily ever after. If it was, then there wouldn't be tens of thousands of detransitioners. When my son called and announced his transition to my husband and me, we asked him not to rush into medicalization (i.e., hormones and surgeries). We asked him for time to allow us to catch up and understand how he came to this decision because this was totally out of the blue. None of us saw it coming. Not even his girlfriend of four years.

Our son did not like being questioned about his decision and promptly cut us out of his life. He was estranged from the family for eight months. He was coached by his new trans community that he didn't need us, that he had a new, better family now. He was advised by his new "family" to only make a certain level of income so that he could be eligible for Medicaid and other government-funded subsidies. He stopped working and then claimed that he was not able to get side jobs because the world is transphobic. He took self-defense classes because he was now female and, therefore, a potential victim of male aggression. He spent most of his days training his voice to be more feminine. He practiced walking "like a girl." Endless hours each day were spent on clothes and makeup. The cocktail, consisting of estrogen, progesterone, "T" blocker, and antidepressants, kept him in tears and in bed. He wouldn't answer texts, emails, or phone calls. He didn't thank us when we sent him a birthday present. He didn't acknowledge our birthdays. He didn't even call when his grandma died.

He became a very hateful, bitter, and cruel person. He was not anything like the son we raised. He posed for highly sexual and provocative partially nude photos and posted them on social media. He talks about becoming a model and getting a "sugar daddy." He partied his days away, keeping himself numb. He lost his girlfriend because she no longer wanted a "lesbian relationship." He developed unhealthy eating habits and is now most likely anorexic, although we have no way of addressing that issue. He had facial feminization surgery thanks to the taxpayers of New York.

He claims he is happy, but, despite that claim, we can see that he is isolated, with very few friends. He continues to be depressed and lonely. His life is performative. It must be exhausting. My heart breaks for him. He needs help but will not receive it because society believes he is being his "true self." I wonder how this can be ignored while everyone pretends that all is well. Society doesn't care about him, but I do. He is my son regardless of his age. It is obvious he is in pain and suffering. But we are not allowed to talk about it. That would be transphobic. Expressing concern for our child is being turned into hate speech.

Almost three years into this journey, he is now talking again, but I'm not sure it's any better this way. We are constantly walking a fine line. We are not allowed to ask questions or talk about his health or life decisions. If we say one thing that is perceived by him as "trans critical," we are promptly cut out again. What we have is not a relationship; it is a set of hard-and-fast rules that must be obeyed.

It's like a stranger moved in and evicted our son, and we all are required to pretend we don't notice, like when a lead actor is changed in the middle of a television series. We continue to tell him how much we love him. We do and always will. He is forever a member of our family, and we all suffer alongside him. What is so hard to explain is the pain we all feel when trying to find our family member behind the surgically altered face, behind the chemically altered body, behind the unnatural voice and body movements, behind the makeup and clothes. We can't help but wonder: when this stranger moved in, where did our son go?

42

When Love Is Called "Abuse"

On my birthday, I missed my kids, so I decided to send them both cards. I went to the store and carefully picked out the cards, and wrote out messages of joy, compassion, love, and support. The one for my younger son, who is at boarding school, would be delivered by his dad. The one to my nineteen-year-old, I decided to hand deliver along with some birthday cake and fresh blueberries.

I wasn't sure exactly where Tracy was living, but I followed the crumb trail of medical appointments, soup kitchens, and laundromats, all tied together by Uber rides. I hadn't seen Tracy since the Spring of 2021. Tracy likes to claim poverty, but we parents still get all these bills. So, I followed that residual parent-child bond of financial support, which led me to a neighborhood I'd never visited before—a typical urban landscape of small bungalows on wooded lots. A modernist five-story building showed some recent investment in the neighborhood, as did the small, tightly remodeled duplex that housed the nonprofit that runs the shelter houses. My teen was living in one of those houses, according to the trail of Uber pick-ups, but I didn't know which one. I asked some people on a stoop if they knew Tracy. "No, I never heard of a Tracy," answered the lady with pigtails. She was wearing a gray hoodie and clearly didn't want to talk with me. I had no idea at that moment, but later on, I learned that this lady on the stoop is one of the staff at the shelter. She knew my teen, suspected who I was, and lied to my face. I drove around the corner, back to the program office, and, when no one answered my knock, I left the small package for Tracy leaning against the door.

Apparently. this delivery of cake, fresh blueberries, and a card represents heavy criminal activity for which I am now expecting a summons by the police. I only hope that Tracy has to appear in court to make the allegation. I think I have that right, as a criminal defendant, to see and hear my accuser.

Is that the only way I have to speak with my nineteen-year-old? Through the court? Enforcing this family separation is wrong and damaging to my teen's mental health.

If going to court on charges of stalking and harassment is the only way to see Tracy, I'll take it. But I hope to just chip away at this wall of hostility. I hope we don't go to court. I hope that Tracy's heart begins to open up, that love blossoms again where I know it used to flow freely, that the unrelenting hostility will give way to renewed family relationships.

My dread and disbelief overflow and combine with my certain knowledge that my nineteen-year-old is in very real danger. I can't get anyone to help me, and I can't do anything myself. Even the smallest chink in the facade might be enough to allow in some light, some hope for Tracy.

This is a state-enforced family separation happening in a deep-blue city. We got here through the blind worship of the medical right to privacy that works to the detriment of family relationships and to the detriment of my teen's health and welfare.

The ascendant trans policy holds that parents are harmful, toxic, hateful, and abusive of their children. Parents are automatically guilty of this if there is the slightest mention of it by a young person. Because of "abusive" parents, children as young as five are endorsed by all sorts of authorities—teachers, counselors, social workers, therapists, and doctors—to lie to their parents, to hide significant dimensions of their lives, and to effectively lead a double existence. My teen, who shouted at me that turning off the wireless modem was abusive and a violation of his human rights, and then told teachers or counselors at his high school that his mom is abusive, was believed and endorsed and pushed along in that unreasonable hatred. My role as mom, my authority and my duty to provide a safe and wholesome home, all of that was thrown out the window. Never was I, the mom, ever engaged in any open discussion by any of these authority figures who endorsed my kid's allegations—I was just silently shunted aside. The adults in charge of helping my child to grow up endorsed unreasonable hatred and distrust of me.

That first allegation of abuse, back in high school, was so confusing to me that I did little in response. To this day, I continue to be confounded and confused by my teen's choices and behavior. A massage therapist who helps me with my sciatica told me about her own thirty-year-old daughter and how when she goes off the rails, she also alleges abuse by her parents. Most teens don't go around alleging abuse, especially when, objectively speaking, there is no abuse.

Kids get angry. Kids get over it. It's the adults who endorse the unreasonable anger who are taking a difficult situation and making it much, much worse. I am not someone to fear. I am Tracy's mom, and I love my teen.

In the spring of 2021, my teen ran away from home. Tracy told the family who took him in that I was abusive, just like he told his school. When I went to that family's house (because my teen fled in an Uber, I knew the address), both parents looked terrified of me. To me, this was odd and unexpected. I was holding a box of cupcakes that I'd brought as a gift. I thought we'd all sit down with a cup of coffee and a cupcake and talk for a few minutes before Tracy and I returned home. Back then, I thought it was a temporary break, that my kid would settle down soon. That was nine months ago.

That morning on the doorstep, where I stood with the cupcakes that I brought as a present, I learned that these parents had referred my kid to a homeless shelter. They never even bothered to talk with me. They blindly took Tracy's wild statements as fact. They threw me, Tracy's mom, in the trash. They assumed my teenager would be better off in a homeless shelter than with me. They think I'm an abuser. If those parents had reasoned with Tracy, endorsed me as a mom, and encouraged reconciliation, this could have all played out much differently.

The night before Tracy ran, I tried for us to have a conversation about what the word "abuse" means. We needed to have that conversation because Tracy had begun to more and more frequently make unreasonable allegations of abuse. This is an important conversation if your kid thinks turning off the Internet is abusive and is willing to denounce you to school authorities for it. And there were other instances too, the most recent being a report to child protective services (CPS) for abuse because of an argument with my younger son. Instead of helping me in a difficult situation, Tracy called CPS and alleged I was an abuser. That investigation went nowhere because there was nowhere for it to go—no signs of abuse, no records of abuse, no abuse. But still, if you want to see your mom as your enemy and as an evil, toxic person, you're going to see all of their parental actions through that lens, and that's where Tracy's thinking had gone.

When exactly Tracy decided that I was toxic and evil is unclear, but I know this developed, in part, via online chat rooms sometime in the second half of his junior year and continued into the start of his senior year of high school. Then Covid-19 hit in the last semester before he left for college, and this walloped hard at all the groups and activities that normally helped hold Tracy's world together. In the online world Tracy increasingly inhabited, denouncing parents as toxic and evil was the norm.

In December, at the end of his first semester in college, I received a call from a psychiatric hospital saying I needed to come pick up my son. The hospital only disclosed depression as the cause of hospitalization. That was an obfuscation of a much more complicated situation. The following May, my son told me he wanted to be a girl. That's when I first met Tracy.

My son was an A student, a varsity athlete, and a talented musician. Tracy dropped out of college, punched holes in my walls, lives in a homeless shelter, refuses all contact with me, and is intently focused on rapid trans-medicalization.

It's been nine months since I've seen my teen.

The city will not even admit that my child is living in one of its homeless shelters, much less help me to reestablish a relationship. When I point out that Tracy has a trust fund and a home, the shelters respond by saying that anyone who is not the owner nor on a lease can claim to be homeless. They say, well, if a person claims they are not safe, that's sufficient. If a person says they want no contact with their mom, then no contact by you is allowed.

When I ask, "How can I clear my name? I am not abusive!" I get silence.

When I say, "Well, Tracy is still on our family insurance policy, and yet you've signed Tracy up for Medicaid, and we get the bills for that, too," I get silence.

That my child is suffering is extremely clear. No one's best life is to live in a homeless shelter. No one chooses to drop out of college to live on welfare. We have to presume that this action was forced somehow by circumstance. But forced by what circumstance? No one cares. No one who knows any of the details will listen to me. And no one will provide adequate care for my teen or allow me to take care of him, as I want desperately to do.

As I contemplate the painful situation for Tracy, I suddenly get a text from a program manager for the city shelter. She won't tell me anything in any straightforward way because, according to city policy, she is not even allowed to admit Tracy is in the system. But through a series of confusing texts, it becomes clear that my teen wants to file stalking and harassment charges against me because I brought over some birthday cake to share on my birthday.

Excuse me very much for loving and missing my child. Excuse me for wanting to see my kid and wanting to know how my fragile and hurting kid is doing in this rough-and-tumble world. For wanting to help him.

At what point can we say that false allegations of crime meet the criteria of "threat to self or others"? The harm is to me but also to Tracy, because such false accusations can themselves be a type of criminal behavior. So-called caring professionals taught and encouraged my teen to lie. They separated my family. They continue to harm my son by preventing me from helping him.

My teen is fueled by anger that generates unreasonable fear. It's the oldest of psychological mechanisms, to lash out unreasonably at one's mom. That's what's happening. I know that fear is unreasonable because I raised my kid with loving kindness and dedication. My kid had every possible advantage, but he still had specific challenges, as many kids do.

In my "blue state" case, I am "abusive" for taking away the WiFi, for ending a dinner because of improper use of electronics at the table, and for seeking treatment for my depressed child. There simply was no "abuse" as the word is generally accepted and understood. The state colluded with my teen's allegations and demonized me, the mom, while allowing Tracy's enduring trauma injuries to remain without treatment.

I will resist the alternate path—to wash my hands of what seems a hopeless situation and walk away. My son is in danger, and I will never abandon my maternal love. I won't be tricked into acting like my teen's enemy, nor forced into callous indifference.

If I'm hauled into court, I'll have my say. If I'm brought before the judge, I'll demand to confront my accuser, my teen, and I'll say, excuse me for loving you. Excuse me for wanting ethical medical care that helps you get past this fear reaction.

I'll admit to the crime of loving my teen and doing my best to get him the help he so desperately needs—and deserves. And I will never agree to stop trying to help Tracy.

43

Ambiguous Loss

What do you call a loss that is unresolved or enigmatic? A loss that is lacking in clarity, in certainty, in resolution. One that doesn't allow for the typical markers and rituals that help a person process a loss, delaying and complicating grief. Though I have a PhD in psychology, my experience lies outside the realm of the clinical and counseling professions, so I did not have a name for this type of loss. That is, until I came across therapist Pauline Boss's concept of "ambiguous loss"—a concept that I have found captures, almost perfectly, the grief I've experienced since my (now) fourteen-year-old daughter abruptly came out as a transgender male a year and a half ago.

Though I have never—not for even one minute—believed in the authenticity of my child's transgender identity, my husband and I eventually decided to affirm "him" in making a full social transition, at home and at school. Outside the context of this essay, I use only male pronouns when referring to my child, and no longer address her by her birth name. But I can assure you, my child's transgender identity truly did come on very suddenly, a few months into the pandemic, with no prior signs of gender dysphoria or of nonconforming behavior whatsoever. It also, I should add, emerged shortly after the appearance of several significant mental health issues that brought about changes in our child's personality that we could not have anticipated.

So, to say I was blindsided would be an understatement. It was as if I had woken up in a parallel universe, where I had a different child—a child with a different name who had different pronouns, different hair color, different clothing, different interests, even different mannerisms. A universe where, if a person says they are transgender, the only appropriate response is to affirm. One where, at best, I was expected to carry on as if nothing had changed. At worst, I was expected to actually celebrate the loss, to banish my child's "deadname," to think of her as "She who must not be named." To celebrate a new person.

To have my sense of reality turned upside down in such a short period of time made me wonder if I had slipped into an episode of the *Twilight Zone*. The experience has been jarring. My daughter is gone . . . but not gone. And I don't know where she is. I see pictures of her on the wall, come across old photos of her on my phone. I see her name on old documents. I see her old clothing (blouses, bras, and, yes, bikinis) in closets and makeup in drawers. I miss her, but I can't say so. I want to say her name, but I cannot.

I run into acquaintances who ask how she's doing, and I'm unsure how to answer. In the occasional conversation with a stranger, someone happens to ask if I have children, and I'm not sure whether to say I have a daughter or a son. I sometimes have conversations with other mothers, mothers who share struggles that are unique to having daughters (menstruation, particular body-image concerns), and I have to pretend that I have no frame of reference. I find myself looking forward to doing mundane tasks that I once found a chore, like picking up my child's prescription at the pharmacy, because it is the only place where I can look someone in the eye and say my daughter's name out loud without fear of consequence. It is the loss of a life as I once knew it.

Or is it, really? An added layer of uncertainty lies in not knowing if this is real, authentic, something that will endure. Or, if it is something else. Something that will fade with time and that will ultimately be counted as one more case of gender detransitioning (or not counted, more likely, as who would I tell? Where would I register this information? Who is keeping track?)

It helps my husband to think of it as "a phase." But "a phase" does not do this experience justice. A phase is something one need not worry much about—something that will pass—like a small child who will only eat peanut butter and jelly sandwiches, wear only a certain pair of shoes, drink only from a certain cup. Frustrating, but no harm done. Wait it out.

Except that this phase, this fixation does not involve demands for a particular food, or for a particular pair of shoes, or for a particular sippy cup. No, this phase involves suffocating binders and requests for cross-sex hormones. Hormones that will, over time, permanently alter one's voice and result in loss of fertility. And, for many, this phase involves surgical removal of body parts.

Please understand, I know better than to assume my grief is comparable to that of losing a child to death. To do so would be to draw a cruel false equivalency. But to pretend it is not a loss is to tell a lie, to be dishonest, to not acknowledge what it feels like to watch a person you love change—change so significantly, over such a short period of time, that you no longer recognize them. To watch, even as you affirm them in their new identity, facilitate a successful social transition, and spend every waking hour searching and calling to find the right therapist, the right psychiatric hospital, the right residential treatment facility, the right outpatient program, the right medication . . . to watch them slowly slip away, like a coin dropped into a spiral wishing well, watching as it circles the rim and descends further into an abyss.

I have enough life experience to know that, with time, I'll move past this, come out on the other side. In the meantime, it is a small consolation, but a consolation nonetheless, to have a term, a concept, a name for all of this silent grief.

44

Unmade Memories: A Mother's Sadness

Helping you pick out a tux for homecoming. Coaching you on asking someone to go to the dance with you. Teaching you how to drive. Helping you to dream and plan which college you will be attending in just a few years. These are the sorts of decisions I thought I would be helping you with as you entered your first year of high school.

These are the questions your friends are working through. I see my friends sharing photos on social media of their boys—your friends, who you have gone to school with for years. These kids are attending dances, they are going to school events, and they are participating in clubs and hobbies.

I envy them. I find myself longing for those memories that I no longer think you and I will get to make.

How can my sweet, sweet boy think he was born into the wrong body? How could anyone put that idea into your innocent head?

You showed not one sign of ever feeling uncomfortable that you are a boy.

Did something happen to you at school? Did anyone hurt you?

I can only guess, because all you do is echo that refrain that all parents in my situation seem to hear from their kids: "It is just how I feel."

I wish you would confide in me as you do with those kids who you call friends. Those kids who think they know you, but truly don't. I wish you knew that, in the end, no one could ever love you more than I do, which is with all of my being. After all, I am your mother, the one who,

233

before you were conceived, prayed for you. The one who cried tears of joy at the sight of those two lines on my pregnancy test because my dream of finally becoming a mother was coming true. When you came into our lives, your dad and I could not have been happier. We had prayed for you for such a long time. You and your siblings complete our world—you know that.

I wonder: how did we get to this? Did I give you too much freedom with your phone and computer? Is this my fault? You never gave us reasons to ever worry or suspect that anything bad could ever happen. We taught you to be safe. You always had good grades at school and were a great kid. You're still a great kid, of course, underneath. It's not your fault that you were groomed by strangers. People who had nothing better to do took advantage of you. They saw a vulnerable child.

Never in a million years did I envision that this could happen. That my teen could fall prey to a cult that would convince you to modify your healthy body. I am so upset, furious, to find that we can't even get you the support that you so desperately need. If I take you to a therapist, that therapist will automatically affirm your feelings, cementing your path to surgery and drugs. We can't even count on school professionals because they, too, have been brainwashed into this ideology. I'm afraid, because they can take you away from us if I don't tread carefully.

How can your friends, your true friends, who have known you for years, think that you are right? Don't they remember growing up with you and seeing no signs? Can't they see that this is just crazy? That none of this makes sense. Of course they can, but they feel that they must play along. It's the thing to do.

I wish you would understand that feeling uncomfortable with your body is part of growing up. You are just a child, still growing, and hating your body doesn't mean you have to change it.

For now, I will continue to read more about this monster that has taken over my life and yours. I will continue to love you, and although in the end I will love you no matter what, I hope and pray that you come out of this unharmed and you find yourself again. And that you will still have the chance to make those high-school memories and to have those coming-of-age experiences that I dreamed of for you—and that you deserve. I will continue to pray for all of the children and parents going through this. May God protect our children and end this cult.

45

A Foolish, Pointless War

Above all, I love my daughter. And, to me, there is no cause worth her life.

Canadian psychologist Jordan Peterson speaks about young people creating wars when none exist. Some kids join the circus, the merchant navy, Médecins Sans Frontières, or a touring rock band. They might marry young and badly, join a priesthood, become a Scientologist, join a commune. Or, as in my daughter's case, embrace gender ideology. Gender is our children's generation's war, it seems. In this sense, our pain and sadness is perhaps similar to mothers of previous generations, whose children have gone off to fight in a distant war.

Some kids, away at the war of their own creation, get hooked on drugs, booze. Some of them don't come back home. Some return, damaged, wiser, enriched, or all of these things.

My daughter has gone off to fight in her war. There are times my brain switches off, and I forget that's she's gone, that she's left our family.

Her war is a foolish, pointless war, in my view. But aren't they all, from a parent's perspective? Many individuals, institutions, and governments speak of transgenderism as a human rights concern, thus worthy of fighting for, but I steam about the damage I see it causing to humanity on so many levels, physical and psychological. They think my daughter's war is worthy of her sacrifice. I do not.

When children go to war, life doesn't stop for the rest of us. It never does. There was a period of a couple of years when I didn't know what to do with myself except to cry. My marriage suffered, my other child suffered, I had self-destructive thoughts. None of this brought my daughter back.

In times of war, when our children leave, communities often band together for support. That's my focus now. Parents are all stronger together, and I am grateful to everyone, including Genspect, who has held hands together with me. We are on the home front, waiting and hoping for our children to come back to us.

I know that all generations need a war, a cause, to set themselves apart. I hope I'll be one of the lucky ones whose child comes home from the faraway fields of battle, scarred but stronger for the fight.

46

How Trans Destroyed My Family

My story is depressingly similar to so many others.

Two and a half years ago, just after the first lockdown in New Zealand was lifted, my much-loved teen told me that he was transgender. I was blindsided.

My son, whom I had raised single-handedly from the age of four when his father died, had shown no prior sign of any interest in anything feminine. He is on the spectrum (with what used to be called Asperger's) and was always a little awkward, socially inept, and solitary—but also extremely clever. And, of course, he was on his computer much of the time, more so during the enforced lockdown. He was also like many kids who were indoctrinated into thinking that a gender change was the panacea for all the difficulties and angst of puberty. Like many others, he was probably finding information and support on platforms such as Discord and TikTok. He told me that he had met some trans people online on a gaming site and "suddenly things made sense."

When he came out to me, I was at a loss as to what to do. I had never really thought much about transgender. I'd read books by people like Jan Morris and others and had been sympathetic to their difficulties, but I didn't know any trans people in person, and I had no idea that the trend was spreading in our schools in the rapid way that it was.

As far as I'm concerned, people should be able to live their lives in any way that makes them happy so long as they're hurting no one, and I believe that there are some who genuinely feel that they are the opposite gender. However, I had always imagined that such people were adults when they decided on that path. Now here was my teenager telling me that he wanted to be a girl. And as I began to devour everything I could on the subject, I became very disturbed at just how widespread and insidious the gender issue had become and how apparently intelligent, professional people were encouraging it among our kids.

We went to my son's doctor to talk over the situation and get advice. He was unsympathetic to my worries. He couldn't discuss my son, he said. Anything they talked about would be confidential because my son was over sixteen. Basically, my son could do whatever he liked was the message I received. We left with a referral to a gender clinic.

When we finally were given an appointment at the clinic (it took several months), my son was immediately affirmed and called by his preferred pronouns and his new name. I was told that, when asked, he had said that he had been suicidal and had thought of harming himself. I didn't believe this; I was convinced that he had been coached. Of course, the old chestnut, "Would I rather have a live daughter than a dead son?" was trotted out, though, at that stage, I didn't know that this is a story repeatedly told to parents who question the process. I told the doctor at the clinic about my concerns, the suicide of my son's father when he was four, the depression in his wider family, his ASD (autism spectrum disorder). It made not a whit of difference. He received no counseling, just affirmation.

I tried to be positive and supportive. I took him to appointments, even to the fertility clinic to store his sperm. The whole process was excruciating. How could puberty blockers be "totally reversible" if this was necessary? He wouldn't discuss the situation with me. Worried about the possible adverse effects on his health, I pointed out that perhaps he was actually gay, that anything he might do in the future—the hormones, the surgery—would be cosmetic only and also harmful, and that he could never truly change sex. In response, he told me that I was a transphobe and that he had thought me better than this. He said that the only difference between men and women are hormones. As my son is someone who is scientific, I found it impossible to understand how he could possibly believe this.

He was almost finished at his high school and looking forward to university after doing extremely well and gaining several scholarships.

When I later helped him move his belongings into the halls at his university, I was a proud mum, hopeful that he would put all this behind him. I didn't want him to go, but I had thought it would be good for him to be with others of his age rather than to live at home. I didn't realize when I said goodbye to him that I would not be seeing him again.

I have neither heard from nor seen him since. He doesn't reply to texts, phone calls, or letters. I am bereft. I lie awake at night and think of the funny little boy I raised and my heart breaks. He has cut not only me out of his life but others close to him as well: his Big Buddy, who has been his mentor since he was seven, his music teacher, and his older brother and sister. I assume that he is being influenced by others. I know that activists tell kids that if their parents aren't 100 percent on board with their transition they should be excised from their lives.

He and I have been through so much together in the past fourteen years, and I never imagined that something like this could happen to us. The only positive thing to come from it is that I have made many friends—parents like me, others who sympathize, and members of organizations like Genspect. I have had so much support and information from abroad.

We may be a small country at the bottom of the world, but we are just as embroiled in this ideology as North America and Europe. Discussion and debate is a thing of the past. Too many good people are afraid to voice their feelings. All I can hope is that one day this mad craze will be over—that one day the scales will fall from people's eyes and the whole situation will be recognized for what it is: this century's "The Emperor's New Clothes." And beyond all else, I hope my son comes back to me.

47

Layers of Sadness

In 2021, my nineteen-year-old son walked from his college campus to Planned Parenthood and was prescribed wrong-sex hormones on his first visit, no therapy required. There was no differential diagnosis. Some days, it's an effort to walk my dog and cook dinner, let alone write an essay about the nuances of what my family is enduring. But I can write about sadness in bullet form, which is apropos, since my family has been fired upon by insidious gender ideology. Like a spray of bullets, it hits us randomly from all directions.

- *Our voicemail:* On our landline voicemail is a recording of the last time our son called saying, "Hi, it's Mark." When my husband and I chose his name, we were grateful for our miraculous healthy baby boy. Sometimes when I'm alone in my house, I listen to this phone message, which was received more than a year ago. My husband and I have a tacit agreement not to erase it, even though our son wants to erase himself.

- *My husband:* My husband is heartbroken. He's angry with the zeitgeist undermining his effort to be a good father. He says it feels like a knife in the back that his son disregards his parents' guidance and instead defers to the trans cult. He feels rejected as a male role model, another layer of sadness. I tell him the cult could have snatched our daughter instead. He gets it, but this doesn't change the fact that his precious son was stolen. To distract himself, he goes to the basement to throw something away and sees a robot project he and Mark had worked on. Then he cries, and I crumble too, with his tears.

- *My daughter:* Two years older than Mark, she and her brother were buddies growing up. She misses her brother. She misses our close family. Fixated on his female fantasy, Mark has threatened to shun his sister if she cannot endorse his delusion. With her peers as well, my daughter worries she will be canceled if she does not speak enthusiastically about her brother as her "sister." I'm sad that she is caught in the crossfire of gender ideology.

- *My son's bedroom:* A month ago, I faced my fear and opened the door to my son's bedroom. I sat on his bed, looked at his posters still tacked on the walls, and endured another wave of grief. To cope, I decluttered. Since this horror began, decluttering has helped lighten the load. My mind was numb during the hours I consolidated my son's stuff. The worst part was his laundry basket filled with the khaki pants and polos he wore before his awful stereotypical female wardrobe. Do I launder them? Do I give them away? I folded and returned them unwashed to his dresser and closet, feeling grim and sad.

- *Photos:* I'm sad every time I walk by the family photos that hang in the hallway. Do I take down these photos of our family on a boat ride, at the beach, of my son as a toddler grinning with his sister on a carousel? No. Though my memories are tainted, I do not deserve to have them deleted. Some days, I allow a glimpse of my handsome son in his senior photo before he graduated high school. This photo, now in a drawer, used to be on the fridge, but it was too painful there. In the living room, my wedding photo pains me too. On that special day, it was inconceivable that my future child would try to escape his own body and that his self-harm path would be sanctioned. I struggle to hold on to the reality of the goodness of my family and the meaningfulness of years filled with the daily effort of raising my son. My confused son deadnames his birth name and devalues his family. Along with the present and the future, the trans cult stomps on my memories. There is sadness in every direction.

- *My son:* Mark is an exceptionally intelligent, quirky person with a great smile. He has a history of speech delay, affect-dysregulation, anxiety, constrained food preferences, and rigidity and had difficulty making friends. He is likely on the autistic spectrum. He was unlucky to be a teenager in the digital age when this social contagion spread. In high school, he flirted with the trans cult, but my husband and I thought we had helped him find his way back to material reality. Of course, his anxiety has not magically gone away with wrong-sex hormones, and a selective serotonin reuptake inhibitor (SSRI) joins his mix of daily pills. Mark was a tall teenager on the verge of thriving as a young adult. Today he is a tall, gullible young man who believes his longer hair, small HRT-induced breasts, and costume of dresses or skirts fools others. During his formative college years, his mind and body have been hijacked by an evil mind virus that was and continues to be aided and abetted by Planned Parenthood, other institutions, and many gaslit people. It's terribly sad.

- *My town:* When I drive by the high school on the way to the grocery store, a cloud of sadness fills my car. Just a few years ago, I drove my son each day to high school. Despite his anxiety, Mark was enthusiastic about school, earning all As and participating in clubs. I delighted in his zest as he scurried into the high school and later chatted about his day at dinner. Senior year, I beamed when he played the suitor in the school play, wearing my husband's suit jacket. Driving home from the grocery store, I see high schoolers file out. I notice teenage boys who look okay, and I envy their parents. Why did my son succumb? The dark cloud follows me home.

- *The empty nest:* My empty nest is soiled. After decades of being involved, caring parents, this was supposed to be our golden years. Now it's a challenge to not have them be our sad years. Because we cannot affirm his delusion, our son is largely estranged. The sparse connection when I reach out to Mark is a diminished remnant in cruel contrast to the closeness my family shared before the trans cult infected him. It feels like a long nightmare that I can't wake up from. Actually, it's sleep that offers an oasis, though less so on nights when my dreams are filled with helpless distress.

- *The future:* The part of my son obsessed with his womanhood fantasy is murdering the rest of him in slow motion. Instead of blossoming as a young man, Mark falls deeper into the dark abyss of gender ideology. Maybe if his fantasy crashes into reality, or his brain matures, or after enough societal backlash, he will desist. Or—maybe he won't. Despite this profound loss, I know I need to reach for as much well-being as possible—for my daughter, for my husband, and for myself. But my heart feels like lead, and I grapple one day at a time with feeling okay. Because what's been inflicted on my son and my family is sad. Unceasingly sad.

48

I Wish I Didn't Know

There are days that I wish I didn't know everything I do about gender ideology, elective youth medicalization, radical transgender politics, and the terrifying changes they have made to our society as a whole.

I wish I didn't know that my fourteen-year-old daughter is currently on a path that could see her heavily medicated and surgically modified before her eighteenth birthday. I don't want to think about my child becoming a permanent medical patient if she persists in her socially induced, self-proclaimed transgenderism. I wish I didn't have to sit, worry, and wait while she spends time with her affirming father, wondering how much deeper she is sinking into a dangerous ideology while she's gone. I want to be rid of my understanding that, as a Canadian mother, I have no right to protect my child and that, if her other parent decided she would be better off on testosterone and would benefit from a double mastectomy, I would be legally unable to challenge the decision.

There are times that I would love to unlearn that laws are being put in place to ensure affirmation for all children who claim to be born in the wrong body, tying the hands of well-meaning therapists and doctors and freeing others to eagerly accommodate irreparable changes to young bodies under the guise of inclusivity. I wish I didn't know that my government has made it illegal for parents, like myself, to access talk therapy, exploratory therapy, or any other type of therapy that is not all-affirming for our gender-questioning kids.

Today I feel the weight of the awareness that government policies are being introduced and pushed into law by radical trans activists in order to forward their own agenda and that, as a result, misgendering the child I gave birth to could essentially constitute a hate crime or even a "thought crime." I don't want to know that school curriculums for all ages have been injected with gender ideology and that these teachings are being concealed from parents. I wish I could dismiss the knowledge that my child has been using a new name and new pronouns with all of her teachers, not one of them communicating with me about these changes.

I want to unthink thoughts about children being lured into an insidious cult over social media, sometimes to the point of leaving their families to slide into the slippery embrace of self-advertised, predatory "glitter moms." I wish I was unaware that parents have lost their children to child services or to the other parent in their efforts to stop their underage children from taking hormone medication and being medically castrated while others are fighting to have their children processed into the opposite sex. I wish I didn't know that in some of these cases, the judges were themselves transgender-rights activists.

I wish someone could erase from my mind the knowledge that children as young as eight years old are being prescribed puberty blockers and that girls as young as thirteen are having double mastectomies. I don't want to know that my kid may one day join the rapidly rising number of older teens and young adults who are finding themselves at the end of this rainbow with no pot of gold waiting for them but only a mortifying realization of what's been done to them. I long for the days when I used to picture my healthy child as a young adult pursuing her goals through higher education, career, family, and simple day-to-day life. I wish I didn't know that she may instead put many of these things on hold while she suffers from the side effects of cross-sex hormones and sex-reassignment surgeries or even social and emotional maladjustment.

I wish I didn't have to lug around heavy thoughts about the vast amounts of money being made by the gender industry as they place child after child and teenager after teenager on the conveyor belt to "a brand new you." I wish I couldn't connect the dots from a radical ideology to the media, to my government, to the school system, to the Internet, to social media, and to my child. I crave blissful ignorance of an ever-growing complacency and compliance among parents, therapists, and doctors who submit to the will of the underdeveloped minds of young people rather than save life-altering drugs and invasive surgeries as a last resort. I wish I didn't know that the time-honored commitment to the oath "First, do no harm" does not apply to troubled gender-questioning children.

I wish I didn't know that an entire generation of young people is at risk of a vulturous cult's mindwash that will leave them battered and broken both mentally and physically while it reaps the rewards of financial gain and political advance.

But I do know . . . and so I must act.

Parents on the Parent Underground

49

Parents: The New Resistance of the Twenty-first Century

Code names. Secret messages passed in the dark. Covert operations. Hiding from the authorities. Are we talking about 1944 in Europe? Sadly, no: we're talking about the present day, and our secret resistance is taking place all over the world.

Instead of spies and resistance fighters inside enemy-occupied borders, we are parents of gender-questioning children who are skeptical of the weakly evidenced, affirmation-only approach currently being pushed by activists and activist-captured organizations.

Rather than codes and secret messages, we pass copies of Abigail Shrier's *Irreversible Damage* wrapped in plain brown paper to curious friends. We interact on secret online groups and write articles and letters using fake names and emails to obscure our true identities due to the very real risk of cancellation and doxing.

All we have to do is look at the appalling and one-sided treatment of J. K. Rowling to know we should stay quiet. We don't have her clout or money to fight against cancellation. And we parents must be anonymous or pseudonymous due to unfair accusations of transphobia, or for fear of child services being set upon us, or, worst of all, for fear of losing our relationships with the children we raised and loved since they were in utero or pictures on adoption papers. But we realize it is nevertheless imperative to act. We can no longer do nothing. For there is a bitter war being fought, and at stake are the very hearts, minds, and bodies of our gender-questioning children.

Those on the side of these future adults are the people who care about them most—us, their parents, who hail from every political, religious, and geographic stripe. Those in the enemy camp are activists and those who would profit from our children's mental distress. Trans people themselves are not the enemy—far from it. Indeed, since they have the real-life experience to know what is really at stake, many of them are welcome allies in this fight, joining forces with parents.

Those of us in the parent underground have delved deep into the research with a PhD level of interest. We have seen the comprehensive reviews of trans healthcare out of Sweden, Finland, and the United Kingdom and have realized we have been sold a bill of goods by the very organizations that claim to have our children's best interests at heart, like the Endocrine Society, the World Professional Association for Transgender Health (WPATH), and the American Academy of Pediatrics. We have combed the neuroscience literature and know that brains don't fully mature until the age of twenty-five (and even longer for vulnerable adults).

We parents know our children's every behavior, tic, and nuance since birth and have confirmed or suspect comorbidities with gender dysphoria like autism, anxiety, eating disorders, and trauma. We wonder if our children might actually be gay and if homophobic bullying is making them run from their sexuality. We wonder if gender dysphoria is the cause or the effect.

We parents are the Resistance—and even if we get bloodied, bruised, and battered on the battlefield, we'll pick ourselves up and never stop fighting this war for the best long-term health outcomes for our kids, at least until those kids become full-fledged adults who can truly understand what is at stake: fertility and future children, lifelong sexual pleasure, permanent side effects, experimental surgeries with high failure rates, mental fragility, and much more.

Perhaps some will find the comparison to the Resistance of World War II insulting. But for us parents, it's very real and very apt. Our kids' lives and long-term mental and physical health are on the line. And so we fight for their future selves, for who they may become.

Because we know at least some of these kids—and no one can predict which ones—will decide to detransition (or realize they can't because many of these procedures are irreversible). They will need help picking up the pieces, and you can be sure all the activists will then turn their backs on them and deny their existence.

Only when healthcare for gender-questioning children has been depoliticized, only when neutral and exploratory mental healthcare has been prioritized, only when conversion therapy legislation does not disingenuously conflate ethical exploratory psychotherapy with torture, only when research is conducted fairly by unbiased academics without agendas, only when the related news is reported by journalists in a balanced manner and not influenced by activists, only when detransitioners are recognized and helped instead of vilified, only when legislation reflects reality—only then will we lay down our weapons and make our peace. Until then, expect a fight.

50

Let's Go All the Way to Protect Our Kids

How do we begin to protect our children? Getting rid of the term "trans kids" is a good way to start.

Comedian and political commentator Bill Maher has, of late, become a hero of sorts—at least to parents like myself who have children who are confused about their gender and believe they are "trans kids." I, like so many parents in my predicament, am outraged by the messages being sent by society about gender ideology. Schools and universities, medical providers and medical associations, mainstream media, governmental authorities, and large corporations (and many of our well-meaning neighbors) all send these societal messages about gender ideology. They tell us that there is such a thing as "trans kids." They don't define the term, but they are very clear as to what "trans kids" need.

The most basic message is that "trans kids" must be "socially transitioned." This means they must be told they are the opposite sex and referred to with terminology that, up until recently, referred only to those of the opposite biological sex. For example, if your son is a "trans kid," he must be referred to as your daughter, and you must use "she/her" pronouns when referring to him. You also must provide your son with a new name of his choosing, which is usually either a name society tends to use for biological females or a "gender-neutral" name that is ambiguous. The name you gave your son when he entered this world must be erased from use and considered "dead." On the other hand, if your child is not a "trans kid" and doesn't like his or her name, you may continue to use the name you gave the child and disregard the new name the child asks you to use, because children's feelings about their name are not that important—only the feelings of "trans kids" toward their names are of utmost importance and priority.

You must provide your "trans kid" with clothing that he or she chooses that allows him or her to feel comfortable in their "gender," which may or may not be stereotypical clothing of the opposite sex. By contrast, a boy who wants to wear stereotypically female clothing or a girl who wants to wear stereotypically male clothing but who does not consider themself "trans," does not need to be catered to in their desires regarding clothing, as only "trans kids" need to be given the clothing of their choice. Gender nonconformity is, in these societal messages, in itself not important or worthy of support unless it is accompanied by a "trans" identity. A girl who really hates dresses can be forced by her family to constantly wear dresses, and the family will not be judged—unless that girl thinks she is a boy—making her a "trans kid," in which case you are absolutely required to observe her choice of clothing.

The next basic message about "trans kids" is that they will likely need to medically alter their bodies as they develop so that they can appear as the opposite sex. You, as their parents, must provide for their choice of medical intervention and let the child lead in determining what they want to do. You must not dare question any of their choices. If you do, they will likely try to commit suicide. (Ignore the absence of statistics showing that many thousands of young people were committing suicide before "trans kids" were discovered to be a phenomenon. They were clearly committing suicide, but we somehow missed these many thousands of suicides.)

If your child was prepubescent when they declared themself a "trans kid," you must—if they want it—provide them with puberty blockers, preventing them from going through natural puberty. Natural puberty, it turns out, is only natural for non-"trans kids." For "trans kids," it is unnatural and bad for them and will likely make them commit suicide. You must follow through with cross-sex synthetic hormones while they are still young teens so they can appear as the opposite sex. Never mind that this combination of blockers and synthetic cross-sex hormones will surely sterilize them and likely prevent them from having fully functioning genitalia for purposes of sexual pleasure. These are "trans kids," and the appearance of their bodies as opposite-sexed takes priority over fertility and sexual function, and overall health.

In sum, "trans kids" will never be their true, authentic selves if you don't refer to them as the opposite sex and allow them to medically alter their otherwise healthy bodies to appear as the opposite sex.

Society at large seems very sure about what a "trans kid" needs. However, it's unclear how we arrived at any of these conclusions, given the fact that there is no medical basis for any of the above-stated needs and, in fact, no actual proof that "trans kids" exist.

Here's what we do know. We do know that some adults have transitioned—as in they have socially and medically altered their appearance and refer to themselves as the opposite sex—and are happy with their decision. We also know that some adults have made those decisions and are not happy with them. Perhaps there are more adults who have transitioned who are happy with their decision than unhappy with their decision (though this is not entirely clear, as many studies have a large loss to follow-up). But even if true, we don't have any evidence that children or teens who have transitioned will be more likely to be happy with that choice when they are adults than to regret it, as this phenomenon is new and there aren't long-term studies of this new cohort of transitioned people, and the few studies on this cohort similarly have a very large loss to follow-up. Further, we do know that there are thousands of detransitioners in this new cohort, many of whom realize the mistake as they mature into adulthood.

Even assuming that more adults are happy with the decision to transition than are not, this, of course, is not proof that they could never have been happy without socially and medically transitioning. In fact, many people have cosmetic surgery and are happy with it—but that doesn't mean that we can leap to the conclusion that those people could never have been happy without those cosmetic procedures. There are lots of things that people choose to do that they are happy about, but that is not proof that they could never be happy without making those decisions. Many people live in tiny houses and are happy about it. Could those people never be their authentic selves without their tiny houses? Many people wear makeup and like it. Could they never have been their true, authentic selves without the makeup? Thus, that some adults have transitioned and are happy with their choice is not proof that they could never have been happy without transition, and it is not proof of the existence of "trans kids."

Let's also consider that the social and medical interventions we are providing these so-called "trans kids" have significant negative impacts on these children. Many, perhaps most, of these kids will end up infertile. Many will lose sexual function. Many will have early hysterectomies. Many will have vaginal atrophy. Many will lose several years of their lives because of the life-shortening effects of a lifetime of synthetic hormones, including strokes, heart attacks, and more. There are also issues with bone density and brain fog. The surgeries often cause infections and other complications, such as incontinence.

Thus, given that there is no proof whatsoever that anyone is really a "trans kid" who needs these interventions, we are negatively impacting the health of these children for no apparent reason.

Social transition is also a problem. Many of these so-called "trans kids" are uncomfortable in their bodies because they are either simply gender nonconforming or homosexual. By inviting or even encouraging them to socially transition, we are then causing children who would otherwise simply be nonconforming or homosexual to set out on a path that leads to medically altering their bodies (and a belief that they were born in the "wrong body"), when acceptance of their nonconformity or their sexual orientation could have led to fulfillment and resolution of any dysphoria. In other cases, girls may feel uncomfortable as girls because they are afraid they won't measure up to today's standards or fear objectification, or boys may feel uncomfortable as boys because they are afraid of "toxic masculinity." Some children may have experienced abuse or trauma that leads them to feel uncomfortable in their own body, which they see as the cause of their abuse. Still other kids may be on the autism spectrum or otherwise "different" and want a reason for their inability to fit in. So many children are uncomfortable with their bodies or declare a "trans" identity for so many reasons. They are not given the opportunity to accept their healthy bodies and simply be themselves but are instead ushered into this new identity as a "trans kid."

Having said all of this, I was disappointed when, on a recent episode of his HBO show, Bill Maher and his guests felt the need to say that some kids can be diagnosed as needing the above-described social and medical interventions. The truth is that NO CHILD IS TRANS. There are some adults who have happily transitioned (and some adults who regretted it). But no child can make the complex decisions involved in transitioning, including giving up their fertility, sacrificing their health, and risking serious injuries, to live as if they were the opposite sex. How can a child who has barely lived as his or her biological sex know that they are more suited to life as if they were the opposite sex and understand the risks involved in medical transition? Few adults really know how it will be, but children certainly cannot make those life-altering decisions.

I don't believe we can ban transition for adults, as it, along with many other cosmetic interventions, exists and is one option an adult can choose. We don't ban dangerous hobbies like bungee jumping, so we can't ban transition. But we can and should prevent children from embarking on such dangerous endeavors.

We need to stop this train, stop the celebration of trans-identity announcements, and stop encouraging children to start on this path. We need to go far beyond that and bring the entire machine that allows the "transing" of children to a screeching halt. We don't have to arrest parents who have opted for these interventions, nor do we have to arrest the medical practitioners who have provided such risky interventions. Rather, we should simply stop pretending there are "trans kids" and tell the truth. Nobody is born "trans," because nobody is born with an intrinsic need to chemically and surgically alter their body and live as if they were the opposite sex. There are adults who have determined that living as if they were the opposite sex makes them happy and that transitioning is the best path for them, and adults can make these kinds of choices, if they are fit to choose for themselves. But no child has this capacity—and no child should be permitted—to make this choice.

We are the adults, and it's time for us to say, "No more." Let's go all the way to protect our kids.

51

Waiting for Change

For the past few weeks, I've been holding my breath in a different way than the way I've been holding my breath since my son announced he was trans, demanding that we refer to him with female pronouns and use only his new name, Erin. To never utter the name I love intensely—my beautiful Elliot, my daughter now, magically no longer my son. Holding my breath while waiting for him to see through the fantasy he has been sold—that drugs will take him from a place of deep and inexplicable self-hatred to a place of warm self-love. Or maybe self-tolerance is enough for him. Oftentimes, I held my breath while waiting to see if the wrong pronoun or the wrong question or the wrong book or the wrong article would bring on the screaming, raging monster hidden only millimeters below the surface of his flawless youthful skin or whether the moment would pass unnoticed.

Now I'm holding my breath because change is in the air. I can sense it. Smell it. Feel it in my bones. Words are being spoken and truths told. A few weeks ago, the unimaginable happened. Three top gender clinicians, Dr. Laura Edwards-Leeper, Dr. Marci Bowers, and Dr. Erica Anderson, began talking about the reality that parents like me have been living and breathing and screaming for years. And while the mainstream media in the United States (by which I mean the liberal media that I clung to and funded during the stressful Trump years) has thus far purposely ignored their deeply disturbing message, it was a breakthrough moment. It portends other changes—the upcoming release of the new

World Professional Association for Transgender Health (WPATH) guidelines, guidelines that the gender clinics have been using as a shield, giving them free license to ignore data and deflect questions and concerns. The new guidelines will hopefully reflect the messages these clinicians are sending: that medical transition for children and teens is neither guaranteed to be safe nor effective; that this population should be thoroughly assessed (only by clinicians like themselves, of course); and that they should engage in exploratory therapy (absurdly referred to as "conversion therapy" by trans activists and everyone who unquestioningly follows them) before starting any medical intervention.

The new guidelines are due to land in December of 2021,* so another month and a half or two of breath-holding for that, but there are other shifts I see out of the corner of my eye. Shifts that suggest change is coming. The BBC aired a ten-part investigative series on Stonewall, the LGBTQ rights organization in the United Kingdom that, until 2014, had worked for LGB rights but suddenly realigned to focus on trans rights—a cause that, in some cases, bumps up against the causes of the very people who formed the organization. I have become intensely aware of the political activities in the United Kingdom because, unlike here in the United States, the fallout from trans activists' demands is becoming more visible, and the more that people on the outside take notice, the more they discover they don't support what's happening. The reporter asked the obvious questions that the rest of us cannot ask. The answers were muddled. They made no sense in the way that none of this makes any sense. Add to this the Dave Chapelle Netflix piece and the ridiculous, pointless protest that followed. What rights are you fighting for? The right to cancel comedy that offends you?

People are starting to speak up. Despite the news blackout, people are seeing and hearing about what's been happening under their noses while the "be kind" terrorists bully those who don't agree, all while

---

* WPATH's eighth "Standards of Care" guidelines, which are really just activist-driven recommendations, weren't released in their final form until September 2022. The final version removed most age-limit recommendations for irreversible cross-sex hormone treatments and "gender-affirming" surgeries, thereby protecting clinicians who would otherwise treat children under recommended age limits from liability. The removal of a chapter on ethics and the addition of a chapter on "eunuchs," among many other changes, further reflect the reality that activism and ideology drive the guidelines.

shrieking about their vulnerability. This may seem beyond our child-centered world, but the more the world sees the emptiness behind this insidious plague of a movement, the closer they are to seeing what's at the bottom of it—the children they are grooming and using and the families they are destroying.

And not just "people" are speaking up. We are speaking up—finding ways to enter conversations, voice concerns, spread information, challenge schools, protest in front of clinics. There is momentum building. I can feel it. Even as I grieve, my skin tingles. I can sense it. Change is coming. Must come. But in what form? And how long will we have to wait? How many of our children will cross over, lost, maybe forever? Or maybe just until they are wholly broken.

And when change comes, what about those out there who have already transitioned? What will it mean to them if they see that they were wronged? Some will have detransitioned through their own pace of self-discovery, but what about those who are on the edge of understanding themselves and their confused motivations? What will it mean to be just waking up only to be blinded by a searchlight? And the parents who thought they were doing right by their children, what about them? To learn that you've consented to treatment that sterilized your child based on misinformation and lies and your best intentions? That you prodded and supported your child down a sham pathway that places tremendous limits on his or her life instead of opening the doors to a brave new world? How could they ever embrace the change that is surely coming?

I need change to come. Viscerally need it. This hell has to end. But what if it slips away silently, the way it started? I can imagine things just sort of quietly ebbing, like some horrific carnival that came to town and set up shop, with its garish tents and promises of redemption, and then stealthily, in the middle of the night, just folded everything up, and loaded it onto the wagons, and rode away. And we were left damaged, traumatized, our children still mesmerized by the fading glow of their tail lights, while most of the people never even knew they'd been here at all. To never have our grief or our suffering recognized and acknowledged as a final insult. I can imagine the medical groups and clinicians in their back-room boardroom discussions, weighing their risks, consulting their counsel, making their decisions, and with a short series of memos, shifting resources and staff away from gender clinics. Slowing, then stopping the flow of patients, referring them elsewhere until there is nowhere else to refer them to. This hell will end with a whisper, or a death rattle, not a bang.

Real change needs to happen. Clinics need to stop treating children and young teens with puberty blockers, and stop treating teens and young adults with hormones, and start seriously assessing them to figure out what in god's name is really going on, and treating them all with meaningful therapy, not "how long have you been trans" therapy. For now, I'm still holding my breath, but change is coming. I can feel it.

52

Yes, There Are Clear Patterns among Male Adolescents with Rapid-Onset Gender Dysphoria

Back in 1992, the "feel bad" movie of the year was called *Lorenzo's Oil*. Based on a true story, this film follows the struggles of a couple battling to find a cure for their son's adrenoleukodystrophy. Desperate for information and ideas, they turn to doctors and scientists who rebuff their efforts: they are told there is no effective treatment and to prepare for his death. Undaunted, the parents badger the scientists, track down scarce studies, and organize meetings until they discover a potential cure: a special oil. Thanks to the parents' efforts, this oil extends the life of their son and helps other children with the disease.

Much as I admire Susan Sarandon's hair, I never wanted to reenact this movie. But sometimes life imitates art. In June 2020, during a dark phase of the Covid-19 pandemic, our then fifteen-year-old son announced to my husband and me that he thought he might be trans. This was not only out of the blue but also out of character. Like any parents, we told our son we loved him, then started to dive deep into the existing research on trans-identified teens. Quickly, we realized that high-quality studies on the topic were thin. The popular "affirmative model" of treatment was based on a protocol developed for people who had had persistent gender dysphoria for years since childhood, not teenagers who suddenly developed it out of the blue. My son seemed to better fit

Lisa Littman's description of rapid-onset gender dysphoria (ROGD). Affirming and reinforcing a false belief that my son was actually a girl inside seemed like a bad idea.

In late 2020, I joined a small group of parents of trans-identified teenage sons in which we offer each other support and share resources. Since then, our group has grown to more than a hundred parents, with members from Europe, North America, and Australia. No matter where we lived, it became clear that our sons shared significant common characteristics. Many of them were smart and quirky and isolated. Their histories and presentations of gender dysphoria were strikingly similar, too. None of them were gender-nonconforming as children. Many of them were sexually delayed and had suffered a recent social rejection. They all made their big out-of-the-blue announcements as adolescents.

To get a better sense of these patterns, I developed three surveys to measure how frequently these issues were present in our kids. These surveys were conducted between January and May 2021 through SurveyMonkey. While this study is not a formal, scientific one, it does gather evidence of some striking patterns within the cohort of male adolescents with rapid-onset gender dysphoria. Some of the significant findings:

- These boys are extremely bright. In our first survey, 44 percent percent of our boys were categorized as gifted (IQ 130–145, n=32/73), 19 percent as highly gifted (IQ 145–160, n=19/73), and 15 percent as profoundly gifted (IQ>160, n=11/73). Our second survey asked for precise IQ numbers and found the average IQ to be 140 (n=19, range 126–175). This appears to be quite different from the historical childhood-onset cohort.

- These boys are socially awkward and quirky. There is a high rate of autism (21 percent), autism-like behaviors (29 percent), and poor social skills (39 percent), and 40 percent have ADHD.

- These boys were suffering mental health issues before their trans identification, and their mental health declined after announcing their trans identification. Roughly 73 percent suffered from anxiety and 60 percent suffered from depression in the six months before they announced they thought they were trans. In the six months after announcing their trans identification, 86 percent suffered from anxiety and 77 percent from depression.

- As identified in previous studies, issues of trauma appear to be a factor. Over 20 percent of the boys have suffered a major trauma, such as the death or illness of a parent or sibling, and 13 percent have suffered a major upheaval such as a move.

- Social contagion appears to be at play, with 42 percent of the boys announcing after a close friend announced.

- Internet exposure appears to be a factor. Nearly all of the boys (96 percent) had been exposed to pro-trans websites.

- Sexuality and sexual behavior appear to be a factor. More than a quarter (27 percent) of the boys demonstrate discomfort with their sexuality, 57 percent are possibly gay or bisexual, and 80 percent have never kissed anyone.

- Around 50 percent of the boys announced within six months of first considering they are trans. Another 24 percent announced within six to twelve months. These boys themselves acknowledge and are aware that this is "rapid onset" and that they did not have these feelings in childhood.

- Trans identification and behavior appear to be loose, inconsistent, and fragmented. Among the boys, a great majority (85 percent) have announced to their parents, but only 46 percent have announced to all their siblings and only 24 percent have told their extended family. Female clothing behaviors (at home 32 percent vs. at school/work 27 percent) generally lag behind female pronoun requests (at home 64 percent vs. at school/work 27 percent).

- ROGD can dissipate. Roughly 42 percent of the boys had a period of desistance that lasted at least two weeks, and 7 percent had desisted for six months or more. Note: as our support group serves families whose sons are actively claiming trans identity, the families with sons who have permanently desisted would not be engaged in our group or taking our surveys.

A few additional notes:

- Though we have not measured it through surveys, our families appear to be generally highly educated and savvy consumers of healthcare information. Parents include doctors, nurses, researchers, lawyers, and other professionals who read the studies behind the headlines and then read the footnotes behind the studies. We tend to be skeptics and "free thinkers." This behavior mimics the high intelligence of our sons.

- Though politically and religiously diverse, our families tend to be "liberal thinkers" in the traditional sense of the phrase and particularly inclusive in our general attitudes and behaviors. We have gay couples and families with gay and trans siblings. We are not bigots.

- Generally, our families follow a "supportive but not affirmative" model. We have offered unconditional love, emotional support, and continued financial support to our sons. No one has shamed or kicked their son out of the house. Some of us have agreed to pronoun changes and minor social transitioning. A few of us have sons who are on hormones. However, most of us have consistently communicated that the trans identification does not seem to match our son's past or present behavior and have firmly stated our opposition to hormones and surgery. We have self-selected away from "gender clinics" and recognize that we may represent a type of family different from those with children treated at gender clinics.

- We have all struggled to find appropriate psychological therapy for our sons. There are very few therapists who will engage in deeper analysis with our sons about their underlying issues, as most just follow a blind "affirmation" model. There are very few therapists who have experience working with profoundly gifted, autistic, anxious, and depressed boys with ROGD. Finding one who connects with a son like this is particularly challenging. Most of our families are muddling through with minimal therapeutic support. Many of us have stories of therapists who misled us about their approach, and our trust in the field is eroding.

- We are aware of a possible connection between selective serotonin reuptake inhibitors (SSRIs) and the development of gender dysphoria in some of our sons. We are also aware of a connection between online "sissy porn" (a subgenre of pornography that involves men who are forcibly feminized or "sissified" to look like women through the use of makeup, lingerie, etc., and who are made to submit to sexual degradation) and anime porn and the development of gender dysphoria in some of our sons. These topics deserve more attention.

- We suspect that social anxiety and isolation lie at the root of gender dysphoria for many of these boys. High-IQ, autistic, ADHD boys are all social outcasts. Puberty further highlights their differences. We suspect that gender dysphoria and trans identification may be unhealthy attempts to find a community.

- Some of our boys struggle with eating disorders, and some of our boys have undergone a severe mental health crisis. We suspect there may be a connection between all of their mental health issues. The health community's knee-jerk diagnosis of gender dysphoria and fast-track to treating it with hormones fails to serve these boys. We need a more thoughtful, nuanced, and flexible model of treatment for our sons.

Research on this topic is severely hobbled for both political and practical reasons. Researchers who have attempted to study this issue have been called transphobic, forced out of their positions, publicly heckled, and had their funding pulled. Practically speaking, there is no way to ethically run a hormone study on trans-identified children (some get hormones, some get placebos, some get none). It is also impossible to run a formal study on children who never present to gender clinics.

Clearly, a teenager who has had gender dysphoria since childhood is different from a teenager who suddenly developed it at puberty, and it is time the medical field acknowledges this different presentation. This recent cohort of trans-identified boys appears to be smarter, more anxious, more depressed, and more sexually delayed and have higher rates of autism and ADHD than previous cohorts. We hope this informal study can spur additional research and conversations. Like Lorenzo's parents, we know there are answers out there—and we won't stop looking until we find them.

53

Parents, Journalists, and Therapists— You Can Still Do the Right Thing

In *Mistakes Were Made (But Not By Me)*, by Carol Tavris and Elliot Aronson, the authors describe how people who start out with very similar positions and ideals can gradually find themselves with diametrically opposed viewpoints and strongly entrenched opinions that they have reframed in their minds as fact. This is because when people make a difficult decision, they subsequently tend to accumulate evidence that tells them they made the right choice. As a result, polarization occurs between themselves and those who made a different decision on an issue that was otherwise a close call.

This is what has happened, tragically, in the trans scandal, to the great detriment of parents and children and, really, our entire society. I am one of many parents who has stood on the top of the Pyramid of Choice. When my young teen child announced he was "trans," I was ill-equipped to make an informed decision about how to proceed. I was familiar with the cultural phenomenon but not at all familiar with how that applied to my child or the medicalization of trans that I would be forced to evaluate. With no notice, I had to pick a direction to slide—"affirm" or "explore/question." I picked "explore/question." Just as the pyramid indicates, I could have gone either way at that point. However, once I opened my mind to questioning base assumptions, I was horrified by what I found. There was an utter lack of real science. I became alarmed about the threat to my child's mental and physical health, became determined not to affirm, and gradually, as I slid down, became an activist trying to protect children from medical harm. But, having stood on top of that pyramid myself, I know in my heart how close I came to sliding down the other side.

Are you a parent that slid down the other side? You are not so different from me; you just made a different first step, and once you took that step, you were committed and followed the logical path. I don't blame you—I nearly did the same thing—after all, medicalizing and affirming your child is billed as the safest choice for your child, and you did what you thought was best. Now, you are as firmly entrenched in your position as I am. You need to believe you did the right thing because the alternative is unbearable to fathom. The cognitive dissonance is something you have to explain away. I get it.

Countless children have been harmed by misinformation in the past; you are not the first parent to find yourself in this boat. Many young adults were misled and hurt, too—convinced that transition was the solution to their problems, only to find out that it was not all it seemed to be. This is not your fault. You are not to blame. You were misled by self-purported experts who manipulated medical journals and traditional and social media to influence you.

This isn't to say there is no one to point the finger at. Jack Turban, Diane Ehrensaft, Chase Strangio, Planned Parenthood, the opportunistic gender clinics that have popped up. I believe that they are culpable—and that time and our legal system will prove this to be the case.

But for the rest of you—it's not too late to do the right thing and help other kids and parents standing atop the pyramid, confronted with no real data, tons of politics and social pressure, and an impossible choice. Journalists, doctors, therapists, transitioned individuals who now have doubts—it's not too late for you, either, if you open your eyes to the viewpoint of those who refused to be pushed onto the side marked "affirm" and who traveled down the other side of that pyramid.

54

The "Lived Experience"
of Rapid-Onset Gender Dysphoria

Transgender activists love to talk about the "validity" of "lived experience" and complain that questioning in any way that sacred thing is an attempt to "erase" them, to "deny their existence"—yes, even to "kill them."

Well, we parents have some "lived experience" of our own to convey to these activists.

Rapid-onset gender dysphoria (ROGD) is real.

This is the term that has come into common usage for a new type of gender distress that was first formally identified and named by researcher and clinician Lisa Littman in her seminal 2018 study. It refers to a new trend in which teens who never had childhood gender dysphoria suddenly begin to identify as transgender around the time of puberty. This phenomenon has since been discussed further by journalist Abigail Shrier in her best-selling book *Irreversible Damage*. It manifests for the first time in adolescence or early adulthood and typically occurs in association with mental health issues, trauma, autism, and/or same-sex attraction. It is much more common in girls (unlike classical gender dysphoria, which presents most often in prepubescent boys), although boys are also being affected. It seems to be spread by social contagion among friendship groups and online. Although it is a new phenomenon, it is rapidly increasing in prevalence in Western countries, and healthcare professionals have begun to express concern about it, including prominent gender clinicians.

The experiences described in the work of Littman and Shrier ring true with the thousands of parents who participate in support groups around the world. As parents, we have begun to speak out publicly about this in increasing numbers. Read the constant flow of parent essays on the Parents with Inconvenient Truths about Trans Substack. Peruse the parent stories on the website of Genspect, a new advocacy organization that provides support to parents. Listen to the parent interviews—there are more being released all the time. Listen to or read the moving testimonies of increasing numbers of detransitioners who eloquently describe the role social contagion played in their trans identification.

Despite this growing number of voices, activists, including many activist clinicians, are fond of denying the existence of ROGD. They are quite happy to erase us—to deny our lived experiences. The explosive increase in the number of teens presenting to gender clinics is implausibly and without evidence attributed to "increased acceptance," which completely fails to explain the reversal of the sex ratio. Parents are derided as bigots by activists, society at large, and even in some cases by family and friends for raising concerns about social contagion and for questioning the advisability of rapid medical interventions in the presence of autism, mental health issues, or trauma.

The hypocrisy of activists is one of the most galling features of this whole debate. The lived experience of a thirteen-year-old girl is enough to justify the removal of her breasts. The lived experience of a "nonbinary" eleven-year old boy is enough for clinicians to seriously consider making an (entirely experimental) attempt to maintain his body in a prepubertal state for the rest of his life.

But the lived experience of thousands of loving, committed, and well-informed parents? That is derided as denial or "anti-trans bigotry" by activists who, I warrant, have never spoken to one parent who is experiencing this phenomenon in their own family. (On a side note, this activist critique of the concept of ROGD is ably rebutted by psychiatrist Roberto D'Angelo.)

Sexologist James Cantor ably summarizes the important issues with regard to the ROGD concept in a piece in *Sexology Today*. He also points out that CAAPS (Coalition for the Advancement and Application of Psychological Science), despite the fact that it is "an umbrella organization of other psychology associations with the expressed purpose of promoting evidence-based practice," has entirely missed the point in its call for the term to be eliminated. This is just one example of many where medical societies, as well as activists, attempt to dismiss this very real phenomenon.

Make no mistake, we do care about our kids' experiences—but unlike the activist clinicians, we care about all of them. For in their other act of supreme hypocrisy, the affirmers will attend only to the part of our kids' lived experiences that fits their narrative. They will ignore the mental illness, the autism, or the history of trauma and abuse that may be behind the trans identity. So, they erase our kids as well. We, as their parents who love and know them best, want them seen as whole, living, breathing people—not as "identities."

It also seems that even the lived experience of trans people is only considered valid if it fits the preferred narrative. As mentioned above, prominent gender clinicians, including Erica Anderson and Marci Bowers, have recently spoken out to express concerns about pediatric gender medicine. This included comments about the validity of the concept of social contagion and their belief that adolescent-onset gender dysphoria can be complicated by underlying mental health conditions. These people are both trans women. Yet, just days after they expressed their concerns, the World Professional Association of Transgender Health (WPATH) released a statement condemning any discussion of these issues in the media. Coincidence? I think not.

One favorite tactic of activists—including self-styled "expert" activist clinician groups—is to claim that there is "insufficient peer-reviewed scientific evidence" for this "proposed phenomenon." They will conveniently forget to mention that Littman was crucified on social media following the publication of her ROGD study, experienced little support from her university, and even lost her job. This leads one to wonder what researcher in their right mind would go anywhere near this topic after witnessing these events?

This situation then allows these same clinicians to smugly claim to support "continued scientific exploration within a culture of academic freedom, not censorship," whilst knowing perfectly well that activists will create all the censorship that is needed to ensure that no more study of ROGD is allowed to occur.

Well, we parents are not having it. ROGD is real. We need no more studies to tell us what we have seen and continue to see with our own eyes. These are our lived experiences. Unlike activists, we do not histrionically accuse our detractors of trying to deny our existence or kill us. However, we do expect to be listened to and taken seriously so that our kids can receive proper care and avoid unnecessary harm—and we will not stop screaming from the rooftops until this happens.

55

Gender Dysphoria: The Science Is Not Settled

Some parents have taken it upon themselves to read the research and understand the science, and we are very concerned by what we've found! Please take the time to read our findings . . .

Gender dysphoria is the suffering from a mismatch between one's body and one's gender identity. There has been an enormous surge in gender dysphoria cases in the past decade, especially among adolescents and young adults, with onset starting strongly at or after puberty. This represents a new and different cohort from previous decades, when cases were mainly adult or child-onset gender dysphoria. The science of how to treat gender dysphoria, a temporary condition for many, is not settled.

Old Treatment Practice

Until recently, it was understood that if someone had gender dysphoria, you would first try:

1. "Watchful waiting" (especially in a person below the age of twenty-six with a still developing and maturing brain)

   - Approximately 80 percent (61 percent–98 percent) of those with childhood-onset gender dysphoria grow out of it; it's a developmental phase for them.

- Socially transitioning young people can make gender dysphoria persist.

2. Explorative supportive psychotherapy
    - This is particularly important because other conditions (OCD, autism, trauma, anxiety, distress) can cause gender dysphoria and were, in fact, often disqualifying for medicalization.

Some people have their gender dysphoria persist even after the first two approaches. In such cases, these adults could then undergo an arduous and aggressive intervention (sterilization, removal or alteration of body parts, lifetime off-label hormone treatment that comes with many significant health risks, including those related to the circulatory, skeletal, central nervous, endocrine, and immune systems and other risks not yet fully understood, especially long-term ones).

- This aggressive medicalization was extended to younger people with the Dutch Protocol, studies of fifty-five stringently vetted kids (with many requirements not imposed today). This was an attempt to streamline the first two approaches by attempting to identify, and then medicalize sooner, the small fraction of eventual persisters.
    - Their mental health outcomes were only evaluated a few years past surgery, not the approximately ten years needed to catch many known problems.
    - Treatment included puberty blockers that have risks to bones, brain, heart, and fertility and have other effects that are not known over the long term.
- The sizable adolescent onset group is a new phenomenon and not well studied or understood; many have mental issues as well.
- For some individuals, this aggressive medicalization is inappropriate, and they eventually no longer want to identify with a gender different from their biological sex ("detransitioners"). No one knows how many there are, especially given the long average time to regret (approximately four to ten years) and the evolving prerequisites for starting medicalization (currently almost absent in the United States beyond self-diagnosis).

- The evidence supporting medicalization is lacking or of low quality. Studies have not been able to show that these treatments are safe or improve mental health over time. Many studies are too short to catch known problems that appear after seven to ten years, lose participants to follow-up, or are otherwise flawed, having evidence of low or very low quality in the GRADE (Grading of Recommendations, Assessment, Development, and Evaluations) framework.

There is a lot of support for protecting the people who have gone through this arduous medical treatment from discrimination and those with this identification. Absolutely. Yes. Of course.

A Fallacy Appears

However, around 2010, there was a change, and a false assumption was introduced. This was the (false) claim that having gender dysphoria is innate and unchangeable—that is, if you experience gender dysphoria, you are immutably trans. Period. Does not change. (Even some physicians inaccurately say it's biological.)

There is no evidence for the claim that a given gender identity will persist for all those with gender dysphoria. It is simply not true that everyone who is dysphoric will be so forever unless they transition. This is why there has long been the usual route of first trying watchful waiting and/or psychotherapy for co-occurring mental health issues, which will resolve gender dysphoria for many. There is no known test to determine who might heal from these first two protocols, which is another reason why they have traditionally been tried first.

With this false premise about being immutably trans, again, which is not supported by evidence, the first two treatment steps became labeled unethical conversion therapy. Those who make this charge incorrectly conflate therapy and unethical conversion therapy and falsely imply that ethical psychotherapy is harmful. Now one is told to "affirm." In spite of having no basis in evidence, this approach was rapidly adopted, and flawed research is quoted to support it, e.g., the flawed research that says medicalization lowers suicidality. This fallacy puts children, adolescents, and young adults at risk. It promotes a harmful, unnecessary medicalization of those who would desist with the first two interventions, including the majority of children. For these young people, aggressive medicalization and surgery would be a terrible mistake. Some of them are coming forward now. (See the subreddit r/detrans for an informal "look.")

Keeping the Fallacy Alive

The false premise of immutable gender identity has been buttressed with untrue claims—that the above first two interventions to heal gender dysphoria cannot succeed and that true detrans people do not exist. The following inaccuracies facilitate this erroneous presumption:

- "The desisters aren't really suffering gender dysphoria—they are just tomboys, etc." (There is evidence to the contrary). There is even a claim that desister studies should be halted.

- "Therapy is conversion therapy." (This is a false equivalence. It is true only if gender identity is immutable, which it isn't.)

- "True detransitioners do not exist—people only detransition or are dissatisfied because of discrimination or lack of funding for treatment." (False.) Another untrue statement, that if someone transitions, they are saved from suicide, is also dangerously told to young people.

These are all false. These are all quoted to support the fallacy that all who feel gender dysphoria will never stop feeling distress unless they transition. That one treatment fits all.

Again, this claim is not true.

Several professional societies do support the current affirmative approach. They do not have reliable evidence that supports rapid affirmation. You can see the low-quality evidence (per the GRADE framework) that the Endocrine Society gives in support of its "standard of care" guidelines. Meanwhile, the American Academy of Pediatrics recommendations conflate being gay and being trans and misquote the literature. A peer-reviewed rebuttal to the Endocrine Society's position statement stated that the guidelines given by the Endocrine Society do not rise to the level of "standard of care" and thus are not authoritative.

Rather, the rebuttal says that they should instead be seen as "practice guidelines . . . suggestions or recommendations to improve care that, depending on their sponsor, may be biased."

Summary and Plea

Some people do heal from gender dysphoria with ethical supportive psychotherapy. It is false to say this therapy is the same as (unethical!) conversion therapy for gays. Trans is not the new gay. One is about sexual orientation, and one is about how you see yourself. For the people who heal with therapy, gender dysphoria is reportedly more like anorexia, something everyone should want people to heal from. Explorative supportive psychotherapy used to be the first thing to try, for a good reason.

One size does not fit all. The urgency to medicalize, without exploration, especially given how many of these young people have mental issues that are known to cause temporary gender dysphoria, is not supported by evidence. Originally a last resort for treating gender dysphoria under careful supervision, this aggressive, dangerous, and experimental medicalization, with irreversible consequences, has been promoted as an "on-demand" commodity. It is now being marketed directly to vulnerable young people in distress (most of whom would not have even qualified for the few earlier treatment studies) as the only option forward, the only way to be "their authentic self."

Those who try to point out the contraindications of the current rush to medicalization are often falsely accused of a phobia of those who have gone through this painful, difficult process. It is not anti-trans to investigate the facts. People are wielding "anti-trans" to make people shut out facts. Please take a look at the evidence. Again, the science is not settled. The physical toll of medicalization is enormous and irreversible. If you care about these kids, please become aware of the serious debate in the research community.

Check out the Society for Evidence-Based Gender Medicine (www.segm.org). Look at what is being said by experts (in books, essays, podcasts, and videos, of which there are many). Look at what's hapenning in the United Kingdom and Sweden. Please investigate.

It's not always easy for parents to speak up, especially in public. Perhaps you can.

56

Real Conversations, One at a Time

When my daughter approached her father and me more than four years ago to tell us that she was a transgender boy, the floor dropped out beneath me. As I came quickly to understand, she was the embodiment of a girl with rapid-onset gender dysphoria (ROGD): well-meaning liberal parents, everything princessy and pink as a child, a chest full of dress-up clothes, and complete impatience for people who saw her short haircut and couldn't see that OBVIOUSLY she was a girl. Obviously! But when she started high school, my cool baby feminist introduced herself as "Tommy" and—again, another cliché—her teachers and the entire school administration conspired to call her "Tommy" and he/him at school, all the while using her real name to our faces, the faces of the only parents she'll ever have.

To this day, it's the betrayal of the school that still angers and frustrates me the most. Because—spoiler alert—our trans-insanity had a surprisingly happy and speedy end. The day after her freshman year of high school ended, I offered to take my daughter shopping for summer clothes. She walked right into the juniors' section of a local department store and picked out some cute shorts, tops, and a new girls' bathing suit. I said nothing, but later that night nearly collapsed in relief and joy when I told my husband about our shopping trip. For four months, our bedroom was the only place we could talk about our daughter, using her real name and sex. It was a haven from the crazy charade we were expected to participate in outside.

But this is a story that has been told many times over on these pages. My essay is about the grass-roots work I'm doing to try to put an end to the needless and damaging medicalization of children with mental health and normal developmental challenges. My daughter desisted, but I know how many other children and parents are suffering because of the reality-denying death cult that is transgenderism.

* * *

I am a North American academic in the field of women's and gender studies, and I am protected by the great privilege of tenure. I used to have a high Internet profile, so when I learned about Lisa Littman's ground-breaking paper in 2018, I went on social media to urge fellow academics to read the paper and, even if they disagreed with her conclusions, to support her academic freedom. I also tried to engage people on what I thought was an obvious feminist point, which is that we should encourage girls to love their developing bodies, not to harm them by wearing chest binders (or, in some ways, the even more disturbing and surely pornography-influenced "packers"). How silly of me to think these were uncontroversial opinions for a scholar to share!

You can guess what happened next. Yes, I was dog-piled and repeatedly targeted via social media accounts for the high crime of "transphobia" over the next three years. I was called all kinds of names and assigned all sorts of evil motivations by these mind readers. I was sent abusive emails and was accused of "erasing the existence" of several people with anime avatars with merely the opinions in my own head. Longtime online mutuals quietly unfollowed or blocked me; I heard from other friends that there were campaigns pressuring my followers to drop me because I'm a "known transphobe." I even lost a thirty-year friendship with a woman I considered my best friend in my field. This is a woman who once scolded me for "not trying hard enough" to breastfeed my daughter, and now she's completely on board with medicalizing teenagers and amputating healthy body parts.

The insane distortions of this movement would be funny if their consequences weren't so horrifying. But fortunately, real-world true believers like my former friend are rare.

Since then, I've completely dropped out of social media. The echo chambers we all fall into are alarmingly distorted and push us all further and further into weird ideological corners we'd never be pushed into in real life. So, after fifteen years online, I went "stealth" and into the real world, having conversations with people one-on-one about transgenderism and its danger to young people. In part, I was inspired by the example of Christopher Elston, or @BillboardChris on Twitter, who goes out in public with his white sneakers and sandwich board sign to have one-on-one conversations in person with passersby about transgender ideology and how it's hurting young people.

First, I started raising this issue with colleagues in my academic department. In dozens of one-on-one, quiet conversations in people's offices, not a single person has disagreed with me, called me a bigot, or scolded me for my thought crimes. Most thanked me for raising the issue, saying things like, "I'm terrified that if I use the wrong word with a graduate student, I'll get fired," or "I'm so glad you brought this up, because I thought it was just me who couldn't make sense of this movement." I even raised the issue with a colleague who has a trans-identified son, and he said that he agreed with me completely and is terrified for his son's future health and well-being. Of course he is—he has eyes and ears and has fathered two children and understands intimately that humans are, like other mammals, sexually dimorphic. That's the real world that most people inhabit, not the online not-so-fun house of make believe and let's pretend.

Next, when corresponding over email with friends and acquaintances, I would ask after their daughters, and a few replied that their daughters now believed they were their sons or were "nonbinary." When I told them that I knew what they might be going through because of my daughter's brief trans identification, and said that I had serious problems with what I see as an Internet-enabled instance of teen contagion and mass psychosis, they (every single one, all of them men) said they agreed and were so happy to hear they weren't alone in their heresy. They were bewildered—like me, they all saw themselves as good liberals and accepting people, but they didn't think their children were transgender. I shared all of the usual resources with them—Genspect, Transgender Trend, 4thWaveNow, Parents with Inconvenient Truths about Trans (PITT) Substack, articles by Lisa Marchiano, Abigail Shrier's *Irreversible Damage*, Helen Joyce's *Trans: When Ideology Meets Reality*, Kathleen

Stock's *Material Girls*, and the *Gender: A Wider Lens* podcast with Sasha Ayad and Stella O'Malley. I reassured them they weren't bigots or hateful people—they were just fathers who loved their daughters and probably knew better what was best for their kids than anonymous anime avatars on the Internet.

I think it makes a difference for fellow liberals, and especially men, to hear this from a woman who is a Professional Feminist. I have come to feel recently like I'm a kind of gender-critical Jehovah's Witness: "Has anyone talked to you about transgenderism today?" But I wouldn't keep doing it if people were unwilling to talk to me. (And believe it or not, I'm not always the person to bring up the subject.)

More recently, I've been having these one-on-one conversations with women and men in my community. Some of them are people I meet with regularly—like a farmer at the farm stand, my stylist, a bookstore owner, a fitness instructor, or local teachers. Some of these people are liberal, some are more conservative, and some are right-wing. But you know what? They all listen, and they open right up with questions, more questions, and these conversations can go on for hours. Nobody in the real world believes in this Internet-driven fantasy life of a few disturbed adults and, unfortunately for us parents, some of our mentally fragile kids. Most are relieved to hear that "even a left-liberal feminist college professor" thinks this is nuts. If more of us speak up to one another, we can make real changes on school boards and in our communities when we see gender ideology taking root.

Most people watching this parade can see that the emperor has no clothes. The overwhelming majority of people see what's happening, and they see how damaging it is to young people, to their families, and to our society when we're asked to applaud lies and participate in harmful fictions. Just as much of the advice at PITT focuses on getting kids offline and into engagements with their real bodies in the material world, so we parents and other adults need to exit the online performative screaming matches and start talking—and listening—to real people in the real world. Real people know a real person when they see one. They can tell when you're being honest about your opinions, and they're more than willing to share theirs if they think you won't scold them for using the "wrong" word, or hiss at them for sharing what they've been told is a "bad opinion."

Meanwhile, you can find me at the farmer's market, at the park, on campus, in the library, at the coffee shop, and on the bus, making authentic connections to real people in the real world. I encourage all of you to do the same, especially if you aren't the parent of a trans-identified child. Many of them are too terrified for their kids to be authentic right now, so it's up to the rest of us to make the real world safe for real people with their real ideas and opinions again.

Parents on Parenting Through Trans

57

How to Be a Trans-Educated Rational Parent

If you're reading this, odds are your child has announced out of the blue that they are trans. Unlike some of the people you've read about, your spidey sense is tingling, and you have a lot of questions. Most likely, you never thought you'd hear something like this from your child because they in no way appear to fit the mold of what you're used to seeing on talk shows or in the news.

The Internet will tell you that you need to celebrate your trans child! It will tell you that doing so might be hard, but that you must accept your child for who he or she is, even if it seems strange.

Do not listen—this is bad advice.

If you are not scared out of your mind about the whole trans thing, you are not up to speed yet. There is a real and immediate threat to your child posed by this new ideology, which is, unfortunately, encouraged and even celebrated by politicians, educators, and many well-meaning but grossly uninformed people.

The Internet is populated with very bad advice from trans activists, pharmaceutical companies in disguise, attention-seeking parents and teens, creepy grooming cartoon unicorns, and medical professionals that don't read source materials.

Many people or even an elite group of people believing or presenting something as true *does not make it true.* The *argumentum ad populum* is an argument, often emotionally laden, that claims a conclusion is true because most, all, or even an elite group of people irrelevantly think, believe, or feel that it is. This argument is sometimes persuasive but normally fallacious if there is no direct relevant evidence presented for the truth of its conclusion.

If you are not careful, you will wind up hurting your child by subjecting them to experimental drugs and harmful procedures and mental angst in the name of transition, all due to the madness of crowds.

Your teen is not an adult and does not have the maturity to make adult decisions. They are not extra mature because they are gender confused. They are probably less mature for their age—or at least have the same level of immaturity as other kids their age—and are thus especially prone to be drawn to gender ideology during puberty.

Do not be bullied into abdicating your parental role to outsiders with unknown motivations who will likely encourage your child to disbelieve and mistrust you. Be strong and persevere because your child needs you to fight for them now, more than ever. In this world, parents are the bad guys, and doctors and therapists are accused of conducting "conversion therapy" if they don't do what your child asks for when they ask for it, up to and including amputating their body parts.

As a loving parent, if you want to do what's best, it's time to get up to speed.

Do not despair!

Odds are your child will get through this just fine. Don't fall into the activists' trap.

Many of us in the Parent Underground are likely a few steps ahead of you, so we can give you some advice. We were told to trust others when it came to our kids. That wasn't good enough for us, so we've done our own homework, educated ourselves, and are stepping up to help our kids and to inform other parents that are scared and feeling helpless, just as we once were. We're as much the experts as anyone else now. We are Trans-Educated Rational Parents. You can be one too.

Are you so sure that "trans" is an immutable state of being when you really stop and think about it?

Your child is still the same person inside and outside. Trust your instincts. They are probably struggling with the usual challenges of puberty, but in an insane cultural environment where a magical fix is advertised.

Our Only Horse in the Race Is Our Kids

To be a Trans-Educated Rational Parent, you must be:

- *Pro–Your Child:* We don't care how our kids dress or how they wear their hair. In fact, many of us encourage our kids to be gender stereotype nonconforming—many of us are gender stereotype nonconforming, quirky people ourselves, like our kids! We don't care about pronouns except that it's clear they are a gateway drug.

- *Pro–Civil Rights and Antidiscrimination:* We are NOT anti-trans. Adults have the right to live their lives as they see fit, free of discrimination—period. Questioning an ideology and seeking information and evidence-based care for our children does not make us bigots. You should rightly be skeptical about an ideology that will not permit questions or research and resorts instead to name-calling if you question. If you are not informed, you cannot help look out for your child and give them good advice.

- *LGB Supporters:* Trans is not the new gay. Gay is a sexual orientation. Trans is telling our kids that their natural bodies are wrong. Gay does not encourage irreversible and harmful body modification. Gay does not require a lifetime of taking hormones and medical treatment.

- *Antimedicalization of Gender Confusion for Youth:* We are scared to death of the experimental, untested, ineffective drugs and surgery wreaking havoc on our children's healthy bodies—and the politicians, doctors, and activists that are cheering our kids on and willfully ignoring the incontrovertible facts about the dangers of medicalization of an identity.

I'm Terrified—What Do I Do Next?

First, take a deep breath and keep the following in mind as you read this essay.

1. *The Gender Unicorn is made-up.* Gender is not on a spectrum, and gender nonconforming behavior should not be used as evidence of a

medical condition. Why is it, then, in today's *Diagnostic and Statistical Manual of Mental Disorders* (DSM-5)? Interesting question with a complicated answer (hint: it's not because of new scientific evidence). You will learn a lot more about this, but that's a start. There are only two sexes. There is no third gamete. Our understanding of basic biology still holds true.

2. *Desistance is not a mythical beast.* You may already have searched the Internet frantically for signs that this might be a phase for your child. Despite what you might find—remember, it's the Internet—know that desistance happens all the time. For most kids and young adults, it's just a phase—unless you affirm.

3. *Detransition is real.* There is a large and growing community of people who transitioned but then, for various reasons, decided to return to presenting as their natural sex. These people often feel very misled and harmed by their experience.

Now that you have these three facts in mind, this is what we advise as Trans-Educated Rational Parents:

Step 1: Opt out of the broken "healthcare" system—it's just a transition conveyor belt. ALERT: DO NOT SEND YOUR CHILD TO A GENDER CLINIC OR AN "AFFIRMING" THERAPIST! If you do this, your child will be on a path to blockers and wrong-sex hormones and surgery almost immediately.

There is no set training to become a gender therapist, and many working in this area do not even know, although it has been known for decades, that gender dysphoria can be temporary and caused by other mental issues (OCD, autism, trauma, anxiety, distress) or be a phase in development. Many thus incorrectly assume that if someone has "discovered" they are transgender that the only route is to make them comfortable with this situation either through affirmative counseling or aggressive medicalization.

In reality, kids are just diagnosing themselves on the Internet, and medical professionals are agreeing with them. They call this the "affirmative approach." Affirmation consists of agreeing with your child and further reinforcing the harmful negative thoughts and dysphoria that are causing distress in your child. In no other area of mental healthcare will a practitioner encourage someone to persist in harmful thoughts.

Clinics are a business. They only make money if your child becomes a medical patient. Influencers and doctors are often on the payroll of pharmaceutical companies directly or indirectly. They have a vested interest in pushing your child to medicalize while downplaying the risks and experimental nature of any treatments. This is big business—especially because this type of medicalization is not a one-off treatment but for life.

There are some wonderful therapists that will look at your child as a whole person, but they are completely booked by the deluge of parents seeking real help for their confused child. Most of us in the Parent Underground can't even find help! So, for now, you will need to be the expert, and you will have to learn to help your child. Sad but true.

Step 2: Don't blame yourself. It's society, not you. Nothing you did caused this to happen to your child. Your teen was not "born in the wrong body," so all your research to try to find a biological cause for this based on some nonsense about gendered brains or speculation about hormones in the womb is a waste of time—there is no way to confirm or even test this.

Your child was subjected to harmful influences unbeknownst to you, combined with very powerful societal motivators. Being teenagers, they are very susceptible to influence and, even more unfortunately, our society has not yet recognized this as the harmful fad it is, so well-meaning schools, religious institutions, trusted medical professionals, journalists, and activists have been providing you and your child with false and misleading information.

Step 3: Turn off the Internet and accept that your kid is doing some very unsavory things. Turn off or restrict and monitor your teen's access to social media and the Internet ASAP, after doing some forensics. Your innocent child is not as innocent as you think, nor is this movement innocent.

While you were stressing about how you missed that your child is a girl in a boy's body or vice versa, what was really happening is that your lonely little baby was watching porn or chatting about dysphoria online with random people. Don't beat yourself up about it. A lot of us parents wasted a lot of time on philosophy before we realized our kids were secretly watching some seriously messed-up stuff. Rapid-onset gender dysphoria is not a feeling from within—at least not without some outside help.

This movement is, at its core, about sex and bodily harm to try to reach an unattainable end state—it's not rainbows and harmless-looking purple Gender Unicorns (an infographic tool being used to teach your kids "the facts" about gender ideology in health class at school—and sometimes even in science class!). Despite your best efforts, your teen has been seeing and doing things on the Internet that will shock you after what probably started out as an innocent query, such as a web search for "why am I different?" or "how do I know if I'm gay?"

Do a thorough forensic analysis before cutting off access. This will help you understand what your child has been exposed to, what you are up against, and why they are thinking that transgender applies to them. Look for hidden apps (e.g., the presence of two calculator apps is a warning sign), virtual private networks (VPNs), and logs showing your child has accessed any of the sites on the list below. Look for alternate logons. Your child has likely adopted an opposite-sex online persona and avatar that you need to be aware of. It will probably be disturbingly cutesy, like anime or a cartoon, and/or highly sexualized. You may even discover, as some of us have, that your child has been interacting with an adult "coach" or groomer. If this is the case, report this person to the authorities immediately. Or, perhaps you will find, like some of us, that your child has a peer group of cheerleaders/influencers. Remember, this is not a harmless phase like goth—this will lead to your child taking harmful, exogenous cross-sex hormones (inducing an endocrine disorder) and/ or undertaking dangerous surgeries. If they follow this path, they will likely be sterile and unable to experience sexual pleasure, and they will have to commit to cross-sex hormones for their whole lives. This can cause brain-function decline and bone-mass degradation, among other horrifying things. Oh, and after all that, they will still hate their bodies. Probably even more than before.

The "resources" for teens—*WARNING: these are disturbing*—that your kids are reading and learning from include:

- Reddit—subreddits abound that your child will have accessed:
  - https://www.reddit.com/r/egg_irl/
  - https://www.reddit.com/r/traaaaaaannnnnnnnnnns/
  - https://www.reddit.com/r/MtF
  - https://www.reddit.com/r/ask_transgender
  - https://www.reddit.com/r/asktransgender
  - https://www.reddit.com/r/traps
  - https://www.reddit.com/r/traphentai
  - https://www.reddit.com/r/transporn
  - https://www.reddit.com/r/GoneWildTrans
  - https://www.reddit.com/r/femboy
- Gender-bending anime
- Discord servers—your child will have quickly been invited to Discord servers that are supposedly help groups or support groups but that are rife with groomers. Some examples of these are transcord, satans children, trans community center, The Cowboys, Chill Frogs, and Trans Realm.
- There are also tons of YouTube hypno meditations and violent pornography sites with negligible/poor underage protections.

Find out who the people your kids are interacting with online are in real life. Parents need to know who is influencing their kids.

Step 4: Get up to speed. Learn from ethical, informed therapists and medical professionals that are interested in the outcome of a teen/young adult with a healthy body and a healthy mind.

Helpful resource guides include:

- Genspect
- *Gender—A Wider Lens* podcast
- Partners for Ethical Care

- Transgender Trend—Resources for Parents
- Parents of ROGD Kids
- "Managing Gender Dysphoria Incongruence in Young People: A Guide for Health Practitioners"
- Society for Evidence-Based Gender Medicine

Step 5: Set firm boundaries with your child. This new pronouncement of trans should change nothing about the rules of your household and age-appropriate behavior—your teen is still a normal teen and should still be subject to your household rules and oversight—now more than ever, in fact, because, as mentioned, your child has likely violated many house rules involving your Internet terms of service.

It is perfectly acceptable for you to take the firm stance that you do not accept the alternate reality your child is presenting. You are the adult, and your child is looking to you for guidance. If you "see" them as the opposite sex, that will further cement their belief—which is a belief, not a fact, and, unlike their real-life body, is not grounded in reality. Contrary to popular belief, doing this is not likely to lead to your child's suicide. In fact, you will likely exacerbate their dysphoria by agreeing with them. It is not common medical practice to reinforce problematic thoughts like dysphorias. So, skip the pronouns and the alternate name, and the clothes and all of that. Some of us took bad advice and allowed this for a time—everyone comes to regret it. Preserve reality for your family.

Remember, as a parent, you are the strongest influence on your child. You have cared for, loved, and supported this child through thick and thin. You are the one responsible for their raising and well-being. You are the one who will be there throughout his or her life, not the coaches and cheerleaders you will discover who have been influencing your vulnerable child. Do not abdicate that because you are intimidated by this new ideology.

Step 6: Question the assumptions and learn to counter them. Learn the common myths and contravening evidence and research. Here are common myths followed by the reality:

- *"Gender" is on a spectrum and you are not stuck with the sex you are "assigned at birth."* False. You are built to produce either small or large gametes. These are the only two options. The term "assigned at birth" is appropriate when used with regard to intersex infants, such as those with ambiguous genitalia, but it has been co-opted by trans activists. If your child's sex was unambiguous at birth, this term does not apply to your child. In such cases, your child's sex was simply observed and recorded.

- *Transgender is not a phase you grow out of or move past.* Being transgender is a fixed characteristic, set before birth, that one can "discover." False. People "desist" all the time, but you'd never know that from reading the limited narratives on the Internet. Approximately 80 percent of children with early childhood gender dysphoria outgrow it by their late teens. Not much is known about the new phenomenon of teens who develop it at puberty or beyond, but therapists in this new gender space will tell you that approximately 50 percent of their patients (and these are the most entrenched individuals) desist and stop feeling "transgender."

- *Go along with your child's new identity or they will kill themselves.* False. This is a scare tactic meant to get your child on the transgender conveyor belt. "Transition" isn't even proven to alleviate gender dysphoria. Ethical medicine does not prescribe life-altering drugs or remove healthy organs based only on a patient's request or under terroristic threats of suicide if medical professionals do not go along. This should be a huge sign to you that something is amiss. Compare it to eating disorders. Would a doctor perform liposuction because an anorexic patient says they look fat?

- *If you are trans, it's always just how you were born, and you will definitely feel happy after "transition."* False. Tell that to the many detransitioners who changed their minds and now have to fight for appropriate medical care for the various mental and physical repercussions of their "transition." Once the initial period of reported euphoria wears off, the irreversible body and potentially mind changes remain.

- *Puberty blockers are safe and reversible.* False. Puberty is a full-body maturation process, which also involves hormonal effects on the still-developing brain in addition to the development of secondary sex characteristics (which are a natural consequence of your biological sex). It is unknown what the long-term effects are of disrupting this process, which cannot be turned off and on and then just resume as if nothing ever happened. There has been no study on whether puberty blockers are reversible when used to block puberty for those who are at the right age to go through it (rather than for those who start puberty too early, a use approved by the U.S. Food and Drug Administration [FDA]). The evidence behind the mental health outcomes of puberty blockers for gender dysphoria (off-label use for treating gender dysphoria) has been judged of very poor quality.

- *Transition "treatments" are effective.* False. They are only occasionally effective, and no one really knows the long-term effects. Also, what are we treating again, and what are the goals of the treatment? I bet you can't answer!

- *Transgender ideology promotion is about civil rights and inclusion.* False. Transgenderism is about money. There are billions to be made selling hormones and plastic surgeries to people who believe that they will make them happy. Right now, this field is entirely unregulated, and so it's like the Wild West. As you might imagine, pharmaceutical companies are taking full advantage, as they have time and time again throughout our modern history. Gender clinics providing patient-requested medical care for an invisible condition have popped up in droves. Spokespersons (i.e., influencers) for mail-order hormone providers like Plume are even invited to speak at schools under the guise of diversity and inclusion programs.

- *Medical "treatments" are only a last resort in transgender treatment. There are many ways to be "trans"!* False. There is no long exploratory period or psychological assessment. There is no longer a requirement to live as the opposite gender for a year or more before hormones and/or surgery. You should be very, very worried because, if your child persists with a trans identification, they will likely proceed to these extreme and aggressive treatments. They can simply walk into a college campus clinic or Planned Parenthood and get these hormones on the first visit. Or they can get a same-day prescription from online providers over Zoom without an in-person visit. They will be asked to sign an informed consent form saying the long-term risks are not known and that there are known dangerous and harmful side effects to this experimental "treatment" for something that has no physical symptoms at all. All this before they can even legally drink in most countries. Oh, and these treatments all have euphemistic names. They have a whole different ring to them when you call them what they really are: "gender affirmation surgery" = castration/sterilization + plastic surgery; top surgery = elective mastectomy; hormone replacement therapy (HRT) = testosterone blockers (for boys) + cross-sex exogenous hormones that are off-label (not FDA-approved for treating dysphoria); and "feminization" surgery = plastic surgery to restructure the bones in a male's face.

Step 7: Help stop the madness—for your kid and others. Our kids are part of the first wave of Internet/societally induced transgenderism. This is a new phenomenon, and our kids are poised to be the unwitting test subjects of drugs and medical procedures that are only now starting to be tested on animals. It's human experimentation on a mass scale. Someday we will say about this new form of transgenderism what we have said about other major medical scandals. As then U.S. president Bill Clinton said when apologizing on behalf of the U.S. government for the infamous Tuskegee experiment, "What was done cannot be undone. But we can end the silence. We can stop turning our heads away. We can look at you in the eye and finally say . . . what [we] did was shameful, and I am sorry."

For now, however, our society has fully bought into and invested in this gender nonsense, and it's going to take a long time to get ourselves out of this. Currently, there are more parent guides for convincing your kids not to get a tattoo because it's permanent and they will regret it than on this obviously much more serious issue!

Eventually, people will realize that this is pseudoscience akin to Flat Earther conspiracy theories. Concerned citizens are starting to raise awareness about the power of this movement and its ability to influence your child and lead them down a dangerous path. Sweden, the United Kingdom, and Finland have been taking a good hard look at the evidence and are starting to realize that it does not support the aggressive interventions that have been recklessly scaled up from careful treatments of a very small number of people in the past.

Your child does not have time to await the return of common sense and rational policy, because as soon as they hit eighteen years of age, they can get harmful, experimental hormones that induce an endocrine disorder and cause brain changes with NO meaningful gatekeeping. Do any of you feel that you would have been mature enough at eighteen to make a decision as big as this, when we know the prefrontal cortex does not fully mature until twenty-six?

You need to act now.

Natural Allies

As part of the last line of defense, parents need all the help we can get as we organize, research, conduct studies, write about our experiences, and align with natural allies, including:

- Liberals devoted to free and open discourse

- The LGB community, which recognizes that sexual orientation has absolutely nothing to do with transgenderism and that the current gender ideology erodes their rights and promotes homophobia

- Feminists who see that the denial of sex poses a real and immediate threat to hard-won women's sex-based rights

- Doctors and therapists who have lived through the repressed memory scandal and opioid crisis and understand their obligation to "first, do no harm"

- The many transgender and transsexual adults who are appalled at the medicalization of our youth for a self-identity that has taken on unmistakable tones of religious fervor

- Black men and women who are realizing that Black Lives Matter, Inc., is more motivated by gender ideology than it originally appeared

Always remember, a few years from now, people will see pediatric "transition" as the horrible experiment it is. Even though you were told it was the only choice for your kid, YOU will be blamed for the damage done to your child in the eyes of history. Of course, you will also be the one picking up the pieces and trying to help your child when all the activists and glitter moms are long gone.

Join Other Parents to Fight Back for Your Child

Bring your brainpower, your passion, and your deep and abiding love for your child to bear to make a difference. We can use all the educated, rational parents we can get! Get connected with other parents that are standing up to gender ideology—you can find parent organizations through Genspect.org.

58

A Tragedy in Slow Motion

I am speaking as the parent of a young woman who declared a transgender identity completely out of the blue at the age of seventeen (a month prior to turning eighteen). So many parents feel that they cannot speak out for fear of harming their relationship with their child. I am speaking because, as I have sadly discovered over the last few years, this phenomenon is much, much bigger than my family, and we most certainly do need to talk about it and raise awareness of what is being done to our children. Our daughter has just turned twenty-one and has been in the transgender bubble for just over three years. She had been estranged from us for the past year; however, she miraculously reached out to us exactly one week ago. For that reason, the last week has been a very emotional one for our family. There has been so much damage done, and the healing process will be a long and rocky road, yet right now, I have a glimmer of hope that I certainly did not have when I started writing this several weeks ago.

Our daughter was raised in a loving, supportive family with three older brothers and a younger brother. They were all raised by us in the same loving way we raised our daughter. We have a fabulous relationship with all of her brothers. Growing up, she was not particularly "girly" and did not like dolls, for example, but I thought nothing of that because I hated dolls as a kid, and I was a bit of a tomboy myself. She loved soccer and handball, and she was a brown belt in Taekwondo. She tried so many extracurricular activities—dance, singing, gymnastics, swimming, and tennis—to name a few. She used to walk with me every morning when I walked our dogs and go to the gym with me as well. She enjoyed shopping with me and choosing her own clothes. We would go and have our nails painted together. We would go to plays and concerts together. We had such a close and loving relationship.

She is very smart and always did really well in school growing up, but she was bullied at school when she was younger. As a result of the bullying and the lack of support from the school, we moved her to a new school when she was thirteen years old. That went well for the first two years, and she had a stable friendship group of really lovely girls. Around the time she turned fifteen, she switched friendship groups. The new group had a girl who "did not identify as a girl," and that was my first introduction to gender ideology. I felt the new friends had a very negative influence on our daughter.

Around the same time she changed friendship groups, our daughter started experiencing mental health problems. For three years, these mental health problems continued. We moved through both the public system (called the Child and Adolescent Mental Health Service, or CAMHS) and private mental health systems in our efforts to find help for our daughter. We collected diagnoses of anxiety, depression, bipolar disorder, and possible borderline personality disorder in that three-year period. We took our daughter to over seventy medical appointments related to her mental health in that three-year period. At all times, we were treated well by the medical professionals who were treating our daughter. We were described as loving and supportive parents. Our daughter did not respond well to medication for anxiety and depression; it actually made her feel worse. When we declined to continue with medication both in the public and private clinical settings, at no time were we criticized or treated badly by the medical professionals who were treating our daughter. CAMHS said they would not see her anymore if she was not medicalized, but by then, we had found a private psychiatrist, and he did not insist on medicalization. CAMHS most certainly did not try to report us to child protection services or bad mouth us because we did not want to medicalize our daughter for her mental health problems. We focused on diet, exercise, love, support, and psychotherapy.

But our daughter's mental health eventually became much worse. We found out that she had been cutting herself and binge eating as well.

She had always been very conscious of what she ate—in a healthy way—as she had been a vegetarian for several years. In hindsight, I believe that this time period was when she started focusing on transgender. She ended up having a four-week admission to the mental health ward of a local private hospital in the winter, as it reached the point that she was refusing to get out of bed and refusing to go to school. When she came out of the hospital after those four weeks, she cut her hair short.

The next few months were extremely traumatic for our family. She barely attended school and became aggressive and verbally abusive toward us and her younger brother. She was lying, stealing, and binge eating and would not do anything that we asked of her. I found out she was smoking marijuana. If we wanted to go out as a family with her younger brother to, say, a soccer match, she would declare she was anxious and suicidal so that I could not go. She became extremely manipulative. The stress we were under was enormous. Our son was thirteen at that point in time, and the distress of her abusive behavior caused him to become anorexic. I remember him curling up in a fetal position on the floor and sobbing, begging her to stop her out-of-control behavior. I guess our son saw that his intake of food was the one thing he could control. We were pretty much shattered as a family. I remember sitting in her general practitioner's office sobbing and begging for help. It really was a nightmare. I believe it was over this time period she started to become engrossed with online trans sites. I later found a history in her web browser full of trans searches and sites.

Then, that spring, she announced, all over social media, that she was, in fact, a male and had a new name. She claimed that she had told people at school months before and had been going by her new male name at school for some time. She told us that everyone at school, including the teachers, was supportive. Considering I had been in contact with the school regularly because of her mental health problems and the fact that she had had many absences from school, I was stunned that no one from the school ever told us about her transgender announcement.

She had a scheduled visit to her psychiatrist the week she announced she was trans, and she told her psychiatrist that she was suicidal, so he insisted that we take her to our local public hospital for admission to the adolescent mental health ward. The psychiatric registrar who admitted our daughter to hospital said he thought that she had borderline personality disorder. After an all-night admission that my husband accompanied her with, I went to the hospital to visit her the following day. When I asked to see our daughter, I was told that I had a son. Already above her bed was the male name.

I was aware that two other girls who attended her drama group were saying that they were boys, so I was very skeptical of her announcement of trans. She had never displayed any signs of gender dysphoria. My skepticism was dismissed by the staff of the mental health ward. As parents who did not immediately affirm our child's declaration of transgender, we were shamed and bullied by the medical professionals in that hospital ward. All of our voiced concerns were swept aside, and we were put down by hospital staff in front of our daughter, accused of being bigoted, not inclusive, and transphobic. We were also told that we must accept that we now had a son, or she would kill herself. They said, "Would you rather have a live son or a dead daughter?" They said they wanted to introduce her to a transgender staff member. The very next day was a Saturday, and I was called by the hospital to come and take our daughter out on day leave. I remember thinking at the time that they could not be too concerned about her being suicidal if they sent her home on day leave twenty-four hours after being admitted.

At a family meeting at the hospital, we were ridiculed for "dressing her like a girl" when she was little. They were not one bit interested in her complex mental health history. We were told that she needed an immediate referral to an endocrinologist for hormones. She was seventeen, and we said no, that we did not agree to the referral and that we were returning to her general practitioner and private psychiatrist. They needed our agreement for that referral. The hospital went ahead with the referral and wrote up her discharge summary, saying that we did agree to the referral for hormones. Our general practitioner recommended we take her to a private psychiatrist in our hometown who specializes in gender. The only trouble was there was a six-month-long waiting list before we could get in to see him.

From the hospital admission onward, our relationship with our daughter deteriorated significantly. She came out of the hospital after five nights and immediately shaved her head. The abuse she directed toward us escalated, and she was pretty much out of control. Her lying, binge eating, and manipulative behavior continued. She had another scheduled three-week hospital admission that spring in the same mental health ward of the same private hospital as she had been in five months earlier, except this time, they pretended she was a boy. There was no improvement in her behavior. She left the hospital on day leave against the wishes of her treating psychiatrist to attend the endocrinologist appointment that had been made as a result of her earlier public hospital admission—the appointment we did not agree to. By this time, she had turned eighteen.

When I went searching, I was absolutely stunned by what I found in the browser history of our daughter's computer. It was almost unbelievable. YouTube videos of young girls singing the praises of testosterone, showcasing the changes to their bodies, and cheering each other on. Bragging about surgeries and showing off the scars of double mastectomies. It was macabre. I felt like I had landed in the middle of some sort of alien world, some parallel universe. How could anyone be cheering all these young people on to do such harm to themselves? I can honestly say I have never been as disturbed by anything in my entire life. I found messages from transgender adults, cheering our daughter on and telling her to get rid of her unsupportive family. "Snip snip the mother f...ers" was one phrase I will never forget. That was from an Australian trans adult who is portrayed in our media as some sort of hero. All I could see were red flags and grooming.

As a family, we were on the verge of breaking down; the stress was just unbearable. We were subject to daily torrents of verbal abuse and she called us the most despicable things. I was told I was a disgusting and pathetic parent, a white-privileged bigot, a boring heterosexual, a transphobe—the abuse just went on and on. It was like someone had put a script in her head because it did not sound like our daughter at all. The things she was saying were just bizarre. She would stand with her face so close to mine and unleash her fury. I remember going out with friends one night and coming home to find my husband hiding in the garden just to escape her rage. We limped through Christmas and the New Year and then went on our annual family holiday. She did everything in her power to spoil the holiday. It wasn't a good time for the rest of us.

She was meant to be in her final year of school that year. However, due to missing most of the previous school year, she could not continue with school. We suggested she do a one-year university course that would give her the equivalent of her school leaving certificate. She enrolled in that course, and on the day she was due to start, she wouldn't get out of bed, telling me she had taken pills. I called an ambulance, and she was taken to the hospital. I think I was just skin and bone myself at that time. I'd lost so much weight with the constant stress. I really don't know how we managed to keep going. When I say it was like living in a war zone, I am not exaggerating.

A few weeks later, after the usual daily torrent of abuse from her, we had to restrain her younger brother from lunging at her. I told her I wasn't going to be treated like that anymore. She left the house and went up the road to her glitter family, a girl she went to school with whose mother would pretend she was a boy. She told the mother her father had threatened her, so the mother took her to the police station, and later that evening, the police knocked on our door, and a DVO (domestic violence order) was served on my husband. The police did not even bother to come and talk to us or to find out our side of what had happened or how she had been behaving toward us. We tried to challenge the DVO in court. However, after the hearing was adjourned three times and by then having several thousand dollars of legal bills already incurred, we just gave up. It was just too distressing and a ridiculous waste of money.

Following the visit by the police we realized that we could no longer have her living with us. A friend of ours owned a house that had rooms he rented out to university students for accommodation, and luckily, one room was vacant, so we moved her in there and paid 50 percent of the rent. It was only a few blocks from our house. She immediately started on testosterone and dropped out of university, but I still had some contact with her over the course of that year. At her request, I went to an appointment with her to the endocrinologist in May. I had not seen her since she had moved out and was not aware she had started testosterone. I later found out she had been started on testosterone at the second appointment with the endocrinologist. She'd seen the endocrinologist the previous December and then was given a script for testosterone in March. No psychiatry, no psychology, no examination of her mental health history. A seriously mentally unwell teenager was given hormones that would make irreversible changes to her body.

My sister, who is a medical practitioner, came to the endocrinologist appointment with us. There was a "multidisciplinary team" of three people at the meeting, the pediatric endocrinologist, a nurse, and a social worker. I explained to them that we were waiting to see a private psychiatrist who specialized in gender. We had made the appointment to see him in December of the previous year, but the appointment was not until June, which was the following month. The multidisciplinary team said, "Oh, we are so pleased to meet you," yet sat there at the meeting and did not bother to mention that they had already started our daughter on testosterone in March. I was suspicious. Her voice had gone gravelly. When I asked whether they were aware of her extensive mental health history, they said no, they were not. This was despite her being referred to them by the adolescent mental health ward of the very same hospital in which the endocrinologist had her clinic. The endocrinologist said, "Don't you just want your daughter to be happy." I honestly could not believe what I was hearing. Then they said they were referring her to an adult endocrinologist as she was now eighteen.

We accompanied her to the gender psychiatrist appointment the following month, and he diagnosed her with complex PTSD, which he said was caused by childhood bullying. He was shocked she had been started on testosterone and said that he would not have recommended it. He then told us he was closing his books to anyone under twenty-five so could not see her again.

By now, I had nearly a year of research under my belt. I remember finding Lisa Littman's research and rejoicing. I remember finding Abigail Shrier's first article, "When Your Daughter Defies Biology." I remember finding 4thWaveNow and Parents of ROGD Kids. I remember being put in contact with an Australian mum, and I ended up speaking with her for hours. My goodness, I was actually not alone in my skepticism. The more I researched, the more gender-critical articles I found, and the more I realized how shocking and widespread this medical scandal actually was.

That September, I accompanied our daughter to an appointment with the adult endocrinologist. I took a stack of those articles I had read to the adult endocrinologist and tried to engage her in a discussion about how concerned we were about our daughter's mental health and how many people were starting to speak out about this social contagion. I was dismissed by the adult endocrinologist, who told me, "Your daughter is over eighteen. She can do what she likes." I remember being in total disbelief. How could a medical practitioner have so little regard for their seriously mentally unwell patient?

Our daughter's life continued to spiral. She refused to spend Christmas with us that year. I actually found out that she was going to get on a plane and fly to another state in Australia to meet a trans person she had met online. A complete stranger. We managed to stop her from doing that.

When the next year rolled around, she was still doing nothing with her life. I encouraged her to seek mental health help and arranged an admission to a different private hospital with a mental health ward. This hospital had been recommended by a friend. She went in voluntarily in February for six weeks. The psychiatrist she was under refused to discuss her trans identification with us or acknowledge our concerns about the global spike in young women presenting as transgender. It was a total waste of time. She was discharged as Covid-19 was closing in on Australia, and I suggested she go and stay with my two sisters who were providing palliative care to our elderly father, who had just been discharged from the hospital after a fall. My sisters saw first hand the extent of her mental health problems. She did not get out of bed before 4 p.m. every day. No matter what they did, she refused to try to help herself. After three weeks with them, she went back to the student accommodation and stayed locked in her room, doing nothing.

In June of that year, I had not been able to contact her for several days, so I went to her room, and, finally, she answered the door. I can honestly say I have never seen someone living in such squalor. No sheets on the bed, a sea of clothes and towels and take-away food remnants. My heart just broke. It took me two days and countless loads of washing to clean the place up.

We eventually had her accepted into a program through the private hospital she had been in earlier in the year. It was a weekly dialectal behavioral therapy (DBT) class that was a forty-five-minute drive. My husband would pick her up, drive her out there, and then drive back for her three hours later when the class finished. After the first week of attending the therapy class, she went back to using her own name. Within a few weeks, she stopped taking testosterone. We could see this huge improvement in her. She was coming over once a week for dinner. Our son refused to see her, so he would stay inside, and we would eat out in our back room and watch a movie. She had befriended a lovely girl from Europe who was living in the student accommodation, and she would come around with her and take our dogs for a walk. But eventually the girl had to return to Europe, and we noticed that our daughter started binding her breasts again.

Then she told us she had seen a local plastic surgeon to have her breasts cut off. We suddenly had an uneasy feeling and wondered if she could use our private health cover to do this. We rang our health fund and found out they had issued a quote to a local private hospital the week before for the surgery. We immediately removed our daughter from our private health fund. We wrote to the plastic surgeon, a long letter detailing our daughter's mental health history and our grave concerns not only for her and her welfare but also for the growing number of young people caught up in what we saw as a social contagion. Our daughter actually gave us permission to speak to the surgeon about her. I asked him whether he was cutting the breasts off young women ten years ago. He sheepishly replied, "No." We made it very clear that we did not support our daughter doing this. He made the comment that we were the first parents to object. I know that the two young women our daughter went to drama group with both had their breasts cut off, cheered on by their parents.

After speaking to him, we wrote a second letter to him, and I delivered it with a copy of Abigail Shrier's book *Irreversible Damage*. We also wrote to the private hospital where he operates. We pretty much put them on notice that our daughter was seriously mentally unwell and that we hoped they had procedures in place to ensure patients were able to give consent. We found out that the surgeon called our daughter after that and told her he would not do the surgery. He still advertises for top surgery on his website. I just find it so abhorrent that surgeons are profiteering from the distress of mentally unwell adolescents and young adults.

I briefly managed to get our daughter to see another psychiatrist around this time. Knowing that he was gender critical, I hoped for a miracle. After several sessions with him, she refused to see him again. He did diagnose her with attention-deficit/hyperactivity disorder and autism spectrum disorder (ASD). The autism spectrum diagnosis really made sense. Hindsight is a wonderful thing. Looking back, I can see that she was always on the periphery of her friendship groups and that she never really felt like she fitted in or was like other girls. This became more obvious as she went through her teenage years. Yet of all the health professionals I had taken her to over those three years, no one had ever considered ASD.

Sadly our daughter became more and more alienated from us. She fell back down the trans rabbit hole, just as we had hopes that she was coming out of it. She refused to see us for Christmas, and in January, she told us she never wanted to see or speak to us again. She moved from the student accommodation and blocked all our numbers.

It is now three years since she declared she was transgender, and she has spent that three years on a disability support pension for mental health. She is not working and not studying. She attempted to restart her studies but ultimately withdrew from every course she attempted.

Throughout 2019 and 2020, I wrote countless letters to the hospital that put her on hormones, to the Australian Medical Association, to our State and Federal Health Ministers, to our Premier and Prime Minister, and to the Australian Health Ministers Advisory Council, and was fobbed off every time. We complained to our Health Care Complaints Commission about our mentally unwell daughter being put on testosterone. They dismissed that complaint. We submitted another complaint about the falsification of our daughter's discharge summary by the hospital—which said that we had agreed to the hormone referral when we did not. That complaint was also dismissed, with the commission saying they ascertained that there was "an apparent agreement."

I have spent three years now reading and researching the enormous spike in young people around the world declaring a transgender identity. I sometimes devote hours a day to research, reading, and activism. I have been able to recognize the evolution of gender ideology and its nebulous concept of gender identity, heavily promoted by mainstream media and social media as glamorous, brave, stunning, and cool. I have come into contact with so many parents like myself, all gravely concerned about the social contagion that our children have been swept up in and the scale of the harm that is being done by irreversible interventions like hormones and surgeries. I have read far too many heartbreaking stories of regret, of young people with maimed and permanently disfigured bodies—bodies that they will never be able to return to how they were. The pattern is the same, over and over again: children and young adults who are mentally unwell, perhaps traumatized with histories of bullying or sexual assault; children who are most likely same-sex attracted; children who are on the autism spectrum and neurodiverse children; children who are misfits or socially awkward. Trans suddenly gives them status and credibility, and they become the center of attention.

It is hard to imagine any other medical condition with a serious, life-altering treatment where the diagnosis is solely dependent on the reliability and accuracy of a child's or young person's self-report. We were supposed to accept, unquestioningly, the crazy notion that our female child became a boy overnight at the age of seventeen and that she need-ed to alter her body to match this invisible internal identity. It was, to us, an obvious mental health issue. Our daughter had serious mental health issues over a three-year period prior to her self-diagnosis as being trans-gender. There were serious red flags waving. These issues, these red flags, were all completely ignored by the medical profession. She has also had another three years of very poor mental health because, in their rush to affirm transgender to the complete dismissal of all of her comorbidities, the medical profession has failed to treat her appropriately.

Parents understand social contagion among teens. We were teens once as well. Social contagions have always existed. What has changed is that today they are influenced by thousands upon thousands on social media and misinformation on the Internet. There was a cluster of girls in our daughter's drama group who declared that they were transgender. Three young women, all in the same drama class, suddenly becoming transgender? Surely that alone should raise red flags with any credible medical practitioner. Yet instead of seeing this social contagion for what it really is, the medical profession has lost sight of the Hippocratic Oath and accepted the self-diagnosis of these young people. It beggars belief.

We all know that puberty is an uncomfortable physical and emo-tional time for adolescents. Yet in order to reach maturity, we have to go through it. Puberty is not a disease, and nor is it optional. It is the only path to our adult selves. To stop this in children is inconceivable. To put a mentally unwell and traumatized teenager on opposite-sex hormones is inconceivable.

What has upset me greatly is the role I have discovered that gov-ernment-funded organizations like ACON and TransHub in Australia are playing in the grooming of young people. These are organizations similar to Mermaids and Stonewall in the United Kingdom. ACON has actively encouraged our daughter to undergo a double mastectomy and given her advice that is, in my opinion, negligent. They told our daughter that "top surgery" is nothing like a double mastectomy (for cancer) and that she does not need her "unsupportive family" because they will not help support her. We know that they have actively encouraged her to stay alienated from us. The negative narratives and victimhood that these organizations promote are harmful to the mental health of our children. They have a spiel that you can make your own chosen family and discard your true family. The true family who actually loves you unconditionally yet wants to keep you from harm.

As a mother, I read to my daughter every single night for many years. I took her to plays, concerts, musicals, and overseas and interstate holidays. She played sports and took part in many cultural activities. Yet I have been labeled an abusive and unsupportive parent by medical practitioners who really don't even know me.

Being a member of parent support groups, both in Australia and internationally, has been crucial in helping me get through the grief, shock, and horror of the past few years. Sadly it has also opened my eyes to how widespread the harm is and how many families have been devastated and broken by gender ideology. Once you know what is actually happening, you can't un-know it. Yet mainstream media refuses to report on this scandal, and most politicians refuse to engage with it. We are truly in a war to save our children from harm. We need to stop the harm now. We are in the midst of an enormous medical scandal.

59

To Help My Son, It's Time to Rediscover Myself

I realized after spending two years of my life being turned upside down by my son declaring he was "trans" that I'm not okay.

I've spent all my time reading and listening to everything I could get my hands on to educate myself. I did not believe my son was "trans," but I wanted to verify this belief. I found an abundance of proof, but I also realized that there were people actually pushing the trans narrative for profit. These people are so engrossed in their ideology that they really do not care that they are harming children. Not just my own but countless other children. Once you know, you cannot look away or unlearn.

I joined several parent groups, and the stories parents tell are unbelievable. But not everyone is listening, and what's happening is worse than I could ever have imagined.

This realization of this teen sexual genocide put me in a deeply depressive state that I could not get out of.

Suicide seemed like a good route for me at first until I realized I had to fight. I had to fight not only for my son but also for every child affected by this ideology around the world. Kids are vulnerable and being taken advantage of by greedy and self-serving doctors, therapists, surgeons, politicians, and educators.

In my fight to save my child, I have changed. I have become so knowledgeable that I now question everything I ever believed in. I accepted the status quo. I voted on party lines. I believed that people were essentially good. I trusted. Everything in my world has changed.

The other night I was in a good mood. I was my happy, silly, old self before gender ideology ruined our lives. A mood I had not been in, in a long, long time. My family noticed and appreciated it. I saw my son grin with joy and that twinkle in his eye I had forgotten about. It sort of caught me by surprise. I had forgotten how much I've changed. I realized—I'm not okay.

But I need to be okay in order to help my son be okay. This was a wake-up call for me. If I can be happy again and show my son my happiness, it could be contagious. I'm not helping him or myself by remaining in a funk.

I need to pull myself up by my bootstraps and appreciate the good things I do have. I need to do this, and I can do this. I must do this. I must do this for my son and for myself.

60

A Mother's Letter to Her Child

My Beloved Child,

I came late to the experience of parenting. I was afraid of the responsibility. I didn't feel I was ready. I wasn't sure if it was right for me or if I was right for it.

When I decided it was time, I cannot describe to you how overjoyed I felt the moment I realized I was pregnant. At the same time, I felt unprepared and afraid about not being a good enough mother, the ones I had read about, who could be there for their child no matter what.

Becoming your mother filled my heart with love I had never known before. You were beautiful and fascinating then as you are now.

I wanted to do everything right. I read the books and probably tried too hard. I can see now I didn't understand the importance of letting you find your own limits with food and nourishment. At the same time, I was clear that I was not going to lead you off course. I didn't swear. I dressed you in mixed colors. I was conscious not to reduce your value to a body image by dressing you in age-inappropriate clothes or buying magazines or watching programs that reinforced this.

I did not want to encourage a path toward anorexia, which had been one of the parenting worries in my time. I worried about how I would teach you about alcohol and drugs, which never go away. I hoped I could encourage you to find your passions and your path in life.

I avoided gender-heavy toys. I bought you trains and cars, no dolls, and then I found you didn't want them anyway. As you grew older, I could see that you weren't overly feminine in the girly sense, the sense that overvalued physical appearance (high heels and short dresses) and "perfect," chauvinistic, patriarchal female presentation over real human values and qualities like integrity and self-worth.

As you reached your teenage years, you confessed some attraction to boys. I was even-handed about heterosexuality and homosexuality. I wanted you to grow up to appreciate people for who they were and to understand that we love who we love.

After the first boyfriend went by the wayside, I wondered what would follow. I was so aware that 98.5 percent or more of your fellow female students seemed to be concerned with having long hair and presenting in very feminine ways. The male students, many of them were sexist. What, I wondered, was influencing this?

I am sorry to say that today the experience of being female does not seem to have moved far enough since my childhood. There are so many pressures on girls to be, well, "girly." Girls and women are still running risks to keep ourselves safe, and there aren't enough men that appreciate that we have a right to go where we want, to do what we want, and to feel safe. There are too many men whose actions have led to the "MeToo" and "Time's Up" campaigns, too many men who mistakenly think it's okay to prey on females, and too many systems that are failing to support our rights and freedom. There are times when I wonder, given the choice, how many women would come back as a man. As a society, we have a lot of work to do to right these wrongs.

I worried how the world would be as you edged closer to entering into it. I was not ready to be plunged into this nightmare.

Since you moved from "straight" to "gay" and then to "trans," I feel as if I have been dragged into a fast-moving car, driven by you at speed in the dark with no driving lessons about safety and no lights on. And I am terrified. I thought I had managed to keep you safe, safe from anorexia, safe from early pregnancy, safe from drugs and alcohol. I have not kept you safe from wanting to make irreversible body and life changes. How long have I got to persuade you to slow down, that there is no rush? We don't have to reach the destination in this way. Maybe there are alternatives to this one.

While you have been online, learning about becoming another gender and finding ways to negate your own, I have also been learning about this. I have joined several parents' groups, searching and searching until I found one with parents who are not affirming their children's decisions to transition but who, like me, are asking questions while standing at the boundary saying, "I love you, and this is dangerous." I've met two people who transitioned. I watch videos, read articles and books, and listen to podcasts. I have attended a meeting with a detransitioner and watched others speak of what happens when you set foot on the path to the cliff while others cheer you along the way, telling you that you are making the right choice. Never before have parents found their love, wisdom, and knowledge of their children and their needs ignored or scorned or found themselves condemned for asking them to wait and wonder.

I understand that it must be so uplifting, encouraging, being told by others online: "You feel miserable, here's why . . . and we're here for you." It must be so much better than your school experience, where the vast majority of students treated you as "other" and not "one of us," as these people in the trans community are saying to you, "Welcome, we want you here." Where will they be, those cheerleaders, when you wake from an anesthetic or weeks and months down the line going for injections or in pain as an outcome of the surgery you chose?

I love you so much. I want to tell you that I am learning that taking testosterone sends you on a high and that it lasts for a considerable time. And then, the "high" begins to dwindle, and your body begins to suffer the consequences of this hormone experiment. I want to tell you that I am frightened you will start taking it when you are away from home and not tell me. I am frightened that you don't want to talk this over with me. You know that I have listened and supported you through everything you have shared with me, and I worry that even though I have actively encouraged you to talk to a therapist that maybe you have not done this. We both know that the first one was affirming and not really present and listening. I understand that you have a hatred toward your body and that I have no clue how to support you to begin to relate to it. I have a background in psychology, yet I feel helpless and clueless.

I want you to hear both sides. I want you to listen to detransitioners. I want you to understand the consequences of the life-changing decisions you want to make. Do you understand that you cannot undo those transition decisions and return to the starting point? Do you understand that taking testosterone and choosing major surgery risks pain, and it might not go away? Do you understand that taking a path to medically transitioning is choosing to become a long-term patient in the medical system, dealing with doctors and specialists who have little or no experience in helping you and who offer no support for the psychological pain you might feel as a result of making such decisions which you cannot fully reverse? I watched a series of documentary videos from Sweden in which a few young people were brave enough to share their experiences of transitioning and discovering how hard it was to live with their choices.

I keep thinking that if you came to me and said you were going to have sex, we would talk about the consequences of becoming pregnant. If you began to rely on drugs or alcohol, I would ask you where you thought it was going to lead. It's my job. I signed up for it.

I will not leave you. I will not do less than have your back. I will always be there for you. Please don't exclude me when you are making frightening life-changing decisions without understanding the consequences. There are things we can do, ways to find support that will help you learn to value who you are. If you feel you are the kind of female who does not fit into the categories being shoved into our faces each day, there are many of us, and we are big, expansive, beautiful souls just like you.

Please don't follow the crowd that is jumping off a cliff called transgender without knowing what happens if you do.

Please take the time to find out the beautiful soul that is you, only you, and no one else.

Please give yourself that gift now before committing yourself and your soul to a life of suffering with the consequences of a decision that will limit rather than free you.

Please let me in long enough to hear me out.

Your Mother Who Loves You

61

Not a Desistance Story

This is not a desistance story—this is a middle-of-the-road story. Or, maybe this is just a journey story, as there is no road and there is no end.

My son is seventeen. It's been almost a year since my son announced, at the age of sixteen, that he was transgender.

"Are you shocked?" he asked, almost cheerfully.

I was shocked. I was also shaken and devastated . . . but also strangely optimistic and confident that my bright, beautiful child would find his way in this world, no matter what gender he chose to live as. Images of him as a woman flashed through my mind. I can handle this, and he can handle this, I said to myself. I hugged him and told him that I loved him. "You'd be an amazing woman with gorgeous hair," I said.

"You've done well, Mom," he said, beaming.

It took me about three days of soul-searching and research to realize that he was a clear case of rapid-onset gender dysphoria (ROGD) and is a part of an alarming trend. He was following the online script. As I came to discover, even his reassuring me that I did well was part of the script. I also learned that the cross-sex hormones were an experimental treatment with life-altering side effects, not "gender-affirming treatment," and they did not necessarily improve mental health outcomes. I deleted the bookmark for the local gender clinic from my browser.

"I'm really worried," I told my son. We had a long conversation, and I laid it all out. The side effects, the social contagion, the ideology, the homophobia, and the erasure of women . . . I told him that while I respected his identity search, I couldn't support cross-sex hormones and surgeries, at least not until he was neurologically mature, which wouldn't occur until he was twenty-five years old. He asked to see an exploratory therapist—whether because he was doubting or to appease me, I don't know.

Ten months have passed since then, and, in that time, so much has changed, and yet nothing has changed. My son is an amazing kid. He is bright, kind, witty, insightful, gentle, creative, easy-going, well-liked. Like many ROGD boys, he was raised in a liberal family without rigid gender roles and stereotypes. There were dolls and trucks, Lego and Playmobil sets, and princesses and superheroes to play with. Also, like many, he has rewritten his childhood and now feels he had known he was a girl since he was nine. He doesn't remember playing with trucks, superheroes, and construction toys. Unlike many boys who question their gender, he is not on the spectrum and is not socially anxious, but due to our local homeschooling community disintegrating during the pandemic years, he's been socially isolated. His confidence suffered. He met his best friends on a Minecraft Discord server. They all identify as trans.

My son hasn't asked me to use different pronouns. He likes his gender-neutral name. He promised me not to rush to medicalize, but I don't know whether he means weeks, months, or years. His sister is gender critical, and they are still close. Now that he's been in therapy for months, gone are his occasional irritability and moodiness that I attributed to him being a teen. He is more focused, more motivated, more outgoing, more assertive and confident. He still thinks, acts, and dresses like the boy (albeit a long-haired boy) he's always been. We enjoy spending time together, we talk a lot, we watch movies and online lectures, we play board games, we hike, and we bike. We laugh a lot. He hugs me often and tells me he loves me. We talk about everything—but not about gender. His therapist tells me that not talking about gender might be a way of helping him focus on other things.

I haven't learned how to talk about gender yet. When he brings it up, I try to ask questions and listen, but it is excruciatingly difficult to hear my bright critical thinker tell me there is no biological sex, that cross-sex hormones are reversible, and that transitioning and then potentially de-transitioning is not a big deal. He told me I'm not a good listener, and I agree. I've been reading books on asking better questions and on being a compassionate listener, but I'm too terrified and numb to actually listen. I have a lot of learning ahead of me.

At this point, I think it is as good as it gets. I've put myself back together, more or less. I don't wake up with the overwhelming feeling of dread anymore. Instead, it is a softer pain, one I'm learning to live with.

If I didn't know any better, I would have thought that being transgender wasn't a defining factor of his personality anymore. I see the same boy who jokes, discusses politics, laughs at silly memes, helps out around the house, gets annoyed with his dad, reads books, and plays board games. But his therapist tells me that while he's made amazing progress, he still thinks he is a girl. His therapist thinks we just need more time—time for him to mature.

Everyone says this is a marathon, yet no one knows the distance. Everyone is a little bit out of breath, but no one is giving up. I remind myself that this is a marathon for my son as well—he is attached to his newly found identity and giving it up can be emotionally draining, confusing, and destabilizing. Just as I lost my footing as a parent, he lost his footing as a young man. He found an escape that, under examination, proved shaky and uncertain, but he is still clinging to it because the alternative is to be lost yet again.

From my position in the middle of the road, I try not to live in the past or in the future. Yet I yearn for the time when we will remember this year or two or three as a minor bump that we weathered well—a part of the journey that made us stronger.

62

Finding Hope on the Road to Ruin

During the last week of school before summer break, my son's fourth-grade teacher asked the students in the class to write something down on a piece of paper. She asked them to write a problem they were having or what was on their minds.

My ten-year-old son thought about it and decided his particular problem may fall under the category of TMI (too much information), but he was feeling brave that day and decided to go for it.

He wrote: "Both of my sisters are trying to change their gender, and it is ruining my family."

Understandably, the teacher was concerned. She told him that she was sorry that his family was going through this and asked my son if he would like to talk to a counselor. He declined. Instead, we talked about it when he came home that day.

My heart is broken for him. He's a sensitive and caring kid and he desperately misses his sisters. He is caught in the middle of this gender war where we all carefully navigate the name and pronoun minefield in our homes all day, every day. It is a nonstop, relentless assault on proper grammar, free speech, and rational thought. It is exhausting.

Inevitably there's a misstep that is unavoidable, followed by an explosive argument. The fallout can last for days or hours or minutes, but regardless of duration, it's always excruciatingly painful.

During and after, my mind is flooded with memories—usually of my daughters when they were babies splashing in the pool together, smiling and laughing, singing and happy. All chubby thighs and rosy cheeks toddling around and nearly falling down. In the before times, it was all so easy to regain your balance and keep going. Not anymore. The force of this flood of anger and hatred knocks me down, and there are times when I am utterly broken.

I tell my son that we can disagree with them and still be okay.

I tell him that this is a difficult time for our family, but in spite of that, we still love each other.

I tell him that this doesn't have to ruin us and that we can navigate this tumultuous sea together.

But, despite my shows of optimism and strength, inside, I am desperately worried about him and for him. As he goes out into the world, he will inevitably see and hear ideas around gender identity—a confusing and damaging concept for young kids. I tell him to just be himself, that there is no wrong way to be. We don't have to fit ourselves into these made-up categories—that is a choice that some people make, but we don't all have to.

I worry that his new school will normalize these ideas, and I intend to go there and ask questions about the curriculum. As parents, we need to do these things now because, in making schools a "safe space" for "trans kids," administrators seem to be overlooking the safety and well-being of everyone else. Where will it end? Some days it's hard to even believe that the schools and doctors whom I have trusted with my precious children are capable of such a betrayal. It's unconscionable.

The trouble is that, as parents who are holding the line on affirmation and social transition, we are deemed abusive. We are fighting against the tide all day, every day. There are so many of us now, but somehow it still feels like a lonely path.

We are told we are "bad parents" for not supporting our kids. We are told that we are "bad parents" for letting this happen in the first place. We are meant to feel ashamed and embarrassed for not completely affirming our kids' new trans identity, which came out of the blue. We have been blindsided but are expected to just shrug it off and fall in line. I can't do it. I won't do it.

Both of my daughters are female, unambiguously observed female-bodied when they were born. How and why could this ever be called into question?

I understand that it might seem easier to my immature fourteen-year-old daughter to opt out of shaving her legs—but she loses me when she declares that she is a boy and has always been a boy. What does it mean to "feel like a boy"? I can't get an answer to that question.

Having been around for her entire life, I know this to be an entirely false narrative.

Sometimes I feel the need to remind her of how much she once loved soccer and singing. I am told that was never the case, despite the many weekends I spent on the sidelines at soccer games in rain, sleet, snow, and blazing-hot summer sun. We drove for hours and got on airplanes to travel to games and tournaments. In spite of video and photographic evidence—it has been forgotten, erased from her own past—but not mine.

If you lie to yourself long enough, you start to believe your own lies.

If I ask about the why and how of it all, I'm just shut down and dubbed a transphobic TERF (trans-exclusionary radical feminist). This doesn't hurt me at this point—I don't care much for the name-calling, but those slurs are truly meaningless and overused.

It's not helpful to blame myself, but I do it anyway.

My older daughter's high school GSA introduced these ideas into our home. It all seemed so benign to me—I was proud of her for coming out as a lesbian and for volunteering to be co-president of the GSA. She seemed very happy.

Then came her downward spiral—depression and anxiety, an eating disorder, inpatient hospital stays, Covid-19, and a new nonbinary identity.

She happily introduced her younger sister to gender. In this, they find solidarity—just two "trans kids" supporting each other in their staunch political views that they don't even realize are political. Capitalism is bad, by the way, and college is racist.

Meanwhile, my fourteen-year-old daughter, a former elite athlete and a happy, social, and well-adjusted kid, has transformed into a complete stranger.

The new version of my younger daughter is sloppy and rude, argumentative and aggressive. She now enjoys manspreading, burping, and farting loudly, sneezing directly into people's faces, and adopting what seems to me like a distinctly stereotypical "male" persona. It's all very performative and utterly strange. I am not at all fond of this new person who seems to revel in slovenliness like a pig luxuriating in the mud. Part of me is thoroughly embarrassed for her.

I find myself reminding my two older children who have been indoctrinated into gender that they don't come from an abusive environment. I see them reveling in the fabricated idea that they are persecuted and marginalized. Is this what happens when you give your kids everything?

This situation makes me doubt everything about myself.

I don't fault the parents who are participating in the gender-affirming model of care because everyone is telling them that this is what is best for their child. Who doesn't want what is best for their child?

My younger daughter was called by her preferred name when she walked the stage at her middle school graduation. My son was squeezing my hand. I wanted to scream. No! You have no business saying that name! What on Earth are you doing?! Please stop! I wanted to disappear. Instead, I silently screamed and gritted my teeth until it was over. I feel ashamed about that. When the graduation is over, we make our way back to the car and get out of there as fast as we can.

In the last week, both the pediatrician and the dentist used my child's preferred name at her request. The pediatrician changed the name on her chart and put it in quotes after her given name.

Well-meaning trusted adults like teachers and dentists undermine parental connection and authority by participating in the social transition of children. Adults can see this, but all my children see is that the whole world is in support of this, with the exception of their parents. This is an extremely damaging belief system.

If only my daughters could see that it is because we love them so much that we have no choice but to question this.

There are days when it seems like too much. I try to remember that there are some things I can't control. But my children behaving in this way in the name of finding their elusive "authentic" selves comes at a cost to everyone in our family.

We all have feelings—and our boundaries matter too.

I want my words to my son to be true. This doesn't have to destroy us. I am determined not to let it. I have to hope that, in spite of all of the forces conspiring to ruin my family, against all odds, we will pull together in the end. Although the future is uncertain, that hope is everything.

63

Becoming a Light for Our Wayward Son

At the tender age of fifteen, our sweet, nerdy son announced, completely out of the blue, that he was "trans" and needed hormones. I feel like a broken record—he has autistic-like personality traits, a tendency to black-and-white thinking, and hyper-focus. A sweet and empathetic character, he is a quirky, brilliant, STEM- and computer-focused social justice warrior. He is also one of a significantly increasing number of teen boys and young men, tragically overlooked, who are identifying as "trans." Also, similar to many other trans-identified male teens and young adults these days, his "trans" persona appears to be more like an anime character than an actual woman.

About a month ago, my now eighteen-year-old son started taking spironolactone and estradiol. They were provided by a World Professional Association for Transgender Health (WPATH)–aligned physician after only one visit under the informed consent model. "Informed consent" is neither informed nor real consent for these confused kids. Many of them have never lived life in the real world on their own before deciding to take on the heavy burden of medicalization. They are naïve and tender, often a year or two behind in social and emotional development. My son spent the better part of three years in his room, alone, online for school and for socializing, because of Covid-19 and lockdowns. While his trans ID came out before Covid, we had noticed strong signs of desistance two years ago, only to see the trans ID come roaring back when he hooked up with a toxic friend or two online during the long winter of school closure.

I would argue that these are kids who have missed out on a solid two years of crucial, in-person social development. I'm not a mental health professional, but that seems obvious to me—so how in the heck can a physician decide, on the first visit, that these kids are able to give so-called informed consent? I don't care that the magical age of eighteen has been reached; my son is acting much more like a fifteen- or sixteen-year-old emotionally and mentally right now, clearly exacerbated by the pause in development caused by Covid.

Is our child listening to anyone cautioning against medicalization? Heck no! Although our relationship is pretty good all things considered, he has completely shut us out from the gender conversation and has latched onto the idea that transition is what he is going to do, no matter what. Unfortunately, by the time Covid restrictions eased, he was well and truly indoctrinated and has now constructed a super strong steel castle of defense around this identity. If we keep directly pushing against this, we risk estrangement.

How do we now parent a newly minted young adult who knows everything, won't listen to anyone, and who is embarking on a risky pathway of using harmful medications for a self-perpetuating mental condition? This is a shattering situation as we watch our child head off on a very risky path. I wish I had a road map, but I feel like, once again, I am flying blind into a hurricane. Our focus is changing from setting guardrails around medicalization to working on staying connected, becoming a safety net, and setting out a lighted pathway home in the event that he detransitions. We have to take a step back to preserve our relationship, even while we want, more than anything, to stop the madness. Even Dr. Erica Anderson warns against simultaneously starting college and medically transitioning at the same time. I doubt our son would listen even to her.

How am I coping when our fears of medicalization have come true? I try to focus on the positive things happening each day and give myself breaks from "transworld." Even the smallest little things help lift my spirits and bring hope. While this may seem trite or trivial to some out there who are engaged in activism, this is what keeps me going and enables me to write articles like this. Sometimes if I can just sit outside with my dog, mentally let go of all things trans and watch the bees buzzing around the flowers for five minutes, I count that as a win for the day.

Positive signs in our broader society are encouraging. I recently had a conversation about gender issues with some friends who are very progressive. Our conversation was wide-ranging, covering the potential harms of medicalization, what is happening in schools today, the violent threats against J. K. Rowling for sticking up for women's spaces, and more. I was stunned by how much we agree on gender issues. This is a conversation I would never have dared to have three years ago because it likely would have imperiled our friendship. The tide is indeed turning, and everyday liberal-minded people are seeing through the lies now. I find this immensely encouraging. When more liberal, democratic voters see through the gaslighting, a real sea change is inevitable.

What next? We are laying out breadcrumbs for our child to follow his way back to us when he detransitions. I want to sincerely thank the person who wrote the essay on the Parents with Inconvenient Truths about Trans (PITT) Substack from the perspective of one who detransitioned and found a safe harbor with her mom. I plan to follow that advice as we move ahead into an uncertain future. Every piece of advice I have read from detransitioned people has been like pure gold to me, and I am eternally thankful to you all for your courage and bravery in speaking up from your hearts.

We are enlisting help from lifelong friends in creating a support network so that it will be in place when our son detransitions. Our friends say they will tell our son that, if he should ever decide to detransition, he can go to them and tell them—no judgments or questions asked—and they will give him the unconditional love and support he needs. This way, if he is afraid to tell mom or dad, he can go to them first, if that is more comfortable. I would encourage parents in a similar situation to consider enlisting loving extended family and friends in building an a priori detransition support network for your child, just in case. I think more people than we assume see that trans is not always "for life." Like my friends, they may be very happy to provide nonjudgmental and loving support when your child detransitions.

Even though I am bracing myself for rough waters ahead, I am making small steps of progress in my attempts to set up a loving and supportive landing spot for my child. Therapists, scientists, and physicians—you all have to step up to the plate here quickly before we lose a generation of sweet, brilliant young men to lifelong complications from inappropriate medicalization! For me now, though, every day is a battle between fear and despair, and hope and light. But I'm holding out for the light—because love always wins.

64

Reflections of a Father

What's the most difficult thing about being a parent?

All of us are familiar with the par-for-the-course difficulties: the sleep deprivation, childhood illnesses, and the myriad humdrum worries that assault us in the quiet moments. Will my child do well in school? Will they make friends? Will they forge a rewarding career and find a person with whom to spend their lives?

But perhaps the most difficult moments for me are when I start to believe that I've failed my child. Maybe I didn't protect them when I should have, or maybe I was overprotective when I should have let them learn the hard way. Maybe I didn't say the right things. Perhaps I didn't hold them to the right standard, or I wasn't consistent. Maybe I didn't support them when they needed it. And I probably allowed them to do things that were bad for them.

One thing becomes apparent to all parents: you're going to screw up, and you're going to screw up repeatedly. You can't predict or know it all.

I certainly didn't foresee the consequences of modern technology and how it would impact our culture. I suffered from a failure of imagination. I assumed the Internet would make education and information available to all. I believed it would give rise to improved standards of living, make our society more equal and just, and make our world a better place. I assumed it would connect people who were far in proximity but close in ideals, thereby strengthening some social bonds. And, to some extent, it has.

But I was naïve. I assumed this neutral medium would skew toward the best humanity has to offer. I believed it would somehow force the darker side of human nature to the periphery, much like a city council creates zoning ordinances to ensure certain business activities are located far from schools and neighborhoods.

Well, I think it's safe to say that I blew that one. It turns out that the Internet, much like the TV, was merely an amplifier. In the case of TV, we had intermediaries who determined what passed the smell test. With the Internet, we pretend we have intermediaries and tools. Screen time, anyone? In practice, most kids (who typically are far more tech-savvy than their parents could ever be) have unfettered access to the darkest corners of the human psyche.

But wait, there's more! Remember the early Internet companies hell-bent on securing "eyeballs"? Turns out the owners of those eyeballs need to buy something, or there's not much of a business model.

Corporations figured it out. They were highly incentivized to develop algorithms designed to keep your attention so they could sell ads. Remember, if you don't know what the product is, you're the product. The business model isn't that different from good old-fashioned TV. The longer someone sticks around on your digital properties, the more ads you can sell. We've unleashed Darwinian code that survives only if it keeps you addicted to social media. If it doesn't work, new algorithms will replace it. Billions are at stake.

Here's the thing: we are sailing through uncharted territory. It's been said before, and it'll be said again. As trite as it may sound, it's true.

In my head, I can already hear the rejoinders and visualize the eye-rolling. "Isn't it true that people believed that the novel would corrupt the youth?" Indeed, there has been a long list of moral authorities bemoaning the newest development and how it would utterly ruin society. It was chess one day (yes, the board game that you would be delighted if your child would play), novels the next, and, of course, TV and music. Surely you've seen *Dirty Dancing*. How quaint that in recent decades the main threat to our children, and thus civilization, was good ol' sex, drugs, and rock 'n' roll. I recall with some humor the days when parents would lose their minds over the possibility that playing a record backward would expose their children to satanic messages. Go back far enough, and people lost their minds when someone asked a few inconvenient questions and allegedly corrupted the youth. Socrates was put to death for it.

Certainly each of these developments changed the existing culture and posed challenges for parents who were trying to prepare their children for bright futures while simultaneously trying to protect them from harm. And, looking back, a lot of the fears appear downright silly and unfounded. Did these technologies, the printing press, the TV, change society? Of course. Did they destroy civilization? No. Arguably, such inventions allowed for new art forms and enabled civilization to flourish.

So, it's really no different this time, right? What's with the hysteria? Aren't you happy people have more freedom and the possibility of discovering their authentic selves?

My response is this: do you think an evolutionary algorithm expressly designed to maximize corporate profit is going to provide you with a glimpse of your authentic self? Or will it lead you into a morass of addictive groupthink, wherein you are subjected to relentless comparisons in which you will never appear to measure up? That will inexorably grind away at your self-esteem until you believe yourself inferior? That will expose you to social contagions that pretend to offer solutions to problems you may not know you even had? That will cause you to discard reason and logic if the pain will just go away?

We already know the answer to these questions. And we know that social media causes depression, low self-esteem, and anxiety, among other things. And yet, we keep looking to the cause for the cure. Sound like addiction to you?

I used to smoke. It took me many years to quit. It was difficult, and after much soul-searching, I understood why. The mechanism of action is simply this: use something that creates a need that did not exist before, and the only way to satisfy that need is to use the thing that created the need in the first place.

So here it is in a nutshell: social media purports to offer our children the solutions to problems that social media platforms and algorithms created in the first place.

Depressed? Anxious? Maybe you aren't thin enough. Maybe you need to learn how to dress better. Maybe you're not doing this one simple trick that will solve every problem that ever existed in all of human history.

Or, maybe you weren't born in the right body.

Does it sound like an addiction to you? Does it sound just a little bit insane?

This is the reality we live in today.

And if you have the audacity to question someone's reality? Cue the name-calling. Suggest that there is a reality that exists beyond what they directly perceive or believe? Fascist. That reality appears to contradict their personal beliefs? Transphobe.

Kind of sound like a cult? Or maybe Cult 2.0?

The bitter truth is that some have accepted the narrative that reality is what each person believes it to be. Perhaps there is a physical, absolute reality that underlies our beliefs, and perhaps not. Even if there is, how could we know it? Our senses can deceive us. Our minds are fallible. In this world, wouldn't it be immoral to impose our beliefs on others? Would not each and every person be entitled to their version of reality? Who are you to deny them their authentic selves and their happiness?

It's hard not to be sympathetic to such well-intentioned beliefs. And yet, every single day, we acknowledge a physical reality. We have no choice but to acknowledge it. Gravity, it would appear, is real. So is the material world. Our feet stand upon it.

As parents, we owe it to our kids to not only tell them about the nice things in life and the ideals we strive to uphold but to tell them about the reality of life as well.

Don't want to brush your teeth? Your teeth are going to fall out.

Poor diet and no exercise? You're going to gain weight.

Don't wear your seat belt? You might be severely injured in a car accident.

Don't do X? You might experience consequence Y.

Helping your child navigate reality is your sacred duty as a parent. We all know this intuitively. We live this every single day.

Great pep talk, huh? Just like you shouldn't sugarcoat the reality of a consequence-based world for your kid, I won't sugarcoat this. We've been presented with a near-impossible task. We've unleashed systems that are expressly designed to exploit weaknesses in our psyches so that the largest corporations that have ever existed can make even more money. And everyone around us, if they even bother to consider it, responds with the equivalent of the shrug emoji if we bring it up. Back to doom-scrolling!

This is hard stuff. It's hard for people who've been around the pro-verbial block and understand a little bit about how the world works. Imagine how hard it is for someone approaching, or going through, pu-berty.

So what now? This is not like the good ol' days. This is not sex, drugs, and rock 'n' roll. And we as parents are profoundly ill-prepared to deal with this reality. Most of us aren't skilled coders, or professional debat-ers, or psychoanalysts, or trained in evaluating scientific literature. And, certainly, very few of us are all of these things at the same time. We're outmatched. We face a juggernaut that controls vast sums of wealth and twists and perverts the narrative such that people are ostracized for even asking basic questions about reality. What is truth? What is a woman? What is gender? How do people who transition fare ten years down the road? How many people detransition? Does the risk of suicide recede after transition or increase? Why are we allowing the medical establish-ment to pathologize normal human development?

Science still exists, but it is used as cover. Inconvenient conclusions are repressed, just like the speech that questions the preferred narrative. If we truly cared about people, wouldn't we ask the difficult questions? Wouldn't we ask if our social constructs are in some way, at least margin-ally, related to reality? Wouldn't we do the most important thing of all: follow the money?

After all, who stands to gain here? It's simple: massive technology companies and the medical-industrial complex. They're the ones who will make money off of Cult 2.0, all while denying responsibility and tarring us, the parents. We're transphobes who harm kids by questioning their true identities.

Ultimately, who stands to lose in this horrific equation? Our chil-dren.

Sometimes, it's not the outcome that defines our success as parents but our actions in the most difficult moments. Did we tell our kids the truth, even as they raged against us, called us names, and threatened us with self-harm? Did we push back on the nonsense while acknowledg-ing the suffering? Did we seek to understand the source of their pain while standing firm that no person is born in the wrong body? Did we help them understand that medical transition can lead to a lifetime of dependency on the medical-industrial complex? Did we help them do the hard work of working through puberty and finding true self-acceptance, which would not only deny industry the chance to profit off them but also enrich them with a lifetime of fulfilling experiences?

Is there a happy ending to this story? I wish I could tell you that there is. But like so many engaging novels or movie plots, the ending comes after a long struggle. There's no shortcut to happiness or fulfillment. As we've told our child: the only way out is through.

At the end of the day, we all know intuitively that we just have to do our best. We have to act with good intentions. We have to be fair, and just, and kind. And we have to be honest about reality. Keep engaging, help them experience real life, push back on social media use, and explain the why of it all. While our outcomes will vary, our actions together will help create a more fair and just world.

If you've acted with good intentions and did your best with what you had, and loved your child no matter what, you've been a good parent. Life has a way of tempering idealism. We work with the messy reality we're confronted with, not the perfectly edited movie that plays out in our hopes and dreams.

Finally, as bleak as it may seem at times, remember that we parents have one critical ally that will see us, and our children, through: we have truth on our side.

65

The Gender-Critical Parents' Guide to Trans

One of the most difficult things about parenting a gender-questioning child today is the information asymmetry. Once a gender-questioning kid has self-diagnosed themselves, courtesy of big tech, they have access to the entire world of transgender ideology with its seemingly endless stream of videos, articles, and social media influencers. These resources show them exactly how to act, what to say, and how to move forward (or move their parents forward) with treating and medicalizing their self-diagnosed ills.

Parents, on the other hand, are typically far less informed about gender ideology and much less tech literate. Gen X parents, like myself, can certainly applaud themselves for being in the know when it comes to tech. After all, we witnessed firsthand the evolution of technology and how it has utterly transformed society. But we're kidding ourselves if we think that we, in the aggregate, have the same tech literacy as our children. They were born into it. They've known nothing else. We pride ourselves on donning a wetsuit and going swimming in the ocean; our children are the dolphins watching us bemusedly as we splash about.

If your child has decided that it's time to go full steam ahead down the trans pipeline, you're probably feeling outgunned and maybe even questioning whether or not you're a transphobe for even thinking this rush toward identity finality is inappropriate. There is no easy way out here. Either you're going to get steamrolled and potentially subject your child to a lifetime of medicalization and suffering, or you're going to be the parent and ask the tough questions that allow the child to actually experience the difficult yet rewarding work of identity formation.

During our journey with our gender-questioning kid, my husband and I have observed behaviors that you may also encounter. We hope that these tips will help you shepherd your child through adolescence.

Just remember: you're the parent. And it's okay to say no.

1. *Family Photos: Down the Memory Hole.* Many kids who are exploring a trans identity want to erase their past in the belief that it will make it easier to adopt a new self. This fundamentally flawed notion assumes that transformation requires destruction. This "all-or-nothing" belief is fairly common in adolescents. It's normal to want to alleviate your child's distress, but don't be tempted to indulge this attempt at erasure. Family photos belong to the family, not just the child going through a period of uncertainty. Gently remind your child that the photos are shared memories, and no one person can tell the rest of the family what should be remembered. Further, if they do become trans at some point, it was a journey, and attempting to negate part of the journey is to deny the fullness of the self.

2. *Pronouns: Staring into the Pool of Narcissus.* Oftentimes gender uncertain kids will ask you to use different pronouns in the household. Much has been written on why this is problematic. Explain to your child that asking others to use a different pronoun is awkward and imposing. As a gender-critical parent, you should focus on helping your kid develop resilience and self-confidence. Teach them that if you can't be happy unless the outer world acquiesces to your worldview, you're not going to be happy.

3. *Name Games: Thanks for the Suggestion, Mom & Dad.* Guess what? Hating your given name isn't uncommon. Aversion to a particular name is *nomomisia*, and dislike of your own name is *autonomomisia*. We've all surely met people who've chosen to go by a middle name or some other name for at least some portion of their lives. If your kid prefers a nickname or some other version of their given name, does it matter? This can be tricky: is it a normal, healthy development of the self, or is it just another facet of the erasure phenomenon?

4. *The Affirmation Trap*. Yes, the dreaded "A" word. Identity-seeking kids often want immediate affirmation. If you don't immediately affirm, you're labeled as transphobic. Worse, parents are told that in failing to immediately affirm, they could harm their child psychologically and cause them to commit acts of self-harm. While we should affirm that a person's lived experience is real, and meaningful, we shouldn't fall into the trap of affirming every ephemeral belief about oneself. We, as humans, are meant to evolve throughout our lives. Help your child learn to understand that our self-conceptualization is fluid and ever-changing and that knee-jerk affirmation can lead to rigidity and suffering.

5. *Cross-Dressing*. One thing kids are told online is that cross-dressing will alleviate dysphoria. However, for kids identifying as trans, cross-dressing is part of a social transition that can solidify a trans identity and lead to medicalization quite quickly. If you allow your child to cross-dress and they receive positive feedback from peers and schools falling over themselves to appear "inclusive," the child may be naturally inclined to seek out the next steps. Remind your kids that gender-bending isn't especially new (see glam and even heavy metal rock stars from the 1970s and 1980s for some high-profile examples) and help them explore the root causes of their discomfort with their bodies.

6. *(Mis)behaviors*. Along with cross-dressing, kids might want to try and change their bodies. While some might suggest such behaviors are harmless, breast binding and experimentation with false breasts can have repercussions. Breast binding restricts breathing, damages breast tissue, and can even break ribs. False breasts are simply one more step toward medicalization. If a child feels accepted with these behaviors and is dependent on outside approval, they'll keep pushing down the pathway to medicalization.

7. *Threats of Self-Harm*. The online "how-to" guides encourage gender-curious kids to keep the suicide card up their sleeves. If mom and dad don't quickly capitulate and get on the affirmation train, the kids are told that talking about self-harm will get their attention. There is some good news here: suicide is the most exaggerated

threat and the most refuted, thankfully. Discuss with your child the cold hard facts: the suicide rate of teens identifying as trans is not improved with medical and surgical transition. It's a difficult thing to hear when they've been told that transitioning is salvation, but trans-identified individuals have some of the highest rates of psychological comorbidities and suicide rates. If you believe your child is really suicidal, take them to the emergency room or call 911.

8. *Can We Try This at Home?* Maybe your gender-questioning child isn't quite ready to assume a trans identity in the larger world. Some gender-questioning kids would prefer to "try on" their new identity at home but maintain their natal sex outside of the home. You may feel relieved that your child feels secure enough with you to ask this, but don't amplify the cognitive dissonance. Even more importantly, don't be the bridge to the child's other family members, such as grandparents. Learning how to present yourself to the world is a critical life skill. Help your child develop a coherent and healthy self-image.

9. *Depression and Withdrawal.* Many gender-questioning kids have underlying depression and anxiety, which may manifest as withdrawal from their friends and family. They may believe transition will alleviate these symptoms, but the uncomfortable reality is that social, medical, and surgical transition probably won't help your kid. To paraphrase Thoreau, you're just hacking at the branches, not the root of the problem. Help your kids discover outside activities, create opportunities in real life, and stay away from gender clinics and affirming therapists. Sadly, our current medical-industrial complex has no incentive to explore the underlying cause of distress.

10. *Sexuality, or the Lack Thereof.* One of the pillars of gender ideology is the notion that gender identity is an internal feeling unrelated to sexuality. Kids, often without any sexual experience, are taught to conflate gender identity and sex. The kids are told "genital preference" is transphobic and "gender attraction" is the polite way to discuss sexuality. These notions prey on internalized homophobia and harken back to the 1950s when homosexuals were punished via medicalization. Teach your child about homophobia, internalized homophobia, and the history of gay conversion therapy/punishment.

Remember: you're the parent. Your child may be facing difficult questions about their identity. They may be gay or gender nonconforming. Indeed, some of them may suffer from serious dysphoria that needs mental or medical support. As the parent, your job is to guide them through the difficult waters of adolescence and get them safely to the shores of adulthood.

Science tells us that the frontal cortex is not fully developed until our mid- to late twenties. In every other aspect of life, this is well-recognized and embedded into our healthcare, financial, and social systems. Try to sign up for a mobile phone contract at age seventeen, and you'll be reminded of this fact. You, as the adult in the room, have the fully developed frontal cortex and the reasoning powers that come with that. Use them.

The family unit is under threat as never before—specifically from gender ideology. Maintaining family cohesiveness can be difficult when a child identifies as trans, but it's not impossible, and in fact, a strong family bond can be protective. Members of strong families communicate with each other, all parents are on the same page, and firm but loving boundaries are clearly articulated and enforced. Adolescence is a time of identity exploration and tumultuous hormonal fluctuations. Help your child see that families are forever but that clothes, bodies, and identities change over time.

To our own child, we said early, and often, "There is nothing to do now, just be." It wasn't easy, but it worked. Our child's need to identify as trans subsided as he became more comfortable in his body and mind.

Parents on Desistance

66

Just a Phase

We should never "transition" kids, teens, or young people.

When my son was thirteen, he announced he was trans. He told me that he told his friends. He had sought advice online and reached his conclusion. He was sure, he said sadly. He wanted new pronouns, a new name, new clothes.

I cried. I hugged him. I told him that, of course, I would love and support him no matter what, that he was my precious child, and that I would do anything for him. I said all this because it was true. And also because I thought I had to "help" him be his authentic self, and if he said he was "trans," then, of course, he was a girl trapped in a boy's body. Difficult for him, but that's how it goes sometimes. I believed what I had heard from my usual liberal media sources and peer groups. Why wouldn't I?

But then I thought about my son castrating himself and messing with his endocrine system, and it just felt . . . off. It didn't seem like something to jump right into without really understanding what this was all about. Also, he was just a kid. I was still reminding him to brush his teeth every day!

So, after I picked myself off the floor, I decided to try something other than immediately "transitioning" my teen, socially or medically. I said, hey, you're a kid, and your focus should be on school and being healthy. And you're going through puberty, which is a confusing time for everyone. Let's not label you right now. That's too constraining. Let's just keep with the status quo and see how you feel when you're an adult. These are adult matters and adult ideas that you really don't need to concern yourself with at this moment, at your age. He agreed to give it a try because he respected me and trusted my judgment, but he also told me that he would never change his mind. This was just how he is, and I would have to get used to it eventually. We ended the conversation with an awkward hug and an understanding that, for now, we would agree to disagree.

During the following year, I discovered and removed his secret access to porn, his access to online "friends" who were helping him find his true self, and his video games with girl avatars, and dropped the "affirming" therapist who told me I could have a living daughter or a dead son. With the time this freed up, my son got involved in school activities, spent time outdoors, and developed some new skills. He made some new friends. We didn't talk about trans. He didn't push, and neither did I.

I gradually, very gradually, noticed a change in him. He had confidence, stood taller, and took pride in his appearance and academic prowess. I kept a vigilant eye on his online activities, preserving the appearance of freedom for him while safeguarding him from real harm. And during this time, he became more mature in his interests and viewpoints as he progressed naturally through puberty, that age-old real transition from childhood to adulthood. I held my breath but never brought up trans. Neither did he.

One day, at fifteen, he told me that he no longer felt like he was trans, almost as an aside.

He just simply didn't feel that way anymore. That was it. No fanfare, no crying, no drama. It was so anticlimactic. This trans thing was such a huge deal to me that it had dominated every waking moment of my life since the day he made his trans announcement. I was so worried about him and his health and future. For him, though, it was no big deal, and he was willing to just forget about it and leave it behind like a pair of old socks.

The whole process from "I'm a girl—deal with it" to "yeah, I don't care about that anymore" took about a year and a half. I've since met others with the same story. Their kids, so sure of their trans identities, so sure they would die if not affirmed and transitioned, simply grew out of it when left alone. If anyone tells you that kids don't ever change their minds, they just "know" when they're trans, that's a willfully ignorant lie. It happens all the time. There is no evidence that trans is an innate state, and I have now personally seen kids change their minds on this topic. Honestly, this should be absolutely unsurprising to any and all people who have kids or have been a kid (aka everyone). We are all in a state of flux, evolving, growing. It's the nature of humanity and especially the nature of young humans whose brains are still forming and maturing.

My son grew out of trans, but he's still a vulnerable teen susceptible to fads and contagions. He still needs to be reminded to brush his teeth. He may change his mind again or latch on to a new harmful fad like drugs, or eating disorders, or gambling, or . . . who knows? That's why kids need their parents—to guide and protect them while they figure themselves out.

And all this is why we should never enable the social or medical transition of kids, teens, or young people.

Parents in this mess often hear, affirm your child's trans identity or her or she will commit suicide—it's a matter of life or death—it's really just that simple! It's time to realize that if activist teachers, LGBTQ+ clubs and support groups, affirming doctors and therapists, celebrating journalists, and gender clinics leave the kids alone and stop interfering with their identity-formation process, everything will work out fine—it's really just that simple.

67

The One-Way Street

My son decided he was "trans" two years ago. But since that time, he's changed his mind. He now knows he's male and has stopped talking about gender. He is now concentrating on his next journey—college. But there's a problem: how does he walk back from the trans identification after socially transitioning in school?

He is still in high school. When he announced he was "trans," he was celebrated. Turns out, trans is a one-way door. You are celebrated as "trans," but it feels humiliating to take it back once that phase of your life is over, and you want to move on to something new. Violet in *The Incredibles* could just put her hair back and don some preppy clothes— and voila, she's transformed from a sullen emo kid to a popular, preppy, confident kid who gets the guy! That doesn't work with trans. You can't just cut your hair and change your name back and boom! You're not trans anymore. That is, sadly, not how social transition works. So, my son continues to use his girl name and to wear his hair long. Maybe he feels he has no choice. Maybe he's afraid to let anyone besides his parents know that he has accepted his body and is no longer "special" the way the school and his peers clearly wanted him to be.

There was plenty of help for my kid to become trans. He talked to the school counselor first. This counselor helpfully, in her mind, and se-cretly (from his parents) changed his name and pronouns. She thought she was safeguarding our son from us, his loving parents. My son has realized that his parents were there for him, always, and now that my

344

son no longer considers himself to be trans, he has not gone back to this counselor for guidance—he came to us, his parents, instead.

Why are there no resources for him to feel comfortable at school if he no longer identifies as trans? Why the eagerness to "trans" kids but not to "untrans" them when appropriate? Why is there not a D in LGBTQ for this growing group at schools? It doesn't make the GSA groups very inclusive without it. Kids have always tried on different identities. Schools are idiotic if they believe that trans is any different. They must see that the overnight 4,000 percent increase in trans-identifying teens will eventually slow down, and the fad will burn out, as more and more kids change their minds and "trans" loses its rainbow luster.

If you celebrate a child deciding they are trans, shouldn't you also celebrate them deciding they are not trans and accepting their body as they were born? This is something to be celebrated too. Or does that not fit the school's agenda? No wonder my son is afraid to tell anyone.

He's in limbo, waiting for college to start. It will be his first chance to remake himself again with his legal name and male pronouns. Far from authenticity, he is forced, for the rest of high school, to live a lie and to act out a trans identity to hide the truth. Just think about the tragedy of that and the hypocrisy of all the trans celebrators with their predetermined conclusions and their self-righteous determinations of the only acceptable outcomes for our kids being "transitioned." They should all be ashamed.

Shouldn't resources for desisters and detransitioners also be at colleges? Why are there signs displaying sayings such as "Are You Trans?" but no signs asking, "Are You a Detransitioner?" Where is the inclusion here? I can't believe my son is the only one going through this right now. Scratch that—I know for a fact he's not. I have met plenty of parents of young people now who once believed they were "born in the wrong body" but grew up a bit and discovered they were wrong about that. Shouldn't there be a group for them too? They may be apprehensive about telling anyone, just as it seems my son is. Shouldn't we be providing an easy path in both directions if we insist upon an easy path to trans?

It makes me think society is trying to trans all kids; otherwise, there would be things available for kids who had a change of heart.

Let's be honest. What is the real agenda behind transing children, teens, and young people?

68

To My Daughter's Therapist: You Were Wrong

It has been some months since you and my daughter had the last of four sessions. In the third session, I was invited to sit in on a discussion of the effects of T, testosterone, on a human female body. You smiled calmly as you led us through a series of PowerPoint slides, explaining that my daughter's reproductive organs would atrophy, that she would grow a beard, that her voice would deepen, and that "the phallus" would become enlarged. I sat listening, summoning all of my own skills as a clinical psychologist to not let a tirade loose at you in front of my brittle and fragile seventeen-year-old.

Between your third and fourth (and final) session with my daughter, you and I had a one-on-one conversation wherein I believe you recognized that this mother and this family were not going to easily or willingly surrender this child to whatever gender transition services you were prepared to refer her for after just three forty-five-minute meetings.

I asked what it was specifically about my daughter that convinced you that medical transition would be the right course of action to relieve her distress. You said, "He has gender dysphoria." I said, "She has an eating disorder, body dysmorphia, and ADHD, all of which seem to have some overlapping features with gender dysphoria. Why wouldn't you assess for and treat those before triggering any kind of medical intervention?"

I asked you what happens if my daughter, upon taking T and going through the changes you described, is not relieved of her dysphoria.

What if her feelings and symptoms of self-loathing, dissociation, anxiety, depression, and self-harm become exacerbated? You visibly cringed at my questions and responded that most people who transition are satisfied with their results and don't regret their decision. I asked where I might find peer-reviewed longitudinal studies that suggest that affirming and facilitating social and medical gender transition produce happy, well-adjusted teens and young adults. You said you would gladly send me links to those studies. The links never came.

I was clear, perhaps brutally so, that affirmation of male gender identity would not be the focus of your subsequent sessions and that you would instead help her explore her discomfort with her now almost fully developed, curvy female body. You would talk with her about her anxiety, her depression, her giftedness, her sense of alienation from her peers at a highly competitive suburban high school, and the impact of the pandemic at such a pivotal point in her life. In other words, you would work to slow the transition train way down.

Thinking back to that conversation, I feel a delayed sense of dread as that was before I knew that major medical and mental health associations, the law, and key players in our state and federal government had also adopted a gender identity–affirming stance, albeit for their own personal and political purposes. At the time, I was unaware that, in some instances, parents had been reported to child protective services just for refusing to address a child by his or her chosen name and preferred pronouns. In a way, though, I'm glad for my ignorance because I believe my forceful early pushback saved my child's life. I would not take any of it back.

With an abundance of unconditional love, real psychotherapy, solid psychiatric care, and some long-overdue changes in her personal and social life, my daughter is coming into her own as a quirky, witty, gender-nonconforming young adult. She is grieving as she sheds her preoccupation with chemically and surgically transforming her body into something that would never result in her being male. She will not have to live out her life in a Frankenbody. No dry and shriveling vagina. No beard or male-pattern baldness. No irreversibly thickened vocal cords. And no enlarged and exposed clitoris. You called it a phallus, but she would never pee or ejaculate from her clitoris. It is anatomically impossible.

A critically important thing that we learned along the way is that my daughter, like many other young people who declare a transgender identity in adolescence, is on the autism spectrum. She was diagnosed by an experienced child and adolescent psychiatrist and is now coming to understand how certain aspects of her autism resulted in collapsing and narrowing her focus into gender identity as a way of explaining and coping with what made life so difficult for her during her middle and high school years. She is learning to reconcile being socially awkward and having idiosyncratic interests and will be better for it as she inhabits her full adult self at some time in her late twenties. She is a brilliant and beautiful human being whose entire future came so close to being stolen from her by the gender-transition industry. It is alarming that an entire generation of gifted children who may be on the autism spectrum is being sterilized in what amounts to a eugenics experiment with the participation of big-name medical and professional institutions and to the benefit of a novel category of mental health practitioners: gender therapists like you.

Had my daughter continued on the path she was on when you were her therapist, she would be well into a regimen of weekly testosterone injections and eventual surgeries that would not have resolved her gender dysphoria, a diagnostic category that was included in the fifth edition of the *Diagnostic and Statistical Manual of Mental Disorders* (DSM-5) as a way of validating the experiences of a very small percentage of the population who suffer with lifelong feelings of discomfort and disconnection with their biological sex, all while creating billable codes for gender clinics and mental health professionals (see psychiatrist Jack Drescher's 2014 article "Controversies in Gender Diagnoses": " . . . it is difficult to find reconciling language that removes the stigma of having a mental disorder diagnosis while maintaining access to medical care"). I know this because one of the experts on the DSM-5 workforce on gender dysphoria is a long-time friend who is, himself, appalled at what has come from this diagnostic category that he, no doubt with the most compassionate of intentions, helped forge. It is disappointing that he is hesitant to come out on the side of best and safe practice and to publicly state that gender exploratory therapy is NOT conversion therapy—that, in fact, putting so many young LGB people on a fast-moving conveyer belt to medical transition is the latest iteration of gay conversion practices.

Our daughter was not "assigned female at birth." She was born with the full complement of normal female sex organs and all the eggs that her ovaries will release over the course of her fertile years, regardless of whether or not she ever chooses to become a mother. We expected as much because prenatal DNA testing let us know unequivocally at ten weeks of gestation that we were having a baby with XX sex chromosomes in every cell of her body. And no, she isn't "intersex." Her phenotypic features reflect her Southwest Asian genetic heritage, and she is fine and healthy just as she is. Nothing about her body is or has ever been out of place. If the gender-transition industry is anything, it is profoundly racist and disturbingly sexist.

I believe that the medical fast-tracking of children and young adults who self identify as trans is a contemporary twist on American individualism taken to its point of absurdity. We are now in a situation where corporate wolves are passing effortlessly as progressive sheep. Even Planned Parenthood, perhaps seeing the writing on the wall that was confirmed with the recent Texas abortion ruling, may be hedging its bets by offering "gender affirming hormone therapy." The needs of institutions for staying relevant and projecting themselves into the future trump any fidelity to stated guiding principles. And a parent's need to protect her child's mind and body trumps any and all political affiliations. Our wallets and our votes will speak for us.

* * *

It is now September, and my daughter and I have been living in a city in the former Soviet Union since mid-August. She is connecting to her roots, her land, and her cultural heritage—to rich and lasting sources of identity that synthetic hormones and manufactured gender ideology were threatening to undermine and replace. She recognizes that going down the path of medical transition would have made her into a life-long patient and held her back from so much joy and freedom that she now has access to. She is coming to terms with the inevitable losses that growing up brings and discovering facets of herself that she would never have had if we had taken your advice and initiated medicalization. Gender ideology would have had to become the central focus of her intellect and creativity for the rest of her life.

It helps that the local language, which my daughter is quickly absorbing and starting to speak, is devoid of gendered grammatical markers. I think she is relieved to not have to ask or answer questions about "preferred pronouns" and such. Here, no one is compelled to participate in a mass delusion that requires thought control and speech policing. They had more than enough of that during seven long decades under Sovict rulc. Simply put, people have more pressing daily challenges and live highly interconnected social lives as a result. When you fall, passersby stop to help you up and dust you off. As do other young people, my daughter feels confident walking around the city on her own at all hours. She increasingly feels safe and at home in this city and in her body. And I grow more hopeful every day that removing her from a culture that would pathologize normal developmental struggles and push costly and irreversible medical treatments will enable and reinforce long-term remission of gender dysphoria and trans ideation from her life.

I took the unpopular risk of holding my child's ambivalence and keeping it alive rather than surrendering her to a process that would make her the docile object of bogus "affirmation" and "celebration." And while I became the target of so much hatred and rage for many exhausting months (affirming and facilitating social and medical transition, by far the less conflictual path for parents who have the financial means, would have gained me temporary status as the heroic mother), she never lost sight of the fact that her father and I were the ones who truly had her back; that approval from social-media groomers, "glitter families," and gender clinicians could never be a replacement for her own self-esteem and her family's unwavering love.

Let me close by saying that things are changing in parts of Europe and in the United Kingdom. In the United States, a growing movement of parents and ethical clinicians, most of whom are lifelong progressives and active supporters of LGBTQ people and causes, are organizing and becoming vocal with their outrage and rejection of gender ideology and the unsupported diagnostic claims and harmful treatment practices it has given rise to. When the lawsuits start coming, this will be exposed as one of the biggest medical scandals in history.

It is only a matter of time.

69

The Trans Detour

My son, James, now in his twenties, is my only child. He identified as "trans" from early 2014 until the autumn of 2017, when he decided that the trans label no longer fit him. Although at that time he desisted from being "trans," he's still struggling to rebuild his broken life.

Why? Because he had other issues that were left unaddressed when he was shoved into the one-size-fits-all mold of trans, with "transition" as the only possible cure.

We live in England, in a rural village. Far from being an absent parent, I'd been happy to stop work to be a full-time mum when our son was born. My husband and I separated when our son was around fourteen years old. We have no religious faith, and we have had no strong allegiance to any political party. I'd accepted our son readily when he came out as gay at age fourteen. My ex-husband was more hesitant at first but ultimately was accepting as well. Among his peers, my son experienced severe homophobic bullying, and, as a socially awkward teen, he found his escape online, with immersion in gaming and anime.

James fitted the profile of today's trans-identifying teens, sometimes termed to be suffering from rapid-onset gender dysphoria (ROGD), in so many respects. He is on the autism spectrum, with the typical black-and-white thinking of autism spectrum disorder (ASD), and was diagnosed with attention-deficit/hyperactivity disorder (ADHD) and obsessive-compulsive disorder (OCD), with fear of contamination and intrusive thoughts. In addition to the above, my son is twice exceptional—he is also gifted. Among the parents I know of trans-identifying teens, this is extremely typical of the teen susceptible to trans.

From the age of fifteen, OCD overtook my son's life until it lost all semblance of what it had been. Irritable bowel syndrome (IBS) triggered severe OCD panic attacks several times each day. By sixteen years old, and within weeks of being diagnosed with OCD, he'd suddenly declared he was transgender. He'd never previously shown any sign of unhappiness about being male, nor did he ever present as feminine in appearance or mannerisms. Just like that, my family was swept up in the madness of trans.

CAMHS (Children and Adolescent Mental Health Services) referred James to the Tavistock as soon as he self-diagnosed himself as transgender. They believed that the gender stuff was the root cause of all this. From the start, the sole focus of CAMHS and Tavistock had been transition. I had been told by CAMHS that it was vital that I shouldn't enable or collude in any OCD behaviors, so I was shocked to realize that they were cheerleaders for his new belief. I was also skeptical—even without any real knowledge of gender dysphoria, I knew from the outset that my son being unquestioningly affirmed was wrong. How would this address the OCD that was dominating my child's existence? To keep a steady ground for my son, I avoided using pronouns altogether and persuaded him to use a gender-neutral new name, which, by the way, he still uses after desisting.

My son remained catastrophically mentally ill and housebound after almost a year of being under CAMHS affirmation-only care. The initial appointment at the Tavistock offered no hope that treatment for OCD would be a priority, despite James being in 24/7 crisis with contamination fears and terrifying intrusive thoughts.

Over time, James realized that neither Tavistock nor CAMHS had any interest in helping him overcome his crippling OCD.

I took a gamble and suggested that if he overcame his OCD, perhaps he'd be better able to cope with transition and his other ongoing issues. He jumped at the overture and willingly agreed to instead see a private counselor, whose remit was purely to give CBT (cognitive behavioral therapy) for OCD.

I'm thankful my gut instinct was right.

Removing my son from affirmation-only care was key to his desisting. Private ethical counseling, which focused on treating his actual mental health issues, helped him begin to find his way back to accepting the reality that he is male. Today, he has desisted. He no longer identifies as trans.

Despite finding self-acceptance as gay and desisting from trans, this is now the eighth year of James living as a virtual recluse, immersed online. He was a gifted spectrum student, but his education ended at fifteen years old. Before ROGD, he was a studious, socially awkward, artistic "super geek." He's made so much progress from how unwell he was when ROGD hit, but he is still struggling with untreated complex mental health issues that have become entrenched. His unhelpful detour into trans stalled any real treatment of the root causes of his distress.

James still sleeps through most days in order to be awake and online at night with his U.S. online "family." He lives an isolated life. He struggles to focus and seems disconnected and dissociated. The only people he sees are his grandparents, who he visits one afternoon per week. He seems to pull himself together for that one afternoon.

My son's silent hostile dissociation from me has continued after desisting. For the most part, he's seen me as his enemy and still does because I dared to gently question gender ideology. He has online friends who've transitioned, so he feels loyalty to their choices and can't join the dots that my being deeply concerned for their health doesn't make me a bigot.

My heart is still heavy with worry about what the future holds. He's now a twenty-three-year-old with untreated mental health issues who refuses to seek help. He stopped seeing his private psych in 2017. And he has replaced "trans" with a new escape-from-reality maladjusted coping mechanism with his online life . . . I just have to hope that in the passage of time, he will continue to evolve and to grow through this.

My heart also aches for all the kids who didn't escape interventions and who thought that trans and irreversible medicalization of healthy bodies was the answer, the quick fix for deep-seated issues.

The fact that he was affirmed as trans, despite being so obviously, SO seriously ill with OCD, still shocks me.

My son wasn't taught about gender at school. He had no trans-identifying friends, and there were no transgender students in his year. His life has been derailed purely from becoming immersed online in his room as a struggling, bullied teenager. Gaming and social media chat rooms led him into the world of trans ideology. And then his disastrous wrong-track, trans-affirming detour further pushed him off-balance. This is now the eighth year of him struggling to rebuild his life.

No child is safe from the trans madness, especially our most vulnerable.

70

Saying Bye to the Gummy Bear Cult

By March 2020, we could no longer leave the house unless we had an "attestation" providing a legal justification for being outside. The European country where we lived as American expats had one of the strictest lockdowns in the world.

Within a week of the restrictions, I lost my sense of taste. I was pregnant but was advised to stay at home because, at that point, the hospitals were full. Patients were being transferred by medical trains across the border. Breathless and coughing, I self-isolated in an empty room in the attic, sleeping on a mattress my husband pulled up the steep staircase. To everyone's relief, in two weeks, I was better.

The routine that waited for me downstairs, however, was a new source of stress. Both my husband and I have demanding jobs. My twelve-year-old daughter and her little brother had Zoom school. His was a half-hour cacophony, with the teacher interrupting the lesson every few minutes with instructions on how to mute or turn on the microphones. My daughter was at the other extreme, with nearly eight hours per day.

We had no childcare. Wherever possible, I would put off doing work and then stay up past midnight to catch up, but that was not enough. My husband and I were regularly in Zoom meetings that lasted past dinner time. I would see my children out the window in the garden eating instant noodles that my daughter had prepared.

In the evenings, we would read or watch videos. One night, I heard my daughter laughing in her room. She showed me a TikTok video of a boy in a bulky dinosaur costume dancing on stage with the caption, "When you didn't get the memo that the school talent competition was for singers." We laughed together.

Around May, when on a walk, my daughter told me that she was bisexual and that one of her new friends introduced her to a WhatsApp group for LGBT kids. My daughter had switched schools right before Covid-19 and had struggled to make friends. I responded that it was hard for her to be anything sexual as she was not yet a teen and had never been in a relationship. I told her that she should keep an open mind, and, of course, that we love her and it makes no difference to us. I gave her a hug and felt her heart beating quickly against me.

As Covid-19 came and went in waves, school in the fall of 2020 was by turn in person and via Zoom. I was busy taking care of the baby I gave birth to in the summer. That year was more of the same, except my daughter was clearly exiting the preteen years. She gained inches, and her body was changing. She cut her long hair to shoulder length and started experimenting with her style. Ariana Grande was forgotten in favor of punk and alternative rock.

My daughter was still part of the LGBT group in school, which did not alarm me. I am liberal and have close gay friends. The only thing I requested (and this was immediately after she told me that she was bisexual) was that she delete the WhatsApp group from her phone, because it included people that she did not know of various ages and from other countries. The group was called the Gummy Bear Cult.

In mid-2021, over the summer, my daughter cut her hair very short and occasionally asked which male names I liked. At the time, I didn't think much of it. In August, she spent a few weeks with a relative, so she had a lot of time to look at social media without parental control. Only later did I learn that she had spent countless hours on TikTok and YouTube. Her whole feed was short clips of trans-identified girls sharing advice or posing to catchy music.

In September, when my daughter started school, an American teacher handed out a worksheet asking the students to indicate their names and pronouns. My daughter put down a male name and "they" pronouns. A month later, I received a text from a male name I did not recognize. It was my daughter.

When I went into her room, I saw school papers that had that same name on them. At that point, my daughter was thirteen. Her style had changed radically. She now wore only boy clothes: high-top sneakers, oversized shirts, and pants. Her hair was short. She did not look or act like her former self, down to her mannerisms, which she copied from the kids on her TikTok feed.

Unlike my daughter, I was a tomboy growing up, and, well into my adulthood, most of my friends were male. I work in a field dominated by men. Whatever troubled my daughter, I was fairly certain that it was not being a boy trapped in the wrong body.

My husband and I knew so little about this that we didn't know how to approach the issue and were even hesitant to talk to the school. Nevertheless, I sent an email to the director saying that we were surprised to learn that our daughter was going by a boy's name. At the meeting that followed, the director was understanding and, to a point, apologetic. Teachers were not allowed by law to change names without parental consent. In fact, not every teacher at the school used our daughter's new name, and there was no question of using the boy's name on any official document or in the yearbook.

We didn't want to embarrass our daughter by asking the American teacher to change course, but we also did not want this to go further. We asked those who were using her newly chosen name to continue to do so and those she had not asked to refrain from doing so.

At home, we did not affirm. I listened to my daughter, but what she said didn't make sense. She said: "Imagine a room which represents everything you can do as a girl. Now, imagine there is this other room where there are things you can do as a boy. Why not be part of the two rooms?" Her argument seemed sexist, and I told her so.

My husband told her that he would call her "they" if she called him "thee and thou." Exasperated, she quickly gave up. However, I mostly used her pet name and avoided saying things like "my daughter" to avoid conflict.

I talked to her every night and tried to keep her as close as possible. Because she broke the WhatsApp group rule three times by reinstalling the Gummy Bear Cult after deleting it, we had an excuse to restrict her phone access.

I tried to find a psychologist, hoping that some expert would solve this for me, but I could not get an appointment. As a family, we finally went to a psychologist who did not speak English. The language barrier did not help, and we decided not to go back. I got on a waiting list to see a psychotherapist in the United Kingdom via Zoom. We did not get an appointment until two months later. Ultimately, the sessions we had did not seem critical to our daughter desisting, but they helped me get through a difficult time.

Unable to find a psychologist, I had the impression that I was waiting for Godot. I had to act, but where to start? I remembered reading an article about a psychiatrist who worked at and was critical of the Tavistock and Portman NHS Trust, which runs the United Kingdom's only gender identity service for children. After a few minutes on the Internet, I found it. His name, David Bell, was the end of the string that I followed and which led me to the names of other psychologists, scientific publications, books, and parent groups. One of the parent groups had a link to a video made by an Australian mother whose daughter desisted. I hung on to every word. Many of the stories were nearly identical to mine.

A parent shared a story written by Ray Bradbury in the mid-twentieth century titled "The Veldt." It is about parents being replaced by the children's futuristic playroom, which can transport them to any location the children like. It haunts me still.

I have a scientific education and was reading not just popular books like Abigail Shrier's *Irreversible Damage* but also the underlying studies. At first, I tried to share the information I found with my daughter but soon realized that it was not having any effect. She lacked the maturity to place her personal experience within any framework. For example, we watched an excellent *Wall Street Journal* investigative video about the TikTok algorithm, but when I asked her if TikTok had any impact on her trans identity, her answer was no, even though her entire feed was trans people narrating their experiences. After a few conversations, I gave up.

The darkest time was in the winter. My daughter looked miserable. You couldn't see her eyes behind her bangs. She told me she felt more like a "he" now than a "they." At some point, I cracked and burst out crying, worried that the road she was on would lead to medicalization. I asked her to promise me she wouldn't do anything until she was twenty-five. My daughter thought I was crazy. I wonder if she realized that the androgynous look that so appealed to her was not natural. Many of the influencers she had followed were clearly on testosterone, or as they would call it, T.

This is where I stopped mentioning anything trans-related entirely. I have not talked to my daughter about her trans identity since.

Instead of trying to reason with her, we followed the advice of psychologists and other parents and focused on nurturing our bond and our daughter's confidence as a girl.

Although my daughter needed her phone for school, every minute she was looking at it, I feared she was on social media. We continued limiting Internet access to mitigate the impact of screen time and social influencers.

I also encouraged her to participate in extracurricular activities. She signed up for a music camp that was run by a former teacher who only knew her by her girl name.

Christmas and February vacations were spent with family, with people who did not suspect that, at school and with her friends, our daughter was anything other than the girl they knew and loved. A parent on one of the forums advised me not to help my daughter come out to her family. If she wanted to, she would have to do the hard work herself.

After shopping with aunts and grandmothers, our daughter came back with a few dresses. At the time, we thought it was to keep up appearances. However, what I noticed at some point in the early spring was that she seemed to live a double life. She would don her boy uniform to go to school, but at home, she would try on my dresses and jewelry and wear night dresses as she cooed over her baby brother.

There was a breaking point when our daughter had a falling out with a girl, one of her closest LGBT group friends. She grew close to a boy from the same group and spent hours talking to him on the phone. It may have been that spending time with a boy made it clear that she wasn't one. In early April, she attended a birthday party of a friend from school wearing my dress.

Every weekend, we have been going to the countryside and spending lots of time together, riding bicycles and walking in the woods. We thought very seriously about moving there full-time for the next school year, but given that our daughter now goes by her girl name, dresses like a girl, and seems happy, we decided to stay.

Moving schools was what, in part, brought this on, and we didn't want to rock the boat again. Time will tell if we made the right decision. I can only hope that we will not share the fate of the parents in "The Veldt."

71

In Like a Lion, Out Like a Lamb

When I had children, I promised myself that I would never lie to them. When my five-year-old figured out it was physically impossible for Santa to fly to each house and drop off presents, I fessed up. When he was six and saw my pregnant friend, he announced with authority, "the baby comes out the belly button." I corrected him and let him know the baby grows in a special place in the woman's body called the womb and exits the birth canal. He argued with me in disbelief at this disturbing news for a few weeks until I finally showed him my anatomy book.

When he was ten, he asked me how *exactly* the sperm gets to the egg. We were driving, and I was trapped; this was a truth I didn't feel ready to share. I felt the blood drain from my head, my breath quickened, and I did what any reasonable parent would do—I turned it around and asked him a question. "That's an interesting question! Did you see something?" Turns out he saw these two donkeys . . . and one was on top of the other from behind . . . and then it looked like . . . maybe his penis was going in! Flustered that he'd seen the real thing, I said, "Yep! Yep! That's how it happens! In humans too!" For months my friends teased me. They said my son would turn his wife around on their wedding night and know exactly what to do. We laughed and laughed. Little did I know groomers on Reddit would subvert my relationship with my son and derail his sex education by leading him to high-speed Internet porn. I found that out much later.

Out of the blue in the spring of 2020, my son came to me and said,

"Mom, I was born in the wrong body." This was after the terror of lock-down and the death of George Floyd. He had been spending a lot of time online, and we were distracted with Covid-19. After the initial shock, our family bumped along for the next seven months, convinced that my son's fixation on "trans" was a phase and would pass. We spent time as a family hiking, talking, cooking, and reading. We went camping and passed time reorganizing the house. There were tears, anxiety attacks, whispers at night. We had no idea what to do. The Internet told me that no one changed their minds once they were trans. Then in December 2020, I read about Keira Bell, a young woman who had "transitioned" as a teen, only to realize that she had been misled. Only after having surgery and taking testosterone did she change her mind and realize she was not "trans" after all. Not only did she change her mind, but by the time I heard of her, she was also actively working to protect other children from irreversible harm caused by transition. Keira Bell's story moved me into action.

I joined a parent support group and learned about things I still wish I didn't know—Internet porn, sissy porn, hypno porn, the Blanchard typology, and Reddit and Tumblr groomers. I started listening to podcasts, reading as much as I could about postmodern theory, and sharing with my husband what I had learned about the underbelly of trans. With our newfound knowledge and data, we immediately limited Internet access to approved sites only and put time limits on our son's devices. Doors were slammed, screaming ensued, but we held our ground. No porn (this was never allowed, of course—we just didn't realize he had been accessing it) or social media. We watched, waited, and prayed. Within a few weeks, the fixation started to fade. The depression lifted, the anxiety eased, and we started seeing glimpses of our son back. We had found the only known weapon to fight trans ideology—limiting Internet access and preventing online predators from accessing our child.

The summer of 2021 passed quickly. We moved and enrolled our son in a new school with in-person instruction to give him a fresh start and, hopefully, a new perspective. He made friends right away and even got asked to go to a festival with a friend! I asked him what his friend's name was, and he said, "His name is Tate, and he's a musician." On the day of the festival, Tate's father came to pick up my son. Being the nosey mom I am, I walked out to the car and introduced myself to Tate's father. The front seat was empty, so I peeked into the car to find an adorable girl, introduced to me by her dad as "Kate." My stomach dropped, and I felt nauseated. Things were going so well, and now trans had infiltrated my life again! I was worried that my son would backslide into the ideology to maintain his friendship.

I let my son go but picked him up from the festival myself. He told me on the ride home that Tate also is known as Kate but identifies as a boy. "It's a thing now—all the kids are doing it," he told me. My son had misled me about "Tate," and he knew it, just as he knew that our policy of "no lying" worked both ways. I reminded him of all the times I told him the truth growing up, even when it was uncomfortable. How can I trust you if you lie, I said. He re-agreed to our pact. We will continue to work on our bond and our trust in each other, and I know we will get there. I am his mom, and he is my son, and our bond is unbreakable, now and always. No cultural contagion will break us apart.

Now we call my son's friend Tate-Kate. We both know she's a girl. Just like my son knows he's a boy. We can have our friends and our space to believe what we feel, but we cannot and do not lie, not to each other, not in our family.

Trans ID is a funny thing. It comes in like a lion and leaves like a lamb. My son came in strong, demanding we accept his wrong-body hypothesis and do something about it. A year and a half later, my son's trans identification left quietly, out the back door while no one was watching. I'm grateful that I had the strength to resist, to do nothing. I'm grateful that my son had the maturity and faith to remain open-minded and to trust that I would not lie to him, not even when he really wanted me to, not even when I was scared and uncomfortable. The way I see it, there is no room for lies between a mother and child. In this case, as in all others I've encountered so far, I'm glad I did not compromise in this. I love my son too much to jeopardize his future for a lie.

72

Our Story of Desistance

Today, our son is a twenty-year-old sophomore at a liberal arts college. He is a walking, talking story of success, with a merit scholarship and straight As. He speaks Japanese and has self-published two novels. He's physically and mentally healthy and self-reliant, in a loving relationship with a girlfriend, with a great friend group. He's thriving.

Except . . . when he comes home. Where he is so profoundly triggered by being back in his neighborhood, his house, his bedroom, that he can't sleep. Why is this? Because, sadly, he's haunted by memories of one three-year period of his adolescence filled with depression, anxiety, and self-harm. The three years where he identified as a girl.

He had always been a special boy—a square peg, a socially awkward kid who preferred the company of adults to hanging out with his peers. He is sensitive, empathetic, mature, and intelligent, but he never quite fit in at school. During his preteen years, he went down the Reddit, Tumblr rabbit hole, searching for his tribe. You've likely heard his story before from other parents, because it's a common one.

At twelve and a half, he told us he was gay. We responded with love and support. But his social anxiety only grew, and he began cutting. At thirteen and a half, he asked for a gay therapist, and our school's director recommended one. After three sessions, our son told us he needed to come out to us AGAIN: "I'm a girl; I'm trans." And again, his revelation was met with love and support. But we also reacted with surprise—and private and confident disbelief.

Immediately, we made an appointment for a family session with his therapist, who told us "to mourn the loss of your son and embrace your daughter." This seemed extreme and certainly extraordinarily FAST. Our son had never exhibited any feminine behaviors or traits. But, even so, we chose to trust the experts and to follow the guidance of this medical professional who immediately chose to affirm our child.

This so-called professional then took it upon himself to reach out to our child's school, telling them to change our child's name in the yearbook, to ask the teachers to use new pronouns, and to give our child access to the girl's bathroom. And the school did all of this without question or hesitation.

We were stunned at how quickly our young, puberty-age son had been told that the reason he felt socially anxious and uncomfortable in his own skin was that he had been born into the wrong body.

Today, our son blames us for not pushing back at this absurd diagnosis. He doesn't understand how we bought into it. Why did we not trust our gut feeling that this was wrong? Why did we let him buy girl clothes he never wore? Why did we send him to an LGBTQ+ summer camp, where counselors tell the kids, "This is where you can be yourselves. This is where you are safe. Your parents don't understand you, but we do." Why did we go along with any of this when he had never shown "consistence, persistence, or insistence" regarding gender dysphoria?

Why indeed? We gave him the simple answer. Fear. He had been cutting. And was constantly sharing statistics about trans suicide rates and that he only had a 40 percent chance of living past eighteen. We went along with it all, knowing it was not his truth, because we were scared he would kill himself. And whenever we sought reasonable counsel and wisdom, we found none.

I saw a therapist for myself who specialized in this field. I found her to be kind, open, very easy to talk to . . . until I told her how uncomfortable I was with the situation and the speed with which everything was happening with my son, and how my mom-gut told me this wasn't his truth—and how I was certain that my son was overcome with depression, not suffering from a gender mismatch. She sternly told me that I was in denial. I needed to immediately get into the meetings at an organization she was affiliated with: Transforming Families. I walked out feeling as though, yet again, I'd gone with an open mind, looking for an evidence-based conversation, only to be punched in the gut.

Throughout this entire time, our child did not change his appearance, grow out his hair, or adopt a new style of dress—other than a small padded bra a couple of days a week and a purse. He did not seek out a new peer group. He did, however, take a feminine name, choose female pronouns, and use the gender-neutral bathroom—coincidentally, all the things his therapist and the school had worked out for him. He was also happy to correct us, disagree, spout statistics, and regurgitate pro-trans activist anecdotes. But by almost every metric, he was living his life as a teenage boy.

Yet, all the while, our son told us that he desperately needed hormones or he "might revert back to being a boy" if he didn't have them right away. We wanted to be able to consult with a doctor, at the very least. However, the word on the street, from two separate sources, was that the specialist at the local children's hospital doesn't give the kids any psychological evaluations, only an abacus where they slide beads to tell her how they identify. Then she puts them on hormones or puberty blockers, depending on their stage of development. So . . . that was out. Instead, I called a local pediatric endocrinologist to have a consultation. This doctor told me what I wanted to hear, which was that she would NOT give our son any hormones. So, I brought him in to see her, pretending she and I had never met.

As recently as last month, we explained most of this to our son. We explained how, though we had always presented a loving and supportive front to him, we had worked behind the scenes to prevent any permanent changes to his body or legal identity. Since learning this, his anger toward us has lessened.

At the time, we'd give him reasons like: he was legally too young. Or that our insurance wouldn't cover the cost of hormone replacement therapy. We just needed to buy him time to try on this new label and work through the depression and anxiety component without any gender-based medical involvement. Creating the space and time to explore and grow emotionally.

Eventually, the interest in transitioning began to fade. The purse stayed on the shelf. The bra stayed in the drawer. He seemed lighter, like the depression wasn't winning anymore. Perhaps it was a newfound love for playing guitar with friends in a heavy metal band. Or the satisfaction he found in creative writing. Whatever the reason, we sensed he was looking for a way to realign.

We made an appointment to see his therapist and discuss. The therapist disagreed with our frontline assessment and claimed that our son was in danger of behaving recklessly. And yet we were seeing the total opposite at home, a return to calm, little to no cutting, no more talk about trans activism. The therapist said he didn't agree, nor did he want anything drastic to happen under his watch. He said he could no longer treat our son. We were on our own.

Now, without any professional guidance as to next steps, we suggested to our son that he get some time outside the bubble. How about a summer trip with a teen tour? Our kid was thrilled at the idea of visiting Japan for two weeks. And when he returned home after this adventure, he calmly explained to us, "I'm not a girl; I'm not trans."

Looking back, our son feels he was the victim of manipulation. Instead of being told he was just like every other teenager searching for a tribe while transitioning to adulthood, he was immediately affirmed by adults, therapists, camp counselors, school counselors, people on Tumblr, Reddit, and the Internet, and society at large. They all collectively pushed him down the path of believing he been born into the wrong body. Thankfully he was given the time and space to figure out on his own that this was not the case. But now, even though he never experienced medical interventions, he carries a distrust for the system that rushed to give him a label and that, he believes, failed to support his truth. Which is "I'm not a girl; I'm not trans."

Our son is not the only one who feels let down by the mental health and medical profession. We didn't get it all right by any means, but were it not for our parental diligence, application of common sense, critical thinking, and, yes, subterfuge, our child might be physically scarred for life or dealing with the complexities of drug therapy, trapped in a body he was not born into.

At the moment, our son's trauma consists of anger and nightmares, all unwelcome souvenirs from that scarring three years that were stolen from his childhood. In spite of all his success at college, he remains on antidepressants. We hope that, in time, he will work through his PTSD, casting it aside like he did that padded bra and purse.

73

Anger, Shame, and Then Pure Happiness

Anger and shame: these two emotions have become part of me since my son announced he was trans quite a few years ago. The anger emerged when I discovered that the entire world had been captured by this gender nonsense. Doctors, therapists, schools, friends, and family—all believed that girls could be boys and boys could be girls. I tried to reason with some of the believers using evidence and research and cited the dangers of medicalization and hormones, but they had made up their minds. They would listen politely, but I could read their expressions of doubt, and then they would say something about me just having to accept my son. I've had too many of these conversations over the last few years, and the anger has multiplied with time. Nobody listened!

I brought Abigail Shrier's book *Irreversible Damage* to give to my primary care doctor at one of my appointments. I briefly explained to her that my young son had been taken in by gender ideology and was confused and now thought he was trans. I tried to explain further, but once she heard the word "trans," that was it. She told me to take him to an endocrinologist. I told her that she wasn't hearing me, and I gave her the book to please read. Before she left the exam room, she again told me to take my son to an endocrinologist. That was the last time I saw her. This is just one brief experience of the many that I've had to refuel my rage.

I had a similar scenario with our pediatrician, who I once admired. We stopped seeing him as well. I couldn't risk bringing my son to a doctor who would affirm his new female identity and send us to the nearest gender center. I was already fully aware of what goes on in gender centers, and I knew better.

Yes, soon after my kid made his trans announcement, I did call our local children's hospital and spoke to a social worker who worked for a well-known gender doctor. I was very confused in the beginning and did believe there was a possibility that my son was trans. That confusion didn't last long, though. After a five-minute conversation on the phone, the social worker asserted that I should move quickly and get my son on puberty blockers. She told me with urgency that once my son's Adam's apple comes out and his voice drops, there is no going back. I lived the next couple of weeks in a state of utter panic, weighing these two options. If my son was really trans, I would want to make it as easy as possible for him to transition, which would mean starting blockers immediately, but if he wasn't trans, I would be medicating him for no reason and actually hurting him. I called the gender center back and told them of my dilemma, and the social worker recommended I take my son to a gender therapist to figure this out. She gave me the name of the therapist, who turned out to be the husband of the highest-profile gender doctor in the city and who also just happened to be trans. My confusion began coming to an end, and my skepticism exploded.

The next few years were tough ones. Trying to support my son without giving in to his demands was not an easy task. He was angry that we didn't buy into his new female identity and give him hormones to alter his appearance. We had to go to the schools and insist that the teachers and counselors stay out of our kid's personal gender story. It was then I realized they were very much to blame for the mess we were in. His middle school counselor had seen him multiple times without us knowing. She affirmed him and even showed him "I Am Jazz" YouTube videos that glamorized being trans. If I knew then what I know now, I would have sued the school, but at the time, I was too concerned about my kid to take action.

After many years of struggling with gender dysphoria, our son socially transitioned. We didn't approve, but through this whole journey, we kept telling him that he could dress however he liked but that he was not to take hormones. It is one thing to tell your child it doesn't matter what he wears, but did I mean it? Seeing my teenage son dressed in girl clothes was not easy. My first concern was for him and always has been, but I can't deny the embarrassment and shame I felt. He obviously was severely confused, and he was wearing it on his sleeve, literally. He didn't look like a girl at all. Even with his long hair, it was obvious he was a teenage boy. The first time I saw him in a dress was by accident. I was walking the dog in the neighborhood park and accidentally saw him and some friends. He didn't see me, but I sure saw him. It was heartbreaking. Not only did he look terrible, but I could feel his pain in his body language. I wasn't concerned so much about the clothing but rather about what it meant. I was concerned about his mental state.

It was never easy seeing him dressed this way, but I sort of went numb in order to deal with the feelings. When my son walked from the house to the car, I would pray my neighbors weren't watching. He would occasionally walk down to our local shops and cafés, and I would pray that our friends wouldn't see him. I hated feeling embarrassed of my own child, who I loved more than life itself. It was a terrible feeling. He was suffering, and so I tried desperately to ignore the clothing and not worry about what others thought of him. I would run into other moms at the grocery store, and they would not ask about my son because they didn't know how to approach it. A couple of times, I felt people avoid me because it was too uncomfortable for them. I tried to keep the focus on my son's well-being, because I know that is what mattered.

He graduated high school and went off to college. He presented as female and lived with the girls in the dorm. We were not happy about him going as a girl, but I felt we had no choice. Again, we kept the focus on not medicalizing and keeping him off hormones. We had many conversations about waiting until his brain was fully developed and until he had more life experience before making a decision like that. We showed him articles that explained the risks and dangers of taking cross-sex hormones. Moving him in on the first day of school was hard. Most of the girls were wearing shorts and T-shirts, and my son showed up in a miniskirt. It was very clear he was not really a girl, but everyone politely pretended he was. We moved him in and tried to ignore the stares and prayed for the best.

He finished the year with good grades and a few friends. He moved back home for the summer, and then, out of the blue, he announced that he was going back to identifying as a guy! We were in disbelief and still are! He never told us he was even considering this.

This kid always surprises us!

Since the big announcement, he's been the happiest and most content I've seen since he was a child. He cut his long hair and bought new clothes and began a life as himself—and that's all I ever wanted. It was a very long and tortuous journey, but here we are. I feel like we have our life back, that we can come out of hiding. I only hope that the other kids who fall into this confusion can make it to the other side as well.

74

A Letter to My Daughter

Dear Daughter,

What do I want you to know deep in your core? I want you to know that I love and support you completely, no matter what. You are my child and an important part of our family, now and always. That will not change regardless of name, clothing, pronouns, or gender. I believe I demonstrate that to you daily and hope you can see it. I have loved you from the minute I held you in my arms, and nothing will ever change that. You are as beautiful to me now as you were in those first moments we met. Your beauty is deep in your soul because you are such a loving, strong, and amazing person.

As your parent, it is my responsibility to create an environment that is not only loving but also includes boundaries. The boundaries I create are in place because I care very deeply about your well-being, not because I don't accept you. Among other boundaries, my willingness, or lack of willingness, to use new pronouns should not be the only thing that you judge me on—I have supported you in so many other ways.

I have done a great deal of soul-searching along our journey over the last few years, and that has been challenging. I am not sure you know some of the challenges I have been up against. I have been swimming upstream in whitewater rapids. I realize that I am not presenting the mainstream thoughts about gender. I have a curious mind and refuse to just go along with popular thinking. I am looking at you as an individual with your own set of life circumstances and challenges. I also know that there has been a statistically impractical rise in female-to-male transitions over the last several years. That means that there has not been enough time to research why this is happening.

Right now, there is no proof one way or the other about a "male" brain vs. a "female" brain—research needs to continue. It also means that medical professionals do not know the long-term effects of social or medical transition. There are many people for whom gender dysphoria is not diminished or alleviated by social or medical transition. That is why it is so important for us to continue searching for ways to make you more comfortable with the body that you have. The outcome I fear most is for you to take hormones, have multiple surgeries, and become a lifelong medical patient—only to find that you are still uncomfortable with who you are.

When I am at the end of my abilities to cope, I think of my dad's mantra, "March or die." There were times I didn't want to hear the phrase, but he didn't mean it harshly. It was a call to stand up for myself and my family. I am not sure that I realized it until after he died, but it was his way of telling me to follow my intuition and do the right thing no matter how hard it made the journey. Giving up isn't an option.

I will never give up on you. That includes searching for answers with you about your identity. You are sixteen now, and that means that my role in your life is changing, as it does for all parents during the teen years. But remember, your emotional challenges began when you were twelve years old. You began searching then for a way to feel better, feel complete, feel at ease with who you are. You have always had questions about being adopted and your birth family. And you have the dreaded position of being the "middle" child, which leads to frustration when you don't fit in with the older kids but don't want to hang out with the younger crowd. Adding to the mix, you went through puberty early and had large breasts. On top of it all, your sisters suffered from severe anxiety when grandpa was terminally ill. It was a tough time, to say the least. I don't blame you for searching for answers.

You searched online for friends and for an answer to your discomfort. You experimented with some of the identities you found there, including being bisexual, pansexual, gender fluid, etc. Then you began self-harming—cutting, binge eating, and not eating—and none of it reduced your pain. The more you talked to people on the Internet, the more affirmation and confirmation you got that, yes, this must be why I am uncomfortable—I am transgender.

You asked to see professionals with a specialty in gender. I obliged once and found that therapists, social workers, and physicians are bound by the affirmative approach. If you say you are trans, then you are. I don't think that's what you wanted; you wanted someone to help you explore your feelings and help you figure it out. As a twelve-, thirteen-, or fourteen-year-old, it is nearly impossible not to believe a group of people who are unequivocally supporting your new identity. There is nothing better than having people tell you you're right. Then your doubts started fading, and you became focused on transition. If I just get a haircut, if I just get new clothes, if I just get a new name, if I just bind my breasts, if I just use different pronouns . . . if I do all of these things, then, THEN, I will feel better. But we never should have lost focus on helping you to accept yourself. As you must know deep down, chasing a perceived feeling is impossible. There will always be a higher bar to reach, a greener pasture on the other side.

While I was there giving you an alternative viewpoint, you heard many other people telling you that your parents just didn't understand, they will never understand, and they are transphobic. I was told I was doing irreparable damage by not instantly changing your name and pronouns. I am not transphobic, whatever that means. I am against children, teens, and young adults transitioning. I feel deep respect and love for people with gender dysphoria; it is hell. I know because it's happened to you, my daughter. But to help, to be part of your solution, I won't wade into the unstudied morass of medical transition, not without understanding exactly what the outcomes are. I love you too much to do that to you.

I love you with all of my heart and soul. You are a part of me. I am here with you now and forever.

Love, Your Mama XOXO

* * *

I never gave my daughter this letter, but we did talk about the main concepts over the years, and she seemed open to listening. I did ask her not to start hormones during her freshman year of college, because adjusting to college is hard enough on a good day.

She is no longer in college, but to my immense relief, my instincts in advising caution and setting boundaries were right. She has desisted and is identifying as female—after six very long years, my prayers have been answered.

My daughter has THANKED me more than once for not allowing her to medically transition. She acknowledged that what I went through was awful too. This journey is not over, but hopefully, it will continue down the path of physical and mental wellness.

75

Is Desistance Rare?

"They" say desistance is rare. But is it really?

How many teens fall into the current Internet rabbit hole that is the transgender glitter universe, claim a trans identification, and then later decide it is not for them? We are told that being trans is something you are and not something you do. Well, in our experience, that just is not true.

Our child told us one day that he felt like he was born in the wrong body and that he had a female brain. He spoke of feeling this way for the last three years and knowing the next steps to take. His plan included a change in wardrobe, consulting with medical professionals, and adopting a new name and pronouns. What followed was an obsession with himself, his feelings, and all things "trans." A hoodie became his armor, and sitting at lunch one day, I was heartbroken to see small cuts running up and down his arm. We were confused, hurting for our child, and determined to find him the help that he needed and had asked for. We quickly circled the wagons, and, as a family, we started our search.

At first, I found parent support groups where I was told to hurry up and get him on puberty blockers before he got too tall. This was my first experience with the affirmation model.

Next, I made phone calls to find a counselor, and after a five-minute conversation, I was asked about preferred names and pronouns. It was then suggested that we go ahead and use them right away in order to prevent suicide. This advice was given after five minutes of conversation with me and without any actual contact with our son.

It was all so overwhelming and confusing. None of the advice felt right. It was like stepping into a foreign country that used a different language, and we certainly were not natives.

As we continued to look for support, our son regressed before our eyes. He became disorganized, could not complete simple tasks, and began failing classes. He was spiraling out of control and started hurting himself. We were beside ourselves—we simply did not know how to help or what to do. Finally, after a serious self-harm event, he fell apart and, sobbing, told us he felt "the gender stuff" was coming from the hell that he was experiencing at school. He begged not to return. We also discovered that he had secretly been communicating online with a self-identified trans woman that was "coaching him" and had offered to pick him up if we did not support his plans to transition. We spent a very heart-wrenching and sleepless time searching for help. I considered a career change, homeschooling, and alternative schools. We were hoping and praying our child could make it without failing classes, hurting himself, or running away.

Sheer luck led us to a small "classical" school. It had a homey feel, with no computers, and we felt it had the potential to support his unique intellect without the toxic culture of his previous school setting. Simultaneously, we found a therapist who agreed to help our child navigate his feelings about the why and how of why he felt the way he felt without jumping on the gender-affirmative bandwagon. We enrolled him in private music lessons and found ways to support his mental health, physical health, and critical-thinking skills. He poured himself into music and would initially play for hours each day. Together, we listened to books such as *Freakonomics*, *The Coddling of the American Mind*, and *The Madness of Crowds*. Getting out of the house, spending time away from screens, and being together as a family became our priorities.

Gradually, our child became less withdrawn and shed his surly and caustic demeanor. He began interacting with us and smiling again. He immersed himself in playing music, and I remember being shocked when I heard him singing in the shower. We had not heard singing for months. He began making connections at the new school, and teachers seemed to value his intelligence and encouraged his love of learning. Later, we found nail polish and female clothing in the trash. On his own, he drifted away from the cheerleaders that had given him that nail polish and enjoyed drawing him as a female furry.

We never directly challenged the trans identification. We pointedly did not argue with his reasoning. But we also did not rush to praise him as stunning and brave. We applied the concept of "watchful waiting" while disconnecting him from the dark online world that included groomers who sent him explicit dysphoria hypnosis tracks. We did not know exactly what we should do, but we knew he needed time, love, and support. Time to sort through complex feelings. Time to reflect on the plans he was making without the influence of social media.

Our son now says that he always felt out of step with other kids and never felt like he fit in. He went on to say that in trying to find his place in the world, he was shoving himself into a more confining box, the transgender box, and that now it just did not seem to fit. This was ten months ago. We continue to wait, watch, and love our son. All signs point to positive mental health and growth. He is making plans and enjoying life. How many other teens out there are just like him?

References

Abbasi, Kamran. "Caring for Young People with Gender Dysphoria." *BMJ* 380, no. 8374 (2023): 553, doi:10.1136/bmj.p553.

Abbruzzese, E., et al. "The Myth of 'Reliable Research' in Pediatric Gender Medicine: A Critical Evaluation of the Dutch Studies—and Research That Has Followed." *Journal of Sex & Marital Therapy* (2023), doi.org/10.1080/0092623X.2022.2150346.

Baker, Katie. "When Students Change Gender Identity, and Parents Don't Know." *New York Times*, January 22, 2023, www.nytimes.com/2023/01/22/us/gender-identity-students-parents.html.

Barnes, Hannah. "Gender Identity Services in the UK Are on Pause as Evidence Comes under Scrutiny." *BMJ* 380, no. 8374 (2023): 509, doi:10.1136/bmj.p509.

Bell, David. "Gender Identity Treatment Needs Greater Caution." *Guardian*, January 7, 2023, www.theguardian.com/society/2023/jan/27/gender-identity-treatment-needs-greater-caution.

Bell, Keira. "Keira Bell: My Story." *Persuasion.* April 7, 2021, www.persuasion.community/p/keira-bell-my-story.

Biggs, Michael. "Puberty Blockers." Transgender Trend, www.transgendertrend.com/puberty-blockers/.

Blaff, Ari. "Norwegian Medical Watchdog Encourages Country to Ditch 'Gender-Affirming' Care Guidelines." *National Review*, March 10, 2023, www.nationalreview.com/news/norwegian-medical-watchdog-encourages-country-to-ditch-gender-affirming-care-guidelines/.

Brooks, Libby. "'A Contentious Place': The Inside Story of Tavistock's NHS Gender Identity Clinic." *Guardian*, Janaury 19, 2023, www.theguardian.com/society/2023/jan/19/a-contentious-place-the-inside-story-of-tavistocks-nhs-gender-identity-clinic.

Cantor, James M. "American Academy of Pediatrics and Trans-Kids: Fact-Checking Rafferty." Toronto Sexuality Centre (2018), www.jamescantor.org/uploads/6/2/9/3/62939641/cantor_fact-check_of_aap.pdf.

Cantor, James. "CAAPS, ROGD, and the Science Neglected." *Sexology Today!* August 9, 2021, www.sexologytoday.org/2021/08/caaps-rogd-and-science-neglected.html.

D'Angelo, Roberto, et al. "One Size Does Not Fit All: In Support of Psychotherapy for Gender Dysphoria." *Archives of Sexual Behavior* 50 (2021), doi.org/10.1007/s10508-020-01844-2.

Drescher, Jack. "Controversies in Gender Diagnoses." *LGBT Health* 1, no. 1 (March 2014):10–14, doi: 10.1089/lgbt.2013.1500.

Duval, Derek. "Swedish Documentary: Stopping The Trans Train," Genspect. December 6, 2021, genspect.org/swedish-documentary-stopping-the-trans-train/.

Flier, Jeffrey. "As a Former Dean of Harvard Medical School, I Question Brown's Failure to Defend Lisa Littman." *Quillette*, August 31, 2018, quillette.com/2018/08/31/as-a-former-dean-of-harvard-medical-school-i-question-browns-failure-to-defend-lisa-littman/.

Fox, Angus. "When Sons Become Daughters: Parents of Transitioning Boys Speak Out on Their Own Suffering." *Quillette*, April 2, 2021, quillette.com/2021/04/02/when-sons-become-daughters-parents-of-transitioning-boys-speak-out-on-their-own-suffering/.

Hawker, Elizabeth. "Autism, Puberty, and Gender Dysphoria: The View from an Autistic Desisted Woman." *4W*, March 31, 2020, 4w.pub/autism-puberty-gender-dysphoria-view-from-an-autistic-desisted-woman/.

Hinsliff, Gaby. "Time to Think by Hannah Barnes Review—Inside Britain's Only Clinic for Trans Children." *Guardian*, March 10, 2023, www.theguardian.com/books/2023/mar/10/time-to-think-by-hannah-barnes-review-inside-britains-only-clinic-for-trans-children.

Joyce, Helen. *Trans: When Ideology Meets Reality.* London: Oneworld, 2021.

Kozlowska, Kasia, et al. "Australian Children and Adolescents with Gender Dysphoria: Clinical Presentations and Challenges Experienced by a Multidisciplinary Team and Gender Service." *Human Systems: Therapy, Culture and Attachments* 1, no. 1 (February 2021): 70–95, doi.org/10.1177/26344041211010777.

Launer, John. "Gender Identity, Polemics, and Empathy." *BMJ* 380, no. 8374 (2023): 477, doi:10.1136/bmj.p47.

Levine, Stephen B. "What Are We Doing to These Children? Response to Drescher, Clayton, and Balon Commentaries on Levine et al., 2022." *Journal of Sex & Marital Therapy* 49, no. 1 (2023): 115–125, doi.org/10.1080/0092623X.2022.2136117.

Littman, Lisa. "Parent Reports of Adolescents and Young Adults Perceived to Show Signs of a Rapid-Onset of Gender Dysphoria." *PLOS One* 13, no. 8 (August 16, 2018): e0202330, doi.org/10.1371/journal.pone.0202330.

Mackay, Charles. *Extraordinary Popular Delusions and the Madness of Crowds.* London: Richard Bentley, 1841.

Malone, William J., et al. "Letter to the Editor from William J. Malone et al: 'Proper Care of Transgender and Gender-Diverse Persons in the Setting of Proposed Discrimination: A Policy Perspective.'" *Journal of Clinical Endocrinology and Metabolism* 106, no. 8 (August 2021): e3287–e3288, doi.org/10.1210/clinem/dgab205 academic.oup.com/jcem/article/106/8/e3287/6190133.

Notini, Lauren, et al. "Forever Young? The Ethics of Ongoing Puberty Suppression for Non-Binary Adults." *Journal of Medical Ethics* 46, no. 11 (November 1, 2020): 743–752, jme.bmj.com/content/46/11/743, 10.1136/medethics-2019-106012.

Office of the High Commissioner for Human Rights. "The Right to Choose and Refuse Sterilization." United Nations, June 6, 2014, www.ohchr.org/en/stories/2014/06/right-choose-and-refuse-sterilization.

O'Malley, Stella. "Gaslighting the Concerned Parents of Trans Children—a Psychotherapist's View." *Quillette*, May 4, 2021, quillette.com/2021/05/04/gaslighting-the-concerned-parents-of-trans-children-a-psychotherapists-view/.

Reed, Jamie. "I Thought I Was Saving Trans Kids. Now I'm Blowing the Whistle." *Free Press*, February 9, 2023, www.thefp.com/p/i-thought-i-was-saving-trans-kids.

Respaut, Robin, et al. "Why Detransitioners Are Crucial to the Science of Gender Care." *Medscape*, January 4, 2023, www.medscape.com/viewarticle/986476.

Ristori, Jiska, and Thomas D. Steensma. "Gender Dysphoria in Childhood." *International Review of Psychiatry* 28, no. 1 (2016): 13–20, 10.3109/09540261.2015.1115754.

Sapir, Leor. "A New Low: Advocates of Pediatric Gender Transition Publish a Fatally Flawed Study Purporting to Debunk the Social-Transition Hypothesis." *City-Journal*, August 5, 2022, www.city-journal.org/major-flaws-in-new-study-on-pediatric-gender-transition.

SEGM. "Endocrine Society Position on Gender Dysphoria Treatments Not Supported by Available Evidence: A Recently-Published Rebuttal to the Endocrine Society's Position on Transgender Interventions." Society for Evidence-Based Gender Medicine, June 19, 2021, segm.org/endocrine_society_GD_position_rebuttal.

Seth, Shaniqua. "At What Age Can I Get a Hysterectomy? At What Age Do Doctors Allow Women in the United States to Have a Hysterectomy?" National Women's Health Network, October 13, 2016, nwhn.org/age-can-get-hysterectomy/.

Shrier, Abigail. *Irreversible Damage: The Transgender Craze Seducing Our Daughters*. Washington, DC: Regnery Publishing, 2020.

———. "Top Trans Doctors Blow the Whistle on 'Sloppy' Care," *Free Press*. October 4, 2021, www.thefp.com/p/top-trans-doctors-blow-the-whistle.

———. "When Your Daughter Defies Biology: The Burden of Mothers Whose Children Suffer from 'Rapid Onset Gender Dysphoria.'" *Wall Street Journal*, January 6, 2019, www.wsj.com/articles/ when-your-daughter-defies-biology-11546804848.

———. "Why Marci Matters." *Abigail Shrier* (Substack), October 6, 2021, abigailshrier.substack.com/p/why-marci-matters.

Singal, Jesse. "Gender-Clinic Whistleblower Jamie Reed Has Provided a Detailed Account of Her Most Controversial Claim, Including the Names of Those Involved." *Singal-Minded* (Substack), March 10, 2023, jessesingal.substack.com/p/gender-clinic-whistleblower-jamie.

Stock, Kathleen. *Material Girls: Why Reality Matters for Feminism*. London: Fleet, 2021.

Tavris, Carol, and Elliot Aronson. *Mistakes Were Made (but Not by Me): Why We Justify Foolish Beliefs, Bad Decisions, and Hurtful Acts*. New York: Harcourt, 2007.

Valdes, Leo, and Kinnon MacKinnon. "Take Detransitioners Seriously." *Atlantic*, January 18, 2023, www.theatlantic.com/ideas/archive/2023/01/detransition-transgender-nonbinary-gender-affirming-care/672745/.

WSJ Staff, "Inside TikTok's Algorithm: A WSJ Video Investigation," *Wall Street Journal*, July 21, 2021, www.wsj.com/articles/tiktok-algorithm-video-investigation-11626877477.

Resources

Fair Play for Women

fairplayforwomen.com

"Fair Play For Women is a campaigning and consultancy group which raises awareness, provides evidence and analysis, and works to protect the rights of women and girls in the UK."

4thWaveNow

4thwavenow.com

"4thWaveNow was founded in 2015 by Denise, the mother of a teenage girl who suddenly announced she was a trans man after a few weeks of total immersion in YouTube transition vlogs and other trans-oriented social media."

Gender Dysphoria Alliance

genderdysphoriaalliance.com

"Our Mission: Inform the conversation about Gender Dysphoria; Explain why evidence-based care is so important; Include people who detransition, regret or desist; Support sex-based rights."

Gender Exploratory Therapy Association

www.genderexploratory.com

"We are here because those who are exploring gender identity or struggling with their biological sex should have access to therapists who will provide thoughtful care without pushing an ideological or political agenda. We believe that skilled, ethical exploratory therapy is appropriate for those with gender dysphoria, their families, and detransitioners."

Gender Health Query

genderhq.org

"A resource and community for people concerned about same-sex attracted young people harmed by medical transition for gender dysphoria."

Genspect

genspect.org

"Genspect is an international alliance of professionals, trans people, detransitioners, parent groups and others who seek high-quality care for gender-related distress. Emerging as a leading organisation that offers an alternative to WPATH, Genspect offers a range of education, resources and support for anyone who has been impacted by gender dysphoria. Uniting 25 different organisations in 23 countries, we don't just speak for a few: we speak for thousands."

LGB Alliance

lgballiance.org.uk

"Formed in 2019 and registered as a charity in 2021, LGB Alliance exists to provide support, advice, information and community to men and women who are same-sex attracted."

Parents Defending Education

defendinged.org

"Parents Defending Education is a national grassroots organization working to reclaim our schools from activists imposing harmful agendas. Through network and coalition building, investigative reporting, litigation, and engagement on local, state, and national policies, we are fighting indoctrination in the classroom—and promoting the restoration of a healthy, non-political education for our kids."

Post Trans

post-trans.com

"Hello, we are Elie and Nele, two female detransitioners from Belgium and Germany. Post Trans is a project we have decided to create as we realised that there was a big gap on the topic of detransition. We believe that it is increasingly important to address this issue and to give support to female individuals who stopped identifying as trans. Our goal is to provide a space for female detransitioners to share their experiences as well as giving an alternative narrative to the common discussions on transidentity."

Reality's Last Stand

realityslaststand.com

"Reality's Last Stand is a publication by biologist Colin Wright dedicated to providing weekly news, articles, and other content about the biology of sex and sex differences, gender ideology, Critical Social Justice, free speech, and related topics."

Reddit r/detrans (Detransition Subreddit)

reddit.com/r/detrans/

"About Community: Welcome all detransitioners/desisters and self-questioners. Please self-identify your detrans status with user flair, or your content will be removed (medical or legal professionals, please message mods for an exception). Post anything about gender detransition. Ask questions, share memes, inspire, vent, wonder, etc."

Sex Matters

sex–matters.org

"Sex Matters is a UK-based not-for-profit organisation. We campaign, advocate and produce resources to promote clarity about sex in public policy, law and culture. We have a singular mission: to re-establish that sex matters in rules, laws, policies, language and culture."

Society for Evidence-Based Gender Medicine

segm.org

"Our aim is to promote safe, compassionate, ethical and evidence-informed healthcare for children, adolescents, and young adults with gender dysphoria."

Stats for Gender

statsforgender.org

"Many parents with gender-questioning kids are presented with statistics which make transition sound like paradise, and present any less hasty path as abusive or even dangerous. When kids ask for puberty blockers or cross-sex hormones, parents find themselves cast into PhD level research, scouring scientific papers late into the night, trying to sort fact from fiction. Teachers, journalists, politicians and decision-makers are often confronted with data that make it seem like there's only one option. Yet many are inwardly skeptical of the headlong rush towards transition. They think about people they know who were gender-non-conforming in their youth, and wonder what would have become of them had they grown up in an era so obsessed with gender expression. The absence of a single, easy-to-use portal for statistics and facts about gender has hindered parents and professionals alike. That's why Genspect created Stats For Gender. We believe that the public has a right to reliable data, intuitively categorized, and phrased in simple, jargon-free terms."

Transgender Trend

transgendertrend.com
"Transgender Trend is the leading organisation in the call for evidence-based healthcare for children and young people suffering gender dysphoria and for factual, science-based teaching in schools."

TReVoices

www.trevoices.org
"The medical industry is telling kids that they were born in the wrong body and that medical transition is a miracle cure. Surgery, synthetic hormones, and puberty blockers are prescribed to children worldwide. As a transman myself, having transitioned 100%, I can tell you that the medical complications are enormous, and every study that said it was beneficial has been retracted or modified. But getting this information out is the challenge. Help us educate and save these kids. Every child has the right to enter adulthood with a healthy body and mind. Help us save these children from the monster called 'Big Pharma.'"

Women's Liberation Front

womensliberationfront.org
"Our Mission: To restore, protect, and advance the rights of women and girls using legal argument, policy advocacy, and public education."

Credits

The essays in this volume were originally published on the Parents with Inconvenient Truths about Trans (PITT) Substack. For the purposes of this volume, they have been lightly edited and some of the titles have been changed. You can find the original essays, which often include lengthy comment threads, at the following links:

Parents on Community Capture

1. pitt.substack.com/p/i-suffer-from-parental-dysphoria
2. pitt.substack.com/p/it-takes-a-village
3. pitt.substack.com/p/the-world-needs-all-kinds-of-boys
4. pitt.substack.com/p/letter-to-a-well-meaning-bystander
5. pitt.substack.com/p/dear-parent-do-you-really-know-whats
6. pitt.substack.com/p/what-it-really-feels-like-to-have
7. pitt.substack.com/p/as-a-mother-fighting-for-my-rogd

Parents on Community Influences:
Peer Groups, Teachers, and Schools

8. pitt.substack.com/p/pronoun-bullying
9. pitt.substack.com/p/school-personnel-are-not-qualified
10. pitt.substack.com/p/outside-influences-how-our-spirited
11. pitt.substack.com/p/i-sponsored-a-high-school-gsathen
12. pitt.substack.com/p/30k-a-year-and-my-kid-cant-tell-the
13. pitt.substack.com/p/university
14. pitt.substack.com/p/i-am-not-the-same-teacher

Parents on Online Influences:
Porn, Anime, and Social Media

15. pitt.substack.com/p/brainwashed-yes-content-from-school
16. pitt.substack.com/p/transgenders-connection-with-pornography
17. pitt.substack.com/p/crazy-like-a-trans-gay-fox-girl
18. pitt.substack.com/p/its-been-one-year
19. pitt.substack.com/p/a-clusterfexk-of-doctor-failures
20. pitt.substack.com/p/sex-and-rogd
21. pitt.substack.com/p/death-cults-and-unicorns

Parents on Gender Ideology

22. pitt.substack.com/p/why-our-kids-think-theyre-trans
23. pitt.substack.com/p/trans-a-threat-to-my-daughter-my
24. pitt.substack.com/p/testifying
25. pitt.substack.com/p/true-believer.
26. pitt.substack.com/p/gender-transition-concerns-must-transcend
27. pitt.substack.com/p/early-transition-arguments-pro-and

Parents on the Betrayal of the Medical System

28. pitt.substack.com/p/think-my-kid-is-trans-youd-better
29. pitt.substack.com/p/parents-deserve-answers-before-medicalizing
30. pitt.substack.com/p/doctors-stop-gaslighting-our-gender
31. pitt.substack.com/p/unsafe-parental-disempowerment-by
32. pitt.substack.com/p/a-letter-to-my-sons-affirmative-therapist
33. pitt.substack.com/p/my-daughter-and-i
34. pitt.substack.com/p/why-i-cant-tell-you-my-sons-therapists

Parents on Family, Love, and Loss

35. pitt.substack.com/p/my-new-identity-not-by-choice
36. pitt.substack.com/p/time-accounting-in-the-world-of-gender
37. pitt.substack.com/p/reflections-on-pain-and-things-that
38. pitt.substack.com/p/mourning-the-living
39. https://pitt.substack.com/p/kills-me-every-time

40. pitt.substack.com/p/the-abyss
41. pitt.substack.com/p/behind-the-curtain-the-reality-of
42. pitt.substack.com/p/helping-tracy
43. pitt.substack.com/p/ambiguous-loss
44. pitt.substack.com/p/unmade-memories
45. pitt.substack.com/p/above-all-i-love-my-daughter
46. pitt.substack.com/p/love-and-loss-in-new-zealand-how
47. pitt.substack.com/p/layers-of-sadness
48. pitt.substack.com/p/i-wish-i-didnt-know

Parents on the Parent Underground

49. pitt.substack.com/p/parents-the-new-resistance-of-the
50. pitt.substack.com/p/lets-go-all-the-way-to-protect-our
51. pitt.substack.com/p/waiting-for-change
52. pitt.substack.com/p/follow-the-science-surveys-show-recent
53. pitt.substack.com/p/you-can-still-do-the-right-thing
54. pitt.substack.com/p/rogd-lived-experience-and-the-hypocrisy
55. pitt.substack.com/p/gender-dysphoria-the-science-is-not
56. pitt.substack.com/p/real-conversations-one-at-a-time

Parents on Parenting Through Trans

57. pitt.substack.com/p/how-to-be-a-trans-educated-rational
58. pitt.substack.com/p/living-in-a-war-zone-my-daughters
59. pitt.substack.com/p/to-help-my-son-its-time-to-rediscover
60. pitt.substack.com/p/a-letter-to-my-beloved-child
61. pitt.substack.com/p/not-a-desistance-story
62. pitt.substack.com/p/finding-hope-on-the-road-to-ruin
63. pitt.substack.com/p/becoming-a-light-for-our-wayward
64. pitt.substack.com/p/reflections-of-a-father
65. pitt.substack.com/p/the-gender-critical-parents-guide

Parents on Desistance

66. pitt.substack.com/p/just-a-phase-we-should-never-transition
67. pitt.substack.com/p/the-one-way-street

68. pitt.substack.com/p/to-my-daughters-therapist-you-were
69. pitt.substack.com/p/the-trans-detour
70. pitt.substack.com/p/the-gummy-bear-cult
71. pitt.substack.com/p/my-desistance-story
72. pitt.substack.com/p/our-story-of-desistance
73. pitt.substack.com/p/anger-shame-and-then-pure-happiness
74. pitt.substack.com/p/dear-daughter
75. pitt.substack.com/p/they-say-desistance-is-rare-but-is

About PITT

Parents with Inconvenient Truths about Trans (PITT) publishes stories written and edited exclusively by parents with first-hand experience in the upside-down world of gender ideology.

Founded by Josie A. and Dina S., PITT (pitt.substack.com) is a space for parents who have been impacted by gender ideology to share their uncensored personal stories, experiences, and thoughts, while remaining anonymous to protect themselves and their families. PITT's objective is to inform the public about the devastating impact of gender ideology on families and to end the medicalization of identity for children, teens, and young people.

The essays on PITT are always published anonymously. Any names that might appear on bylines are pseudonyms. Parent authors hail from around the world, including (so far) the United States, the United Kingdom, Australia, Ireland, Canada, Spain, South Africa, France, Italy, Poland, New Zealand, and several countries in Latin America.

PITT is supported, in part, by Genspect, an organization founded by psychotherapist Stella O'Malley that is committed to supporting parents' voices. If you are a parent of a trans-identified child and want a chance to tell your story, you can contact PITT at pitt@genspect.org.